GANDHIAN PERSPECTIVES ON POPULATION AND DEVELOPMENT

Gandhian Studies and Peace Research Series

No.1 : Gandhian Model of Development and World Peace/ **R.P. Misra** (Ed) Rs. 200

No.2 : Conflict Resolution Through Non-Violence: Role of the University - Volume I: Science and Ethics / **K. D. Gangrade** and **R.P. Misra** (Ed) Rs. 200

No.3 : Conflict Resolution Through Non-Violence: Role of the Universities - Volume II: Development without Destruction/**K.D. Gangrade** and **R.P. Misra** Rs. 200

No.4 : The Social Philosophy of Mahatma Gandhi

/K.S. Bharati, Rs. 160

No.5 : Gandhian Humanism/**Mohit Chakrabarti** Rs. 200

No.6 : Gandhian Holistic Economics/**Shashi Prabha Sharma** Rs. 200

No.7 : Gandhian Spiritualism : A Quest for Essence of Excellence /**Mohit Chakrabarti** Rs. 240

No.8 : Gandhian Perspectives on Population and Development/**A.K. Sharma** Rs. 350

No.9 : Thoughts of Gandhi and Vinoba : A Comparative Study/**K.S. Bharathi** Rs. 300

No.10 : Economic Philosophy of Mahatma Gandhi/**Shanti Swarup Gupta** Rs. 400

About the Author

Dr. A.K. Sharma, Professor of Sociology, Department of Humanities and Social Sciences, Indian Institute of Technology (IIT) Kanpur began his academic career with a study of fertility and family planning in rural areas. He has worked at State Planning Institute Lucknow, Indian Institute of Technology Bombay, and Operations Research Group New Delhi. He has rich experience of teaching and research in the field of sociology of population. His books include *Social Inequality and Demographic Processes, Social Demography,* and *Developing the Underdeveloped: A Socio-Psychological Study.* His current research engagements are family planning evaluation, social values, neo-social movements and industrial and organizational sociology.

Gandhian Studies and Peace Research Series-8

GANDHIAN PERSPECTIVES ON POPULATION AND DEVELOPMENT

A.K. SHARMA
Humanities and Social Sciences Department
Indian Institute of Technology
Kanpur (U.P.) 208016

CONCEPT PUBLISHING COMPANY, NEW DELHI - 110059

ISBN 81-7022-533-7

First Published 1996

Published and Printed by
Ashok Kumar Mittal
Concept Publishing Company
A/15-16, Commercial Block, Mohan Garden
New Delhi-110059, (INDIA)
Phones : 5554042, 5504042

IN MEMORIUM

BHOLA NATH MEHTA

1900-1992

PREFACE

Population is one of the most burning problems facing the developing societies. Rapid improvement in mortality in developing countries, in absence of corresponding fall in the birth rate, is causing a rapid growth of population. Social scientists have shown that this growth of population is at the root of socio-economic problems, political conflicts and misery. In this situation all-out efforts are being made to plan population processes in general and reproductive process in particular. Planning involves understanding. Therefore, alternative constructs which are as diverse as mechanistic, bio-social, sociologistic, demographic and behaviouristic theories have been offered to describe, explain and predict demographic phenomena. All of them have their merits and demerits. The present study attempts to discuss population and related issues in the Gandhian perspective.

It is noteworthy that in our age Gandhian theory has become an enigma. There are extreme views on Gandhi's approach to population planning, ranging from total rejection of contraceptive methods to exploring ways of involving Gandhi Khadi organisations in delivering family planning methods at the grassroots level. In these circumstances it is very difficult to claim correctness of any one interpretation. Today we require an open debate on the philosophy of intervention. Yet it should be said that Gandhian holistic theory of population has to be developed in the light of Gandhian thought in diverse areas such as economic development, gender relations, science and technology, urban-rural relations, etc. This study attmpts to explore them.

I am obliged to Drs. B.N. Patnaik and N.K. Sharma who helped in the preparation of this book in several ways. They always readily spared time for discussion and also for the routine work of looking at the manuscript. I am indebted to Drs. R.S. Misra, J.N. Misra, M.A. Ansari, P.N. Rastogi, Lila Krishnan and Raka Sharan for their various suggestions and encouragement. Thanks are also due to the research scholars, Clymes Augustine, Sahatrarashmi, Anurag Dwivedi, Manju Singh and Motilal

Dash, for their suggestions. I am also grateful to Mr. Rajendra Nigam and Mr. D.K. Srivastava for secretarial help, for producing and reproducing various drafts and for doing errands. None of them is, however, responsible for errors, omissions and shortcomings which one may find in this book.

The financial support provided by the Quality Improvement Programme of the Ministry of Education and Social Welfare is gratefully acknowledged.

A.K. SHARMA

CONTENTS

LIST OF TABLES

LIST OF FIGURES

SECTION-A

POPULATION TRENDS, DATA AND MODELS

1

OBJECTIVES AND OVERVIEW

There is no dearth of literature in the field of population studies. Many attempts have been made to examine the complex issue of the relationship between population and development. At the same time there is a feeling in both academic and planning circles that population and development processes are not properly understood, that the mechanisms of population change are not quite known, that we require contextual rather than universal theories of population. Till this day, for reasons of sociology of knowledge, population scientists in India have worked in the framework of Western theory of development and modernization. The well known theory of demographic transition is nothing but a covert structural functional theory of economic development. The theory does not seem to be working and academicians are searching for alternatives. In the present study, an attempt is made to examine population, and those developmental processes which impinge upon population, in the light of Gandhian theory.

Of late, several thinkers and activist groups have turned towards Gandhian thought. They are interpreting and reinterpreting Gandhian thought to develop alternative visions of future society and strategies to transform exploitative capitalist feudal society. The present study can perhaps make some small contribution towards these goals.

The study does not make any claim of originality, objectivity, absolute truth or of providing the most appropriate framework of analysis for examining problems in Indian society. Sociologically speaking, these criteria of knowledge do not make any sense in the post-modern phase and to the author either. Social constructions of social issues are part of society and its collective conscience. At the same time it may be said that we are passing through times when collective conscience is not really collective, rather it is bodly divided. At best it may be characterised as multipartite conscience. Gandhian theory is no panacea for population problems. Yet it is one aspect of reproduction of society. There is no reason why among other paradigms, it should not be constructed and applied. May be in the future a healthy competition between Gandhian and other theories can help in promoting unity and integration of thoughts and raising our capacity to solve our problems.

Population processes are natural part of society. They shape and are shaped by the socio-economic, political and cultural phenomena. Therefore, examination of population issues entails an examination of society and culture. Population studies have shown that economic growth, equality, gender relations, visions of development, urbanization and religion are some factors which impinge upon population patterns. In other words a holistic theory of population should aim at exploring not only the trends and patterns in population but it should also explain major socio-economic and political facts.

Objectives

In the light of the foregoing discussion, the objectives of the present study are listed as follows:

(i) to describe and comment upon the world population trends;
(ii) to describe and comment upon the population trends in India;
(iii) to discuss the dominant theoretical framework of demographic transition in India and problems of data and models;
(iv) to review the existing literature on the relationship between population and sustainable development;
(v) to develop some Gandhian concepts in the light of which social and demographic problems of present day India can be understood;
(vi) to develop an outline of Gandhian theory of population; and
(vii) to examine developmental issues such as social development, feminism, environmental control, urbanization, perspectives on science and technology and role of religious factors in fertility.

An Overview

In order to achieve the above objectives this study is divided into three sections. Section-A has five chapters including this introductory chapter. This Section is devoted to examination of population trends in the world (Chapter 2) and in India (Chapter 3). This also focuses on demographic transition theory and population models developed in the framework of the demographic transition theory (Chapter 4). The last chapter of this section (Chapter 5) focuses on the concept of sustainable development. It also reviews studies on the relationship between population growth and sustainable development.

Section-B has two chapters. They are devoted to discussion of Gandhian theory of society (Chapter 6) and a new Gandhian theory of population (Chapter 7).

Section-C, divided into seven chapters applies Gandhian theory in the following areas: conceptualisation of development (Chapter 8), gender relation and feminism (Chapter 9), environment (Chapter 10), urban patterns (Chapter 11), sociology of science (Chapter 12), fertility among minority groups (Chapter 13) and a holistic theory of population (Chapter 14). Here an attempt is made to remove certain misconceptions regarding Gandhian theory and suggest some guidelines for action.

2

WORLD POPULATION GROWTH

The dynamics of population can be investigated at four levels: the world (or cross-country) level, country level (including regional), community level, and farm or household level. In this chapter are presented facts about growth of population at the world level.

With great strides in technovations in the field of transportation and communication, the world has increasingly become a small village or earth a small spaceship. Population problem has become a global problem. The world economic growth which reached its historical high at 5.2 per cent per year during 1960s, slowed to 3.4 per cent in the 1970s, and 2.9 per cent in 1980s. Even then it remained at a level considerably higher than the rate of population growth. Therefore, the per capita output of goods and services continued to rise, though at falling rates. In these decades many planners and social scientists did not take up the issue of population growth very seriously. Theory of overpopulation was attributed to Malthusianism and the term "Malthusianism" was used in a pejorative sense. After 1990, the world economy expanded only at 0.6 per cent per year, a rate much lower than the rate of growth of world population, leading to fall in living standards, apart from environmental degradation and depletion of natural capital. Researches have shown that population growth has greatly decreased society's capacity to support large population through its negative impact on nature. Population growth has, therefore, become a major issue at the international level. The Rio conference on environment has also recognised the role of population in sustainable development of the world community. In this context it has become important to discuss the global trends in population growth.

History of the World Population Growth

Table 2.1 shows the size of world's population at the beginning of our era, as estimated by the Soviet demographer F.D. Markuzon. According to the estimates shown the world population at the beginning of our era was 326.5 million. It is believed that man separated off from the animal kingdom approximately a million years ago, and thus the world population took about a million years to reach 326.5 million. Commenting upon them Urlanis says that even Markuzon's estimates are exaggerated, particularly for India and Americas. He estimated that only about 230 million people were living on earth at the beginning of our era. Of them about two-thirds lived in Asia (Urlanis, 1978).

Urlanis also maintains that for thousands of years during the Palaeolithic period mankind multiplied extremely slowly; the size of human population at the end of the Palaeolithic period (15,000 B. C.) had reached about three million. During the Mesolithic period (15,000 B.C.—7,000 B.C.) human population rose to 10 million. After that during the Neolithic period (7,000 B.C. — 2,000 B.C.) population reached the 50 million mark. And as mentioned above the world population at the beginning of our era was about 230 million. In the past diseases, accidents, natural disasters, predation by other creatures and the limitation of food supply had restraind population growth. Perhaps breeding was seasonal, offspring being mostly born at that time of the year when food supply was likely to be most plentiful. As time passed, and technological and organisational advancements occurred, world population started rising at faster rates (Garland, 1991).

TABLE 2.1: World population at the beginning of Our Era (in millions)

Part of the World	Population
Europe	35
Asia	220
North and Central America	21
South America	19
Africa	30
Oceania	15
World	326.5

Source: Urlanis, B.T., 1978, "World Population Growth", in Valentey,D.I. (ed.), *The Theory of Population*. Progress Publishers, Moscow, p. 231.

Urlanis claims that during the first millennium of our era population did grow but the rate of growth had declined. For this he presents

Bennett's estimates for the period 1000-1500 A.D. (Table 2.2). To him the cause of this fall in growth rate seemed to be three-fold: slowing down of progress in agricultural technique, wars and epidemics. Consequently, the population rose from 230 million to only 275 million. As a matter of fact Markuzon's estimates for the beginning of our era and Bennett's estimates for 1000 A.D. show a declining population trend during the first millenium.

TABLE 2.2: World Population, A.D. 1000 - A.D. 1500 (in millions)

Year	Europe	Asia (in Russia)	South-West Asia	India	China	Japan	South-East Asia and Oceania	Africa	America	The World
1000	42	5	32	48	70	4	11	50	13	275
1100	48	6	33	50	79	6	12	55	17	306
1200	61	7	34	51	89	8	14	61	23	348
1300	73	8	33	50	99	11	15	67	28	384
1400	45	9	27	46	112	14	16	74	30	373
1500	69	11	29	54	125	16	19	82	41	446

Source: Urlanis, B.T., 1978, "The World Population Growth", in Valentey, D.I. (ed.), *The Theory of Population*, Progress Publishers, Moscow, p. 232.

According to Bennett, world population increased from 275 million in A.D. 1000 to 446 million in A.D. 1500. However, during this period population did not rise smoothly and at same pace in different parts of the world. Between A.D. 1300 and 1400 there was actually a fall in the world population. The reason for this decline is the epidemic of the Black Death which took a heavy toll of life in Europe. Urlanis suggested that the world population in A.D. 1500 was 450 million (*i.e.*, it grew by 64 per cent during A.D.1000-1500). Moreover, while Bennett underestimated the population of Europe, he exaggerated population of both the Americas and Asia by the same amount.

Carr-Saunders (1936) estimated the size of world population to be around 545 million in A.D. 1650. His figures for A.D. 1650 are well accepted. They imply an increase of around 100 million between A.D. 1500 and A.D. 1650, or 22 per cent increase in 150 years.

Around A.D. 1820 human population reached the first billion mark. After that it started growing at increasing rates. During the 19th century, spurred on by the industrial revolution and fall in the death rates in the industrialised nations, growth rates rose to above 1 per cent a year in developed countries. In some parts of the world growth rates may have reached 1.5 per cent a year (Camp, 1991). Consequently, the world population, doubled between A.D. 1820 and A.D. 1930—from one billion to two billion. During this period most of the increase occurred in Europe and North America.

TABLE 2.3: Estimate of World Population, A.D. 1750 - A.D. 2025 (in millions)

Year	Population	Year	Population
1750	791	1960	2,986
1800	978	1965	3,288
1850	1,262	1970	3,610
1900	1,650	1975	3,968
1925	2,000	1980	4,432
1950	2,501	1985	4,826
1955	2,722	1990	5,292
		2025	8504

Source: U.N. 1976, *Prospects of Population: Methodology and Assumption,* p. 116; U.N., 1981, *World Population Prospects as Assessed in 1980,* p. 12: and UNFPA, 1992, *The State of World Population 1992,* p. 44.

Beginning about 1930, the pace of domographic change further accelerated. Due to improving socio-economic conditions and industrialisation, death rates started falling in many less developed countries where the population base was quite large. Thus the third billion was added to the world population in just 30 years, between 1930 and 1960. The fourth and fifth billions were added in 14 and 13 years only. The global population in 1993 was estimated to be 5.57 billion. It is expected to reach 6.3 billion in 2000 and 8.5 billion in 2025 (U.N.,1993). With an annual population increment of more than 96 million people, adding the next billion will take only 11 years. On a finite planet, the implications of such growth are tremendous. Following a "golden age" of increased production the world economic output has started falling. Grain is the most basic economic measure of human well-being. While grain output rose at the rate of 3 per cent per year during 1950-84 (leading to 2.6 fold increase), it rose at the rate of 1 per cent only after 1984. In per capita terms it is declining (Annoymous, 1993). The situation with respect to other products of the economic sectors such as fish and livestock production is not dissimilar.

The Present Demographic Situation

Table 2.4 exhibits some demographic characteristics of the world population around 1993.

TABLE 2.4: World Population Indicators

Indicator	Year	Value of the indicator		
		World	Developed regions	Less developed regions
Population (millions)	1992	5,479	1,225	4,254
	2025	8,472	1,403	7,069
Average growth rate(%)	1990-95	1.7	0.5	2.0
Birth rate per1,000	1990-95	26	14	29
Death rate per 1,000	1990-95	9	10	9
Life expectancy	1990-95	65	75	62
Infant mortality per 1,000	1990-95	62	12	69
Per cent urban	1992	44	73	35
Urban growth rate (%)	1990-95	2.7	0.9	3.7
Fertility rate per woman	1990-95	3.3	1.9	3.6

Source: U.N.,1993, *The State of World Population 1993,* p. 48.

The above table shows that in 1992 the world population was 5,479 million and is expected to be growing at a rate of 1.7 per cent during 1990-95. The birth and death rates during this period would be 26 and 9 per thousand, respectively. Fertility rate is 3.3. The life expectancy is 65 years and infant mortality is 62. Per cent urban is 44 and the urban growth rate during 1990-95 is expected to be 2.7 per cent. The table also shows that there are very great diversities in demographic indicators between developed and less developed regions. In the developed countries, majority of people live in urban areas, enjoy good health and their fertility has gone below the replacement level. On the other hand in the less developed countries most people live in rural areas, depend on agriculture, have much lower life expectancy and have a fertility of 3.6 children per woman. Surprisingly, the death rate for less developed regions is only one point less than that for the developed regions. This is largely due to difference in age-distribution between less developed and developed regions.

Fig. 2.1 shows the relationship between GNP per capita and average growth rate. The average growth rate is average of population growth rates in countries having the same per capita income. As such the graph does not reveal any structural relationship between income and growth rate. However, in the group of low income countries there seems to be a negative relationship between the two. In the rich countries growth rates are below 1 per cent. Israel, Saudi Arabia and United Arab Emirates are some outliers. They all belong to Western Asia.

Fig. 2.2 shows the relationship between GNP per capita, and birth and death rates. It reveals that in most of the countries including both low and high income countries death rates vary within a narrow range of 6-12 per thousand population. Thus there does not seem to be any correlation between income and death rate. However, as mentioned above, absence of correlation between income and death rate is partly deceptive; variations in age-distribution of population hide the significant differences in longevity and life expectancy. The figure also reveals that birth rates are strongly correlated with income levels, particularly in the low income countries.

Literature show that improvement in mortality has been a major factor behind fall in the birth rates in developed countries. This relationship between mortality improvement and fall in birth rate seems to be present at the international level even today. Fig. 2.3 shows how the average fertility rates fall with improvement in life-expectancy at the international level. The average fertility rates vary between 1.5 and 7.3. Average fertility rates are highest when life expectancy is around 46 and lowest when life expectancy is around 79. This relationship has an important policy implication: to reduce birth rates —and through them growth rates —less developed countries would have to intensify their efforts in health and related fields. Fig. 2.4 shows that female literacy also determines birth and death rates.

Garland (1991) has aptly summarized the population history. To quote:

> "In the very early years, nature applied the "Survival of the Fittest" rule to control the health and genetic pool of Homo sapiens; it also controlled the level of population.
>
> Because of changes in technology, social and religious attitudes, that rule became somewhat overwhelmed by the "Sanctity of Life" rule and population control was lost.
>
> The general health of Homo sapiens was improved and expectancy of life extended, but there is the possibility that the genetic pool has been impaired.
>
> Now, the "Survival of the Fittest" rule is re-emerging but not as nature applied it. It is being applied through medical science".

In early 1992, the United States National Academy of Sciences and the Royal Society of London together issued a report soberly warning that "if current predictions of population growth prove accurate and patterns of human activity on the planet remain unchanged, science and technology

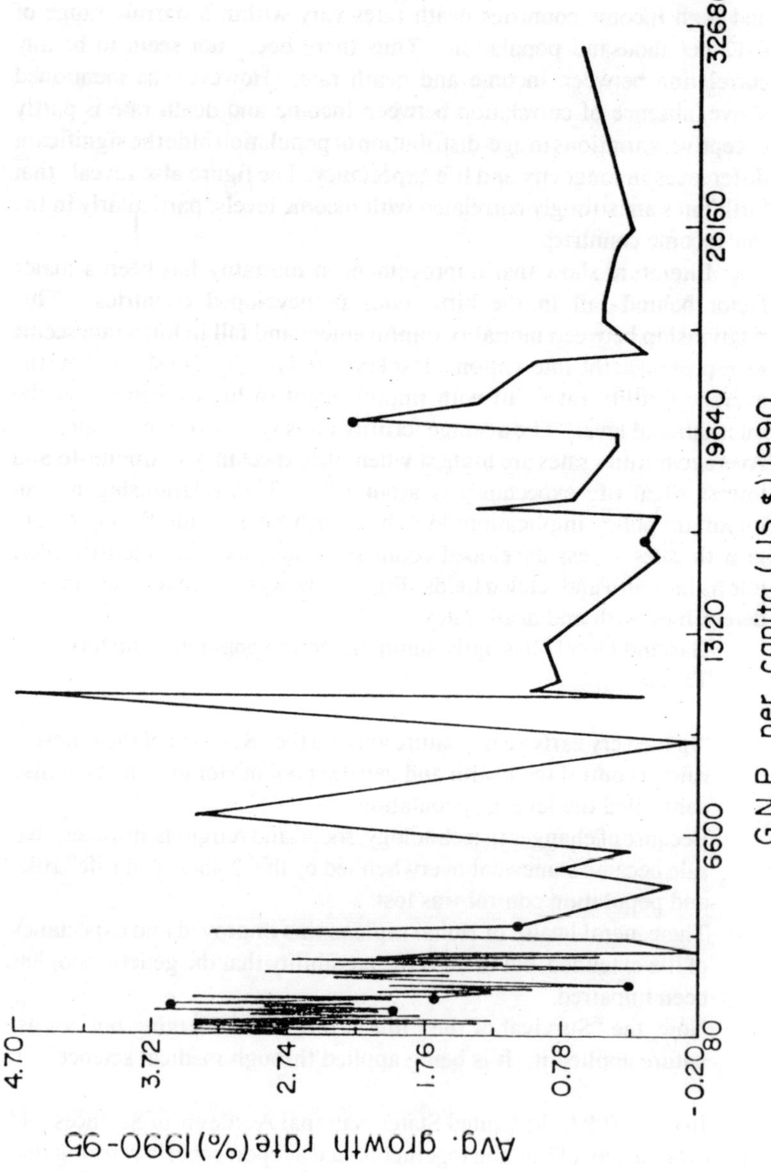

FIG. 2.1: Income *vs.* Growth Rate

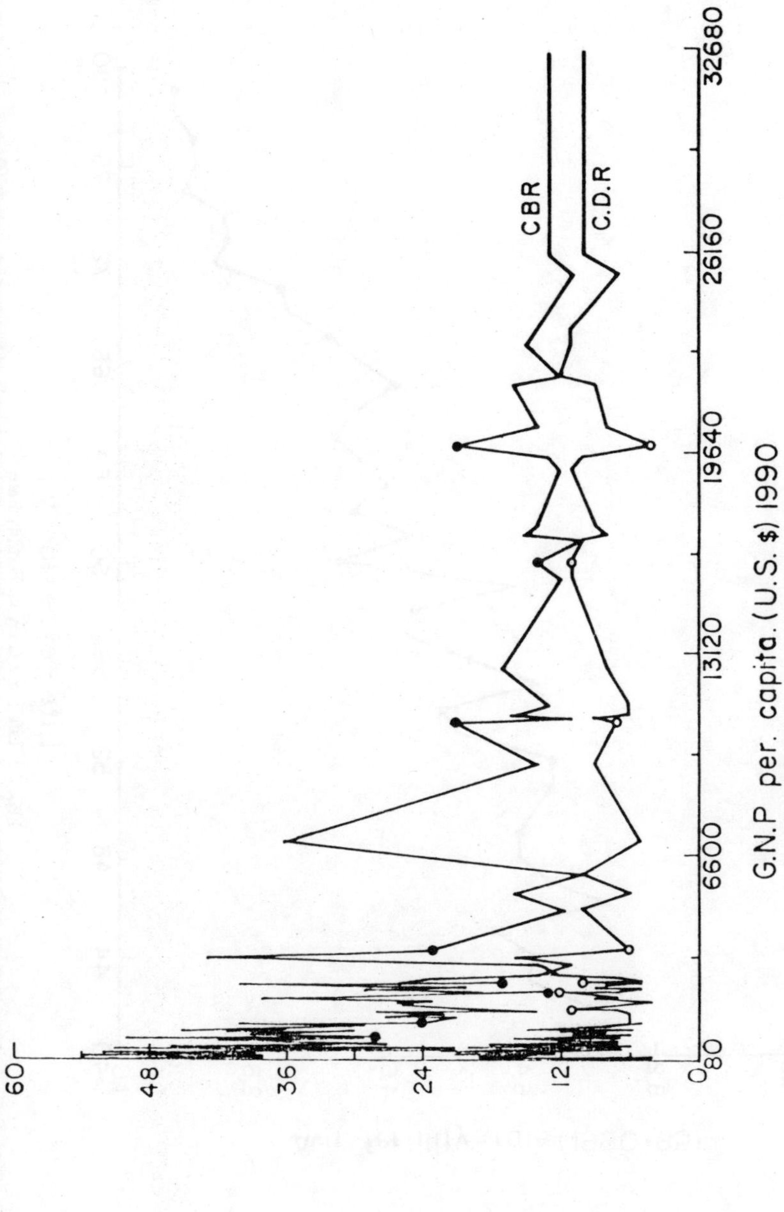

FIG. 2.2: Income *vs.* Death Rate and Birth Rate

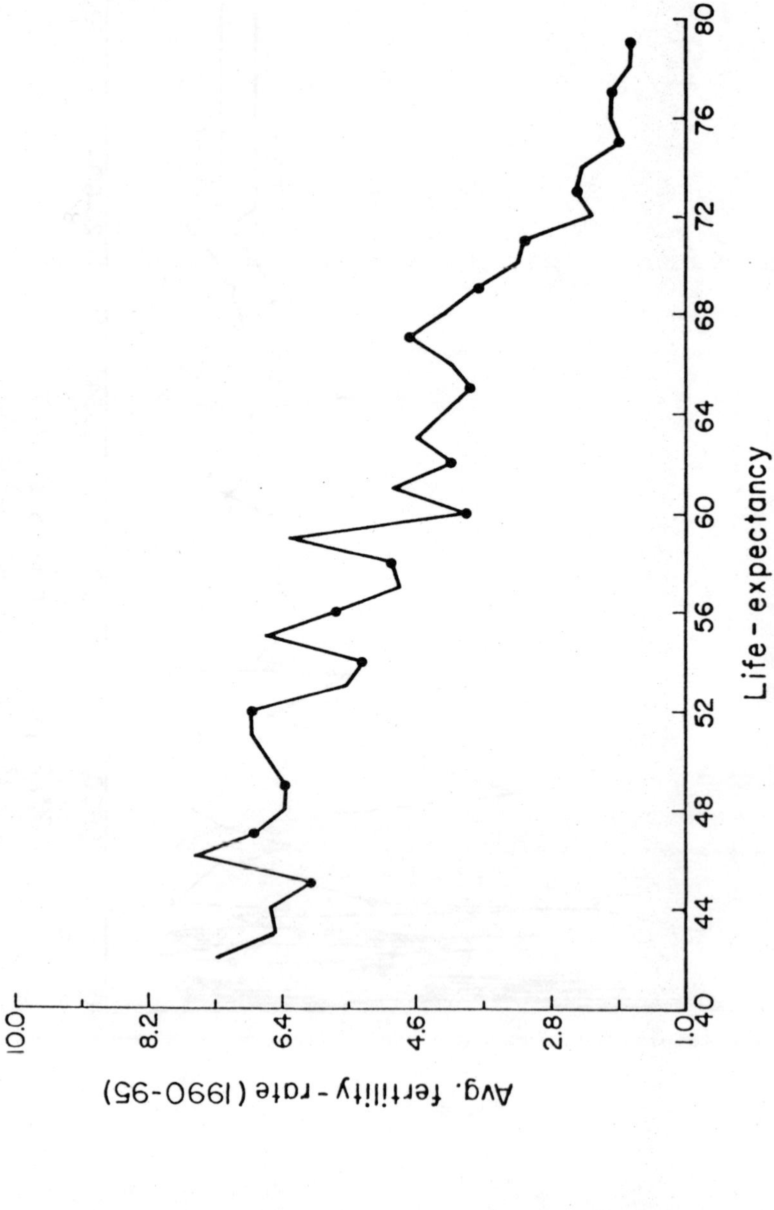

FIG. 2.3: Life Expectancy *vs.* Fertility Rate

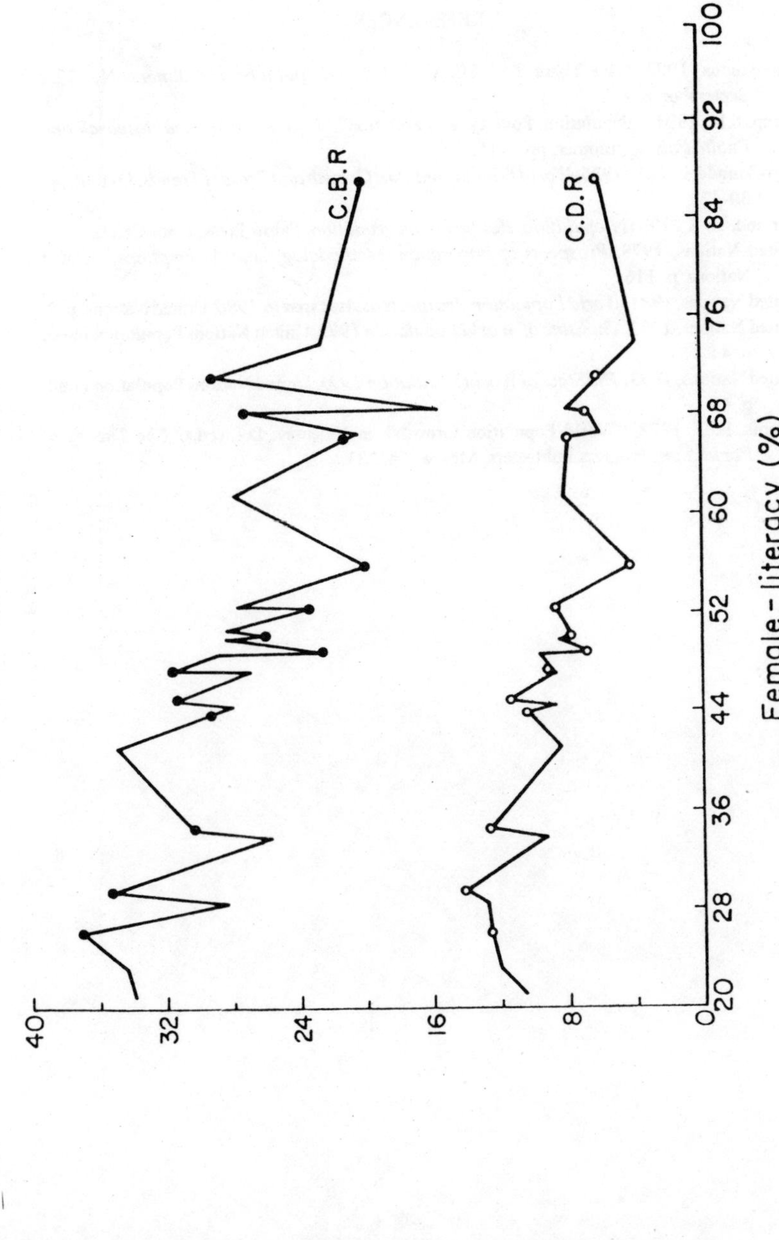

FIG. 2.4: Female Literacy *vs.* CDR & CBR

may not be able to prevent either irreversible degradation of the environment or continued poverty for much of the world" (Anoymous, 1993).

REFERENCES

Anonymous, 1993, "Are There Two Many of Us?", *Population Headliners,* No. 222, September, p. 4.

Camp, S.L., 1991, "Population, Poverty, and Pollution", *Forum for Applied Research and Public Policy,* Summer, pp. 5-15.

Carr-Saunders, A.M., 1936, *World Population: Past Growth and Present Trends,* Oxford, pp. 30-42

Garland, H. K,. 1991, *Population, Resources Degradation,* Palms Press, Dora Creek.

United Nations, 1979, *Prospects of Population: Methodology and Assumptions,* United Nations, p. 116.

United Nations, 1981, *World Population Prospects as Assessed in 1980,* United Nations, p. 2.

United Nations, 1992, *The State of World Population 1992,* United Nations Population Fund, p. 44.

United Nations, 1993, *The State of World Population 1993,* United Nations Population Fund. p. 48.

Urlanis, B.T., 1978, "World Population Growth", in Valentey, D.I. (ed.), *The Theory of Population,* Progress Publishers, Moscow, p. 231.

3

POPULATION OF INDIA

This chapter describes the nature of population movement in India. Readers know that Indian civilization is one of the oldest living civilizations. Thanks to favourable geographical and environmental factors Indian subcontinent has had a flourishing human culture for thousands of years. But we do not have records of distant past. *Vedas,* the oldest books of knowledge, epics, mythological and legal works, religious literature are all that we have to discern any socio-cultural pattern pertaining to ancient India. *Arthashastra* of Kautilya includes discussion on census operation, optimum size of locality and social-structure. *Vedas* include verses on values and social organisation. *Ramayana* and *Mahabharata* are other good literary sources which reveal values prevalent in ancient India. So are *Smritis* and *Shastras*. Yet it must be said that Indian culture did not place much emphasis on history. The central value in India was attached to transcendence. Therefore, the old literary and legal works do not help in construction of objective history of Indian civilization and population growth.

The first population census in India was conducted during the British period in 1872. It was, however, not synchronous. The first synchronous and nearly complete census was conducted in 1881. Since then India has had an impressive record of uninterrupted decadal censuses which have produced rich data on changes in size, composition and structure of population. In addition, in the recent past Sample Registration Scheme and family planning statistics have also yielded estimates of vital rates at national and State levels. This chapter presents estimates of population and data on population processes obtained from census and other sources.

Estimates of India's Population

The earliest period for which someone has estimated population of India is the period of *Mahabharata* War. Based on the description of the size of army that the two warring groups Pandavas and Kauravas had and an assumed persons-soldier ratio, Krishnan (1988) estimated the population of India at that time. The Pandava empire covered the present day territories of India, Pakistan and Bangladesh. The *Mahabharata* War has been dated around 3100 B.C. (Chandra, 1980). Krishnan has written that the Pandavas had seven *akshohinis* of army and the Kauravas eleven. Thus in all 18 *akshohinis* were involved in the war. An *akshohini* consists of 21,870 chariots, 21,870 elephants, 65,610 horses and 1,09,350 soldiers. The chariot-elephant-horse-soldier ratio is 1:1:3:5. Thus in the *Mahabharata* War, 18 times 1,09,350 soldiers (*i.e.* nearly 1.97 million) had taken part. By using the ratio of 15-20 persons to one soldier to reckon the population size, as suggested by Pran Nath, Krishnan has estimated that the population was in the range 29.6 — 39.4 million.

Davis, in his famous work, *The Population of India and Pakistan,* has presented estimates of India's population at various dates between 300 B.C. and 1871 (when the first population census was taken in India). These estimates are given in Table 3.1. Estimates show that after *Mahabharata* War population of ancient India merely trebled in 3,000 years. Also for dates up to A.D. 1845 estimates of India's population have remained within the limit suggested by Pran Nath for the year 300 B.C. They indicate that for more than 2000 years, up to 1845, India's population remained nearly stationary; it rose and fell within a narrow interval of 100-140 million.

TABLE 3.1: Estimates of India's Population, 300 B.C. - A.D. 1871

Date	Population (in millions)	Source
300 B.C.	100—140	Pran Nath
A.D. 1600	100	Moreland
A.D. 1800	120	Playfair (adjusted)
1834	130	M'Culloch
1845	130	M'Culloch
1855	175	Statistical Abstract of U.K. Possessions (adjusted)
1867	194	Parliamentary Papers (adjusted)
1871	255	Census (corrected)

Source: Davis, Kingsley, 1951, *The Population of India and Pakistan,* Princeton University Press, p. 25.

Davis has also estimated population of India and Pakistan in census years between 1871 and 1941. For the period between 1911 and 1941 his estimates match with the census returns. But for the period between 1871 and 1901 his estimates show that census returns suffered from undercount. The highest coverage error was present in the first census in 1871 (Table 3.2). Estimates show that between 1871—1941 the population of India increased from 255.2 million to 388.9 million, exhibiting an increase of 133.7 million in 70 years or an average increase of 1.91 million per year.

TABLE 3.2: Census Returns and Estimated Population, 1871-1941 (in millions)

Year	Census Population	Estimated Population
1871	203.4	255.2
1881	250.2	257.4
1891	279.6	282.1
1901	283.9	285.3
1911	303.0	302.98
1921	305.7	305.7
1931	338.2	338.2
1941	388.9	388.9

Source: Davis, Kingsley, 1951, *The Population of India and Pakistan,* Princeton University Press, p. 27.

In 1947 the British India and princely states were divided into two independent countries: India and Pakistan. Table 3.3 presents census data on growth of India's population from the beginning of this century. The table shows that in 1991 population of India was 844 million and it was growing at the rate of 2.11 per cent per year. In 1991, India's population constituted 16.0 per cent of the world population. There are three great dividing lines in the history of population growth in the present century. They are 1921, 1951 and 1981. Up to 1921 population grew at a very low rate. As a matter of fact during 1911-21 India's population declined by 0.31 per cent. It was due to the great influenza epidemic which broke out around 1918 and which affected most parts of India. On the whole during 1921-51, India's population grew at an average annual exponential rate close to 1 per cent. Although we do not have reliable national level statistics on vital rates during this period, estimates show that rise in life expectancy by more than 10 points (or fall in the death rate by more than 10 points) is the major cause of sustained growth of population at more than 1 per cent (Table 3.4.). In 1951, the Central Government in India started world's first government-sponsored family planning programme. Planners thought that with this the growth rate of population will start declining but contrary to all expectations growth rate started rising continuously reaching a peak in 1981. During 1951-91 the rate of growth of India's population remained above 2 per cent per year. This period is marked by fall in both fertility and mortality rates but mortality rate declined faster than fertility rate. The life expectancy had been rising constantly since 1921 and is expected to rise further (Table 3.5). But appreciable decline in fertility was noted only after 1976. After 1951, the 1991 Census has first time shown a declining rate of growth of India's population. Fig. 3.1 shows the growth of population in India during 1911-91.

TABLE 3.3: Population of India: 1901-91

Year	Population	Decadal Absolute	Growth per cent	Average annual exponential growth rate (per cent)	Progressive growth rate over 1901 (per cent)
1901	238,396,327	—	—	—	—
1911	252,093,390	+13,697,063	+5.75	0.56	+ 5.75
1921	251,321,213	- 772,177	-0.31	-0.03	+ 5.42
1931	278,977,238	+27,656,025	+11.00	1.04	+ 17.02
1941	318,660,580	+39,683,342	+14.22	1.33	+ 33.67
1951	361,088,090	+42,420,485	+13.31	1.25	+ 51.47
1961	439,234,771	+77,682,873	+21.51	1.96	+ 84.25
1971	548,159,652	+108,924,881	+24.80	2.20	+ 129.94
1981	683,329,097	+135,169,445	+24.66	2.22	+ 186.64
1991	843,930,861	+160,601,764	+23.50	2.11	+ 254.00

Source: Census of India, 1991, *Provisional Population Totals,* Paper-1 of 1991, Registrar General and Census Commissioner, India, p. 21.

At the turn of the last century in India, both birth and death rates were well above 40 per thousand population and, therefore, the rate of natural increase (birth rate-death rate) was low. As time passed death rate started declining. By 1941-51 death rate had declined to 27.4 thousand. The birth rate was still around 40 per thousand. The death rate declined more sharply after independence thanks to government efforts to provide good healthcare widely to rural population through the institution of primary healthcare. Economic development and increased rural prosperity also

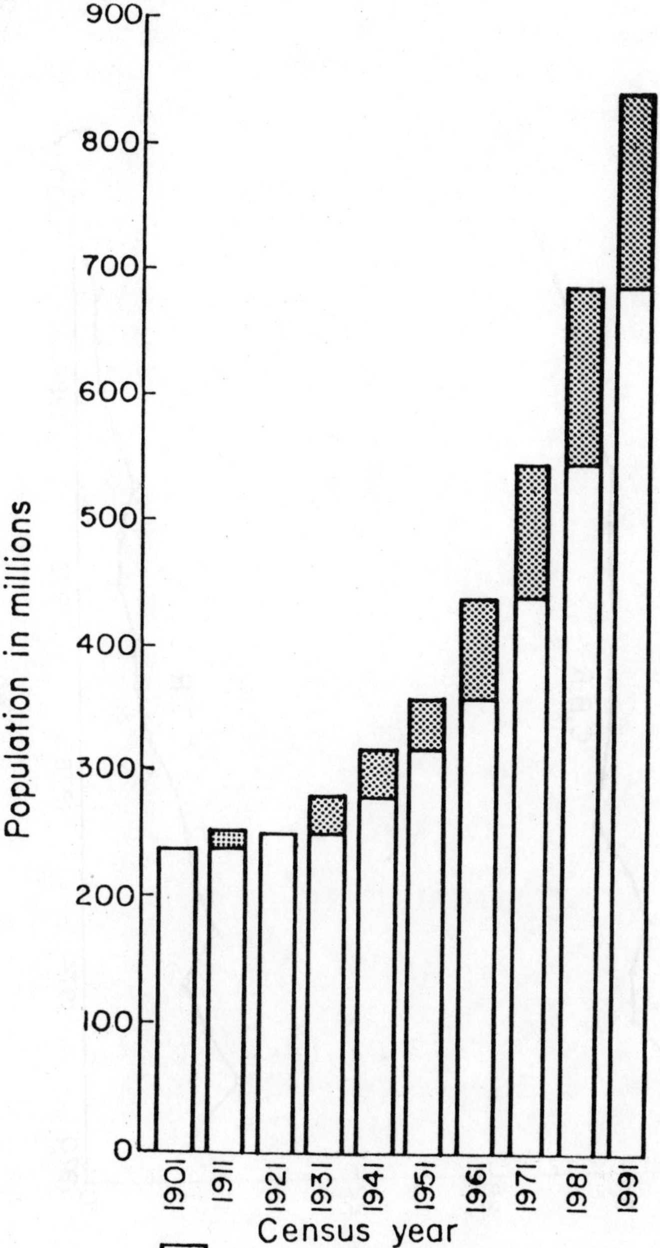

FIG. 3.1: Decadal Variation (Population)

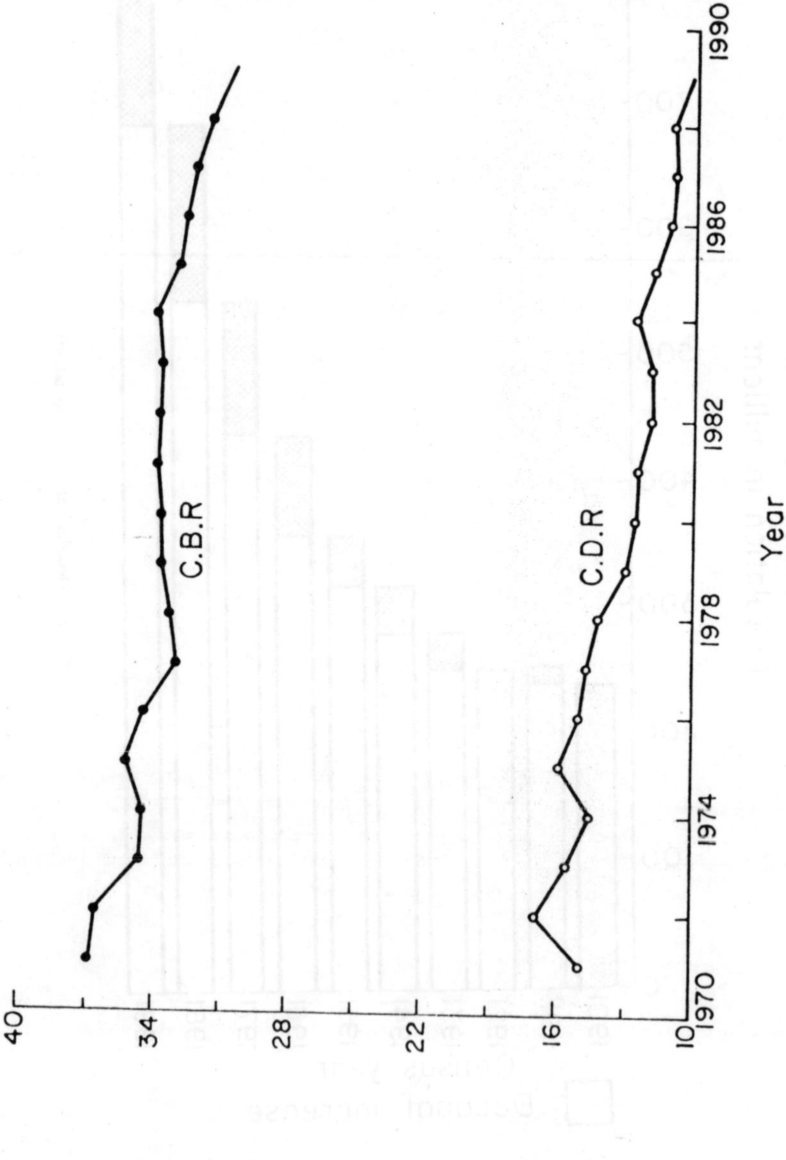

FIG. 3.2: CDR & CBR

helped in raising life expectancy. Estimates show that during 1971-81 death rate had already achieved a low level of 15.0 but the birth rate was still 37.2. Fig. 3.2 shows that although both birth and death rate have fallen after 1976, the gap between the two (*i.e.* the growth rate) has remained somewhat unchanged.

TABLE 3.4: Birth and Death Rates and Expectation of Life at Birth (Census Estimates)

Decade	Rate per 1000 population		Expectation of life (in years)		
	Birth	Death	Males	Females	Combined
1901-11	49.2	42.6	22.6	23.3	22.9
1911-21	48.1	47.2	19.4	20.9	20.0
1921-31	46.4	36.3	26.9	26.6	26.8
1931-41	45.2	31.2	32.1	31.4	31.8
1941-51	39.9	27.4	32.4	31.7	32.1
1951-61	41.7	22.8	41.9	40.6	41.3
1961-71	41.2	19.0	46.4	44.7	45.6
1971-81	37.2	15.0	50.9	50.0	50.5

Source: Ministry of Health and Family Welfare, 1991, *Family Welfare Programme in India: Year Book 1989-90,* Government of India, p. 113.

The Expert Committee on Population Projections projects that during 1991-96 the birth and death rates in India will be 27.5 and 9.4 per thousand respectively. The death rate will continue to decline further. In 2006 the death rate will be 7.8. In the same year birth rate will be 23.0 and the population will be growing at a rate of 1.5 per cent per year.

TABLE 3.5: Projected Values of Expectation of Life at Birth (e°_{o}), 1981-2001

Period	Projected values of expectation of life at birth (in years)		
	Males	Females	Combined
1980	54.1	54.7	54.4
1981-86	55.6	56.4	56.0
1986-91	58.1	59.1	58.6
1991-96	60.6	61.7	61.2
1996-2001	62.8	64.2	63.5
2001	64.1	65.6	64.9

Source: Report of the Expert Committee on Population Projections, quoted in Ministry of Health and Family Welfare, 1991, *Family Welfare Programme in India: Year Book 1989-90,* Government of India, p. 113.

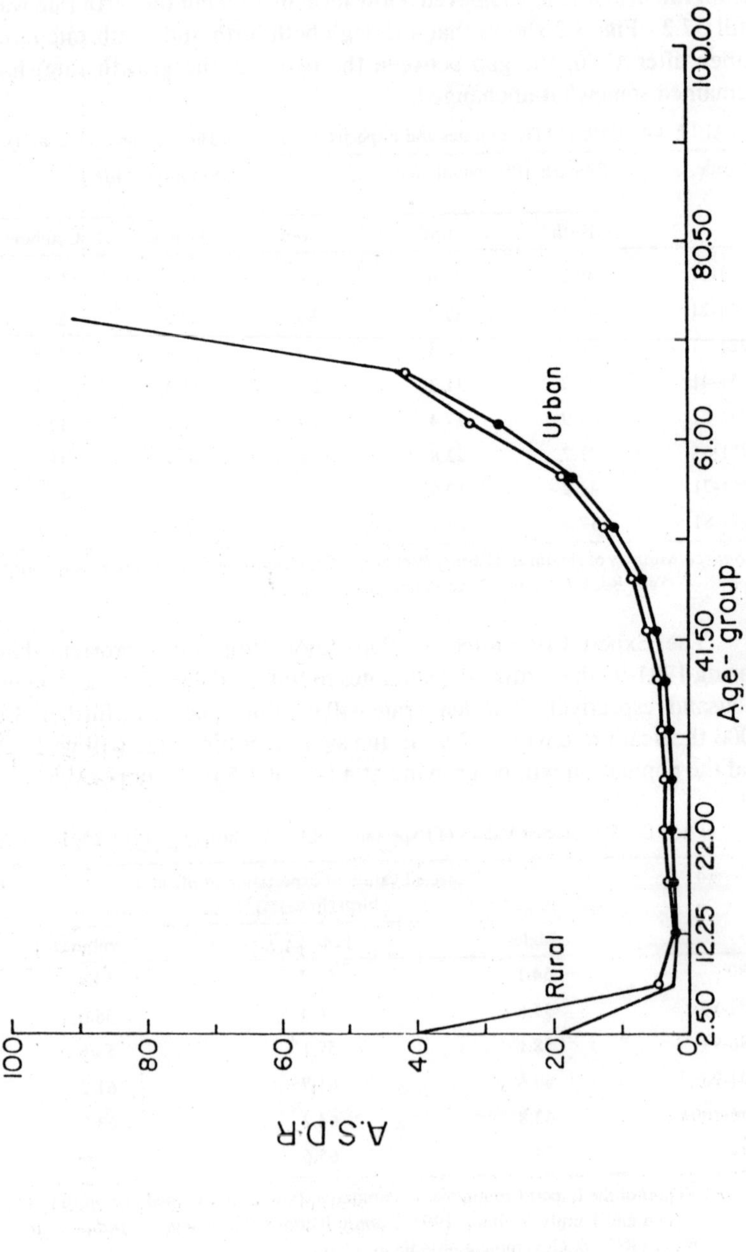

FIG. 3.3: ASDR (Rural & Urban)

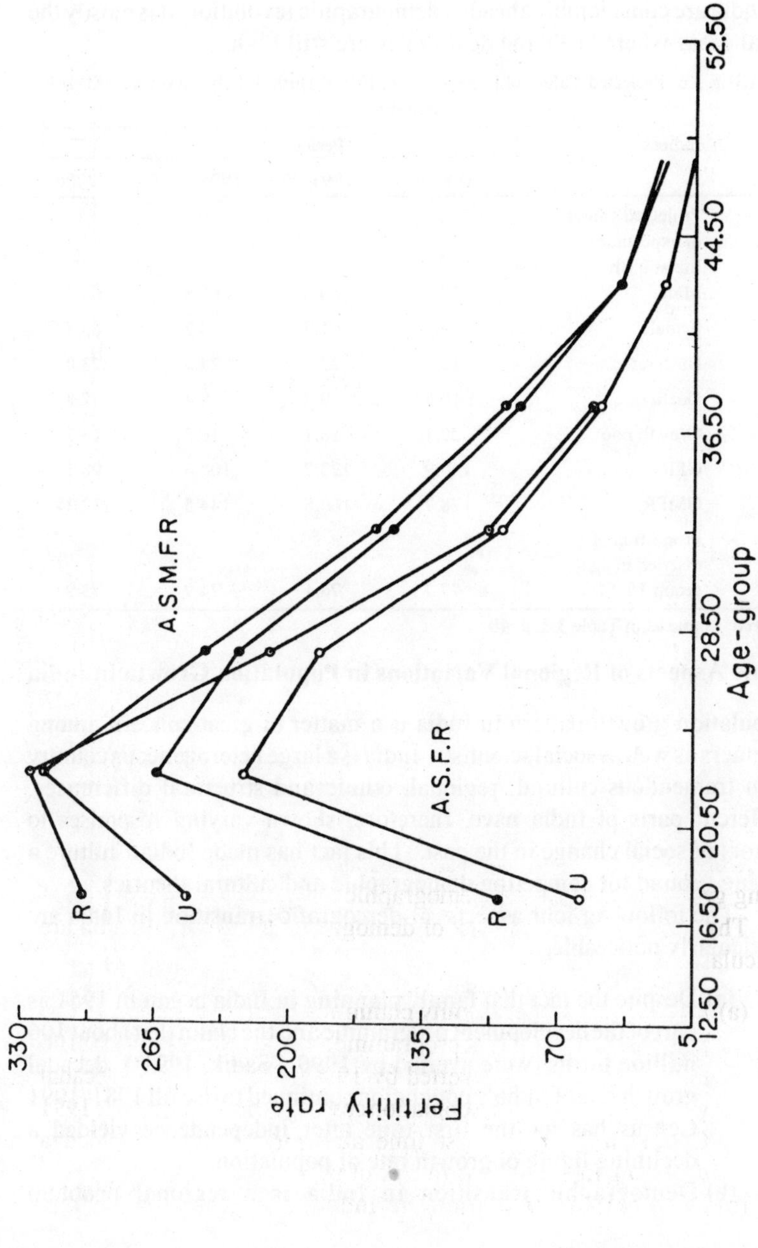

FIG. 3.4: ASFR & ASMFR

Fig. 3.3 shows the current pattern of mortality by age and urban-rural residence. Fig. 3.4 shows the age patterns of fertility and marital fertility separately for urban and rural areas. They clearly show that urban areas in India are considerably ahead in demographic revolution; it is mostly the rural areas where birth and death rates are still high.

TABLE 3.6: Projected Values of Expectation of Life at Birth, Likely Vital Rates, GMFR and GFR

	Indices	Period			
		1986-91	1991-96	1996-2001	2006
I.	Projected values of expectation of life at birth				
	Male	58.1	60.6	62.8	64.8
	Female	59.1	61.7	64.2	65.8
II.	Birth rate	30.9	27.5	24.9	23.0
III.	Death rate	10.8	9.4	8.4	7.8
IV.	Growth rate	20.1	18.1	16.5	15.2
V.	GFR	140.9	122.7	108.6	98.1
VI.	GMFR	178.7	160.8	144.5	132.3
VII.	Proportion of married in age-group 15-44	77.7	76.1	74.9	73.9

Source: Same as in Table 3.3, p. 40.

Some Aspects of Regional Variations in Population Growth in India

Population growth pattern in India is a matter of great concern among planners as well as social scientists. India is a large heterogeneous country with tremendous cultural, regional, ethnic and structural differences. Different parts of India have, therefore, shown varying responses to factors of social change in the past. This fact has made Indian culture a testing ground for competing demographic and cultural theories.

The following four aspects of demografic transition in India are particularly noticeable:

(a) Despite the fact that family planning in India began in 1951 as part of the development programme and the claim that about 106 million births were averted by 1990 (Sadik, 1991), decadal growth rate of India's population continued to rise till 1981. 1991 Census has for the first time after independence yielded a declining figure of growth rate of population.

(b) Demographic transition in India is a regional problem

(Ramabhadran, 1982).

(c) Kerala and Goa States of India have already achieved low levels of birth rate. These are two states in which more than 90 per cent females in the age group 6-14 years are attending school (NFHS, 1995).

(d) National performance in population control is low because of the relatively poor performance in fertility control in the States of Uttar Pradesh, Bihar, Rajasthan and Madhya Pradesh (Government of India, 1985).

Several attempts have been made in the past to explore causes of falling birth rate in Kerala. As a matter of fact, Kerala "experience" has given a new direction to the classical theory of demographic transition (Ratcliffe, 1983). However, few attempts have been made to relate fertility to historicity and develop a holistic understanding of the population growth.

Population totals of 1991 census provide an opportunity to examine growth rates of Indian States for the period 1901-91. Some findings of this examination, plain but hitherto neglected, are given below. Census data on percentage decadal variation during 1901-91 are shown in Table 3.7.

1. Till 1971 growth rate of population in Kerala continued to be higher than the growth rate of India's population. Also except during the decade 1931-41 decadal growth rate for Kerala continued to rise till 1971 when it achieved a level of 26.29 per cent. After that it declined to 19.24 during 1971-81, and further to 13.98 during 1981-91. It is notable that till 1981 Kerala had the highest density among all Indian States. We should ask a question: is fall in population growth rate in Kerala not caused by high population density? May demographic response of Kerala not be seen as response of the highest density State which had undergone the most rapid growth during preceding decades? Kerala's experience confirms the logistic growth theory quite well (Sorokin, 1928). The 1991 density of West Bengal is much higher than the 1991 density of Kerala. Should it be assumed that West Bengal will follow the Kerala line and yield a declining rate in the 2001 census? Urban fertility of West Bengal is already close to replacement level fertility.
2. Demographers have not paid as much attention to Tamil Nadu and Orissa as to Kerala. These are two other States in which 1981 census growth rates were as low as in Kerala. As a matter of fact growth rate of population in Tamil Nadu was lower than in Kerala. Tamil Nadu

does not have high density of population but it has high literacy. Orissa has low values of both density and literacy. Growth rates in these two States have declined further during 1981-91. It may be noted that net (out) migration for Orissa and Tamil Nadu has been lower than for Kerala (Table 3.8). Thus their low growth rate ensues from low value of natural increase rate only.

3. There has been a tendency among Indian demographers to put Bihar, Madhya Pradesh (M.P.), Uttar Pradesh (U.P.), and Rajasthan in the same category. Bose's acronym BIMARU has become quite popular for this group of States. Data show that there are significant differences between these States and it is not quite justified to place them in the same category. Till today population growth rate of Bihar has been lower than the growth rate of India, and even at this relatively lower level, growth rate has declined in the recent past. U.P. also had a lower growth rate than India till 1971. It was for the first time in 1981 that U.P. exhibited a higher growth rate than India. During 1981-91 population growth rate in U.P. has declined. This fall in growth rate began in U.P. at a level lower than the level at which Kerala entered the declining growth phase. M.P. exhibited higher growth rate than India during 1901-11, 1921-31 and after 1951, and a lower growth rate during 1911-21 and 1931-51. During the last census decade growth rate for M.P. has increased. On the other hand, Rajasthan has always had a higher growth rate than India except during the decade 1911-21 when its population declined faster than that of India. However, during 1981-91 growth rate for Rajasthan has declined quite significantly from 32.97 to 28.07. Among the BIMARU States U.P. and M.P. are outmigrating States and Bihar and Rajasthan are inmigrating States (Table 3.8.).

4. The highest rate of population growth is observed for the States of North-East. They are Arunachal Pradesh, Meghalaya, Mizoram, Nagaland and Tripura. Nagaland exhibits the highest rate. Except Tripura all of them have low density of population. Again there is no similarity between States of North-East India. The States comprising this zone are characterised by significant variation in patterns and problems of population (Sharma, 1986). The major source of population growth in this zone is migration. This has serious implications for ethnic composition of population in States.

Among Union Territories (UTs) all are growing at a fast rate. Delhi has the fastest rate followed by Andaman and Nicobar Islands and Chandigarh. Delhi and Chandigarh are metropolitan cities. They already have regionally mixed populations. But rapid growth caused by migration will disturb the ethnic composition of populations in the Union Territories and States of the North-East. Delhi and Chandigarh face the problem of constant rise in density of population.

5. During 1981-91 Himachal Pradesh showed one of the lowest decadal growth rates. Historically, except the decade 1911-21 when epidemics probably did not affect Himachal Pradesh as much as U.P., Bihar, M.P., Maharashtra, Orissa, Rajasthan and West Bengal, Himachal Pradesh had always been growing at a slower rate than India. Improvement in 1991 sex ratio and some data on migration (Table 3.8) show that it is a net inmigrating State. Studies are, therefore, needed to examine causes of low growth rate in Himachal Pradesh. Does it arise due to high mortality, low natural fertility or family planning?

6. Except Goa, Jammu and Kashmir, Karnataka, Punjab, Nagaland, Orissa, Sikkim, Daman and Diu, Lakshadweep, and Pondicherry all States and Union Territories had consistently higher or lower growth rates than India during census decades 1951-61 and 1961-71, which are indicative of trends before fertility transition began in India. Before the onset of the third or declining phase the States and Union Territories growing at faster rate than India were: Chandigarh, Andaman and Nicobar Islands, Tripura, Delhi, Dadra and Nagar Haveli, Mizoram, Manipur, Assam, Haryana, West Bengal, Meghalaya, Gujarat, Rajasthan, Kerala, Madhya Pradesh, and Maharashtra. (Table 3.9). The States with lower growth rates were:

TABLE 3.7: Percentage Decadal Variation in Population: 1901-11 to 1981-91

Sl. No.	India/State/ Union Territory	1901-11	1911-21	1921-31	1931-41	1941-51	1951-61	1961-71	1971-81	1981-91
1	2	3	4	5	6	7	8	9	10	11
	India	5.75	-0.31	11.00	14.22	13.31	21.51	24.80	24.66*	23.50
	States									
1.	Andhra Pradesh	12.49	-0.13	12.99	12.75	14.02	15.65	20.90	23.10	23.82
2.	Arunachal Pradesh	@	@	@	@	@	@	38.91	35.15	35.86
3.	Assam	16.99	20.48	19.91	20.40	19.93	34.98	34.95	23.36	23.58
4.	Bihar	3.67	-0.66	11.45	12.20	10.27	19.76	21.33	24.06	23.49
5.	Goa	2.36	-3.55	7.62	7.05	1.21	7.77	34.77	26.74	15.96
6.	Gujarat	7.79	3.79	12.92	19.25	18.69	26.88	29.39	27.67	20.80
7.	Haryana	-9.70	1.95	7.14	15.63	7.60	33.79	32.23	28.75	26.28

Contd.

1	2	3	4	5	6	7	8	9	10	11
8.	Himachal Pradesh	-1.22	1.65	5.23	11.54	5.42	17.87	23.04	23.71	19.39
9.	Jammu & Kahsmir	7.16	5.75	10.14	10.36	10.42	9.44	29.65	29.69	28.92.
10.	Karnataka	3.60	-1.09	9.38	11.09	19.36	21.57	24.22	26.75	20.69
11.	Kerala	11.75	9.16	21.85	16.04	22.82	24.76	26.29	19.24	13.98
12.	Madhya Pradesh	15.30	-1.38	11.39	12.34	8.67	24.17	28.67	25.27	26.75
13.	Maharashtra	10.74	-2.91	14.91	11.99	19.27	23.60	27.45	24.54	25.36
14.	Manipur	21.71	10.92	16.04	14.92	12.80	35.04	37.53	32.46	28.56
15.	Meghalaya	15.71	7.21	13.83	15.59	8.97	27.03	31.50	32.04	31.30
16.	Mizoram	10.64	7.90	26.42	22.81	28.42	35.61	24.93	48.55	35.50
17.	Nagaland	46.78	8.55	12.62	6.04	8.60	14.07	39.88	50.05	66.86
18.	Orissa	10.44	-1.94	11.94	10.22	6.38	19.82	25.05	20.17	19.50
19.	Punjab	-10.78	6.26	12.02	19.82	-4.58	21.56	21.70	23.89	20.26
20.	Rajasthan	6.70	-6.29	14.14	18.01	15.20	26.20	27.83	32.97	28.07
21.	Sikkim	48.98	-7.05	34.37	10.67	13.34	17.76	29.38	50.77	27.57
22.	Tamil Nadu	8.57	3.47	8.52	11.91	14.66	11.85	22.30	17.50	14.94
23.	Tripura	32.48	32.59	25.63	34.14	24.56	78.71	36.28	31.92	33.69
24.	Uttar Pradesh	-0.97	-3.08	6.66	13.57	11.82	16.66	19.78	25.49	26.16
25.	West Bangal	6.25	-2.91	8.14	22.93	13.22	32.80	26.87	23.17	24.55
	Union Territories									
1.	A & N Islands	7.34	2.37	8.78	14.61	-8.28	105.19	81.17	63.93	47.29
2.	Chandigarh	-16.07	-1.65	9.10	14.11	7.47	394.13	114.59	75.55	41.36
3.	Dadra & Nagar Haveli	19.52	6.99	23.23	5.70	2.70	39.56	27.96	39.78	35.63
4.	Daman & Diu	1.45	-3.26	15.98	17.52	13.55	-24.56	70.85	26.07	28.45
5.	Delhi	1.98	18.03	30.26	44.27	90.00	52.44	52.93	53.00	50.64
6.	Lakshadweep	4.85	-6.31	17.62	14.43	14.60	14.61	31.95	26.53	28.40
7.	Pondicherry	4.39	-5.06	5.93	10.20	11.31	16.34	27.81	28.15	38.60

* In 1981, Census was not conducted in Assam. Based on the 1971 Census population and the 1991 Census provisional results the population of Assam for 1981 has been interpointed. As a consequence of the revised estimates for Assam for the year 1981, the total population of India as of 1981 has been estimated as 683,329,097 as against earlier published figure of 685,184,692. Hence the revised decadal growth rate for India during 1971-81 has been estimated as 24.66 per cent.

@ In Arunachal Pradesh the Census was conducted for the first time in 1961. Hence the growth rates for earlier decades are not available.

TABLE 3.8: Components of Population Growth, 1971-81 (per cent)

State	Annual rates				
	Population	Natural increase	Net migration	Decadal CBR	Change in CDR
Andhra Pradesh	1.59	1.86	-0.27	-6.20	-28.80
Assam	2.22	1.84	0.38	-7.90	-32.00
Bihar	1.90	1.84	0.06	18.00	-6.20
Gujarat	2.04	2.31	-0.27	-9.50	-24.70
Haryana	1.98	2.58	-0.60	-10.10	-28.80
H.P.	2.19	2.08	0.11	-10.90	-29.10
J & K	2.15	2.22	-0.07	-2.90	-16.40
Karnataka	1.75	1.72	0.03	-10.20	-26.80
Kerala	1.46	1.97	-0.52	-13.70	-25.30
Maharashtra	1.63	1.70	-0.07	-4.80	-27.50
M.P.	1.77	2.16	-0.39	-1.80	-6.60
Orissa	1.49	1.66	-0.17	-5.20	-24.30
Punjab	1.62	2.08	-0.46	-12.50	-23.40
Rajasthan	2.48	2.19	0.29	-7.80	-17.70
Tamil Nadu	1.25	1.59	-0.34	-12.00	-22.50
U.P.	1.30	2.17	-0.87	-9.40	-25.30
West Bangal	1.87	2.13	-0.26	9.60	-10.00

Source: Krishnaji and Sekhar (1991).

TABLE 3.9: Growth Rates of States and Union Territories before and after Fertility Transition in India

Rate	Rate after fertility transition (after 1971)		
before fertility transition (before 1971)	High growth	Low growth	Erratic growth
High growth	Chandigarh, A & N Islands, Tripura, Delhi, D & N Haveli, Mizoram, Manipur, Haryana, Meghalaya, Rajasthan, Madhya Pradesh	Kerala	Assam, West Bengal, Gujarat, Maharashtra
Low growth	Uttar Pradesh	Bihar, Himachal Pradesh, Tamil Nadu	Andhra Pradesh
Erratic growth	J & K, Nagaland, Sikkim, Daman & Diu, Lakshadweep, Pondicherry	Orissa, Punjab	Goa, Karanataka

Bihar, Himachal Pradesh, Uttar Pradesh, Andhra Pradesh and Tamil Nadu. After the transition situation changed. It is notable that Kerala and Uttar Pradesh constitute two different classes of phenomena. Kerala grew faster than India before the transition and slower afterwards, U.P. grew slower than India before the transition and faster afterwards. Growth rates in Assam, West Bengal, Gujarat, Maharashtra, Andhra Pradesh, Goa and Karnataka are erratic, i.e., their relationship with the growth rate of India was not the same in tow decades, 1971-81 and 1981-91. Kerala, Bihar, Himachal Pradesh, Tamil Nadu, Orissa and Punjab are the six States which have exhibited consistently lower growth than India after 1971. However, there are wide variations in the growth rates of these states and the low growth in these States may have been caused by different sets of circumstances. Demographic transition in India is a complex regional problem. There is a need to collect socio-economic and anthropological data to explore transition dynamics of India's population at national and sub-national levels.

Bose (1991) has divided States and Union Territories in India into six zones: (a) demographically vulnerable States, (b) demographically progressive States, (c) special category States, (d) city-dominated States and UTs, (e) islands, and (f) residual UTs. Within each zone again there are sub-zones. In the zone of demographically vulnerable States eight States are included. They are Bihar, Uttar Pradesh, Rajasthan, Madhya Pradesh, Orissa, Assam, West Bengal and Haryana. These States have 56.08 per cent population of India (Table 3.10). Among them the first four (*i.e.*, Bihar, U.P., Rajasthan and M.P.) are socio-economically as well as demographically backward. Orissa has a low growth rate but due to its high infant mortality and other forms of demographic misery it is included in the category of vulnerable States. Assam and West Bengal are vulnerable because of illegal migration from Bangladesh. West Bengal also attracts migrants from other states. It has highest density of population and the primate city of Calcutta is decaying. Finally, Haryana is unique. It has low death rate and the second highest per capita income among all the Indian States. Yet its birth rate is very high. Status of women is very low in Harayana as shown by female literacy rate, age at marriage, the gap between male and female literacy rates, etc.

Kerala, Tamil Nadu, Karnataka, Andhra Pradesh, Maharashtra, Gujarat, Punjab and Himachal Pradesh are included in the category of demographically progressive States. They have 40.41 per cent population of India. Interestingly the Vindhyachal mountain range divides India not

TABLE 3.10: Demographic Zones and Sub-Zones

	Category of States		Proportion of population to total population
1.	Demographically Vulnerable States (DVS)		
	1.11	Bihar	39.72
	1.12	Uttar Pradesh	
	1.13	Rajasthan	
	1.14	Madhya Pradesh	
	1.21	Orissa	
	1.22	Assam	14.43
	1.23	West Bengal	
	1.30	Haryana	1.93
			56.08
2.	Demographically Progressive States (DPS)		
	2.11	Kerala	
	2.12	Tamil Nadu	23.20
	2.13	Karnataka	
	2.14	Andhra Pradesh	
	2.21	Maharashtra	14.21
	2.22	Gujarat	
	2.31	Punjab	3.00
	2.32	Himachal Pradesh	40.48
3.	Special Category States (SCS)		
	3.10	Jammu & Kashmir	0.91
	3.21	Sikkim	
	3.22	Arunachal Pradesh	
	3.23	Nagaland	
	3.24	Manipur	1.12
	3.25	Mizoram	
	3.26	Tripura	
	3.27	Meghalaya	2.03
4.	City- Dominated States & UTs (CDS)		
	4.1	Delhi	
	4.2	Goa	1.42
	4.3	Pondicherry	
	4.4	Chandigarh	1.42
5.	Islands (ISL)		
	5.1	Andaman & Nicobar Island	
	5.2	Lakshadweep	0.04
			0.04
6.	Residual UTs (RUT)		
	6.1	Dadra & Nagar Haveli	
	6.2	Daman & Diu	0.02
			0.02
			100.00

Source: Bose, Ashish, 1991, *Demographic Diversity of India: 1991 Census State and District Level Data: A Reference Book,* B. R. Publishing Corporation ; New Delhi, pp. 12-13.

only geographically but also demographically. On the south of the Vindhyachal birth rates are lower, sex-ratios are less distorted, female literacy rate is better and status of women is higher than in the north.

Special category States, viz. Jammu & Kashmir, Sikkim, Arunachal Pradesh, Nagaland , Manipur, Mizoram, Tripura and Meghalaya are those which have their own special problems. All of them need to be considered separately . They have 2.03 per cent of India's population. Often their problems arise from physical inaccessibility, smallness of population size and nearness to international border . City dominated States require special environmental programmes to stall environmental degradation arising out of overcrowding. Among islands and residual UTs also geographical rather than demographic factors dominate .

Implications of Population Growth

There are several implications of the rapid population growth and regional defferentials. In economic terms rapid population growth implies low rate of capital formation and, thus, low growth of income. It also implies large supply of labour force and higher rates of unemployment. In social terms rapid population growth implies greater competition leading to more intense social conflicts, higher speed of urbanisation, greater. impediments to social development and anarchy . In environmental terms it implies higher rates of deforestation, mining of natural resources , water logging , extension of agricultural land, intensive farming , pollution and reduced chances of sustainable development .

One thing is clear. For several decades the country will continue to experience high growth rate. Demographers say that even after achieving the net reproduction rate (NRR) of 1, population continues to grow for several decades due to population momentum. According to the U. N. medium projections, assuming that the replacement fertility in India is achieved by AD 2020-25 when each woman will bear one girl on average in her lifetime, India will have a larger population than China in AD 2035. It will be close to 1,545 million. India's natural growth rate is currently around 1.95 per cent per annum. With this high growth rate and large size , india's population is likely to cross 1.7 billion before achieving zero growth (Pathak, 1993). Therefore in planning for development it is imperative that strategies of development are so evolved that they are based on due recognition of high population growth rates.

Regional differentials in population growth are equally significant. Majority of large States with high rate of population growth are backward States. Due to both population longages and resources shortages (Hardin, 1991) development gap between States may widen further. For similar reasons, socio-economic differentials between ethnicities, status groups, urban-rural areas and classes may also widen. These differences will give rise to social tensions and political instability. It has become much clearer than ever before that population growth in India is a serious socio-economic and political issue and that it has to be dealt with effectively and urgently.

Characteristics of India's Population

Characteristics of population are described in terms of measurements of demographic and socio-economic variables. Among the demographic variables we may include sex-ratio (*i.e.* male-female ratio), proportion of population in different age groups, nuptiality patterns, birth and death rates, etc. Socio-economic variables include religious, linguistic and ethnic composition, literacy, urbanisation, labour force and its occupational and industrial classification, income, etc. Recently, new concept of development has stressed health and morbidity patterns, infant mortality rate and life expectancy at birth (separately among males and females)

Table 3.11 presents data on demographic characteristics of India and some selected other countries of the world. India is world's second largest country and more than 16 per cent world population is living in India. The table exhibits that India's population during 1980-90 grew at a higher rate than the world population. Its N.R.R. is expected to reach unity in year 2015. Its stationary size would be 1,862 million. Thus it is expected to double before reaching the stationary state. Regarding age distribution, the table shows that in India 36.9 per cent population is in the age group 0-14 years, 58.7 per cent in the age group 15-64 years and therefore, 4.4 per cent in the age group 65 + years. In the developed countries percentage population in 0-14 years is only half of that in India. The main reason behind the discrepancy between low income and high income countries in percentage children (0-14 years) lies in the fall in the birth rate, though the fall in the death rate also raises average age of population.

Among the social characteristics sex ratio is of utmost importance. Generally, sex ratio is defined as number of males per 1000 females but in India it is conventionally defined as number of females per 1000 males. According to the 1991 Census sex ratio of India is 929 females per 1000 males. This shows a shortage of 71 females per 1000 males. This shortage of females can in principle be due to: (a) higher mortality among females than among males, (b) higher emigration of females than males, (c) low birth ratė, and (d) errors in census data. In India, the imbalance between population of males and females is due to sex-differentials in mortality and possibly due to errors in census data. As caused by changes in sex-differentials in mortality, changes in imbalance in sex ratio may be seen as indicator of deterioration or improvement in status of women. Table 3.12 presents data on sex ratio in India during 1901-91. It shows that at the turn of the last century sex ratio in India was 972. During 1901-71

TABLE 3.11: Demographic Charactristics of Population of Selected Countries

Country/ World	Population 1990 (million)	Average annual growth rate of population 1980-90	Hypothetical size of stationary population (million)	Assumed year of reaching net reproduction rate of 1	Age-structure 1990(%) 0-14 years	15-64 years
1. Bangladesh	107	2.3	257	2015	42.9	54.0
2. India	850	2.1	1,862	2015	36.9	58.7
3. Pakistan	112	3.1	399	2030	44.2	53.0
4. Philippines	61	2.4	137	2010	39.9	56.8
5. Colombia	32	2.0	63	2000	35.4	60.6
6. Poland	38	0.7	50	1990	25.1	64.9
7. Malaysia	18	2.6	44	2015	38.3	58.1
8. Australia	17	1.5	24	2030	22.1	67.1
9. United States	250	0.9	317	2030	21.6	66.1
10. Sweden	9	0.3	9	2030	17.4	64.6
11. Japan	124	0.6	114	2030	18.4	69.7
World	5,284	1.7	—	—	32.3	61.1

Source: The World Bank, 1992, *World Development Report 1992,* Oxford University Press.

TABLE 3.12: Sex Ratio In India, 1901-91

Census Year	Sex ratio
1901	972
1911	964
1921	955
1931	950
1941	945
1951	946
1961	941
1971	930
1981	934
1991	929

Source: Same as in Table 3.3.

it declined more or less continuously to a low level of 930. In this period life expectancy had been rising constantly. Sex ratio declined becuase males benefitted much more from mortality improvement programmes than females. Between 1971-81 sex ratio improved by 4 points when life expectancy of females reached a level higher than that for males. In the last decade again sex ratio has declined. This decline is perhaps due to sex determination tests, leading to selective abortions of females babies, age-pattern of mortality and errors in census data.

Table 3.13 exhibits that as compared to developed countries India's record in social indicators, *e.g.* literacy, life expectancy and maternal mortality rate is dismal. However, it is somewhat better than in the neighbouring countries such as Bangladesh and Pakistan. There is a mismatch in male-female difference in life expectancy between the World Bank figures and the Govenment of India figures (Table 3.6). Several sources show that female life expectancy in India is now slightly higher than male expectancy. The World Bank figures should be interpreted with caution.

TABLE 3.13: Social characteristics of Population of Selected Countries

Country/ World	Primary enrollment rate 1989 (%)	Adult illiteracy 1990		Life expectancy (years) 1990		Meternal mortality rate (per 100,000 live births) 1980
		Female	Total	Female	Male	
1. Bangladesh	70	78	65	51	52	600
2. India	98	66	52	58	60	500
3. Pakistan	38	79	65	55	56	600
4. Philippines	111	11	10	66	62	80
5. Colombia	107	14	13	72	66	130
6. Poland	99	—	—	75	67	12
7. Malaysia	96	30	22	72	68	59
8. Australia	106	*	*	80	74	11
9. United States	-	*	*	80	73	9
10. Sweden	104	*	*	81	75	4
11. Japan	102	*	*	82	76	15
World	105	45	35	67	64	—

* Less than 5 per cent

Source: Same as in Table 3.11.

Table 3.14 presents data on some economic characteristics of population of the selected countries. India has a low per capita income of 350 dollars. As a matter of fact among 125 countries for which the World Bank has compiled data, India's rank is 21 (from the bottom). Mozambique with a per capita income of 80 dollars has rank 1. The ratio of India's per capita income to that of the world is 1 to 12. The ratio of India's per capita income to that of Japan is 1 to 70. During 1965-90 India's per capita income has grown at a rate of 1.9 per cent per year, a rate higher than the average rate of growth of the world. Also during this period India had more controlled inflation. Still if India continues to make progress at this level, she will take about 40 years to reach the present day economic standard of Philippines and more than 120 years to reach the present day economic standard of Jamaica or Turkey. In our times economic growth has been confined to industrialised nations. For many India is poor because it is still an agricultural country. As much as 31 per cent of the GDP in India comes from agricultural sector. The distribution of income is far form being equal. Although better than in many poor as well as rich countries, in

TABLE 3.14: Economic characteristics of Population of Selected Countries

Country/ World	GNP per capita 1990 (dollars)	Average annual growth rate of GNP per capita 1965-90	Average annual rate of infla-tion 1980-90 (%)	Share of agriculture in GDP 1990	Share of households income, latest		Urbanisation 1990 (%)
					Lowest	Highest	
1. Bangladesh	210	0.7	9.6	38	10.0	37.2	16
2. India	350	1.9	7.9	31	8.1	41.4	27
3. Pakistan	380	2.5	6.7	26	7.8	45.6	32
4. Philippines	730	1.3	14.9	22	5.5	48.0	43
5. Colombia	1,260	2.3	24.8	17	4.0	53.0	70
6. Poland	1,690	—	54.3	14	9.7	35.2	62
7. Malaysia	2,320	4.0	1.6	28*	4.6	51.2	43
8. Australia	17,000	1.9	7.4	4	4.4	42.2	86
9. United States	21,790	1.7	3.7	3*	4.7	41.9	75
10. Sweden	23,660	1.9	7.4	3	8.0	36.9	84
11. Japan	25,430	4.1	1.5	3	8.7	37.5	77
World	4,200	1.5	14.7	10*	—	—	50

* For 1965

Sources: Same as in Table 3.11.

terms of inequality India's situation is worse than countries such as Poland,Japan. Lastly her level of urbanisation is only 27 per cent, nearly half of that of the world population.

Lastly, the latest demographic estimates for India for the year 1993 are summarised below. They are prepared by the ESCAP Population division of the United Nations.

Mid-1993 population (million)	896.5	Projected population in 2010 (million)	1,189.4
Average annual growth rate (percentage)	1.9	doubling time (years)	37
CBR (per 1,000)	30	Per capita income (U.S. $)	330
CDR (per 1,000)	10		
Total fertility rate	3.8		
Infant mortality rate	86		
Life expectancy (years)			
Males	60		
Females	61		
Percentage aged 0-14	35		
Percentage aged 60 +	7		
Dependency ratio (Population aged 0-14 + Population aged 60 +) / Population aged 15-59 x 100	75		
Density (persons per km²)	273		
Percentage urban	26		
Annual growth rate of urban population (%)	2.9		

REFERENCES

Bose, Ashish, 1991. *Demographic Diversity of India: State and District Level Data,* B.R. Publishing Corporation, Delhi, pp.3-18.

Census of India, 1991, *Provisional Population Totals,* Registrar General and Census Commissioner, India.

Chandra, A.N., 1980, *The Rig Vedic Culture and the Indus Civilization,* Ratna Prakashan,

Calcutta.

Davis, Kingsley, 1951, *The Population of India and Pakistan,* Princeton University Press, p. 27.

Government of India, 1985, *Seventh Five Year Plan 1985-90,* Government of India Press, New Delhi.

Hardin, Garrett, 1991, "From Shortage to Longage: Forty Years in Population Vineyards", *Population and Environment,* Vol. 12, No. 3, pp. 339-49.

Krishnaji, N. and Satya Sekhar, P., 1991, "Population and Agricultural Growth", *Economic and Political Weekly,* Vol. 26, No. 26.

Krishnan, P., 1988, Historical Demography through Literature: A Preliminary Report on Indian Historical Demography", *Demography India,* Vol. 17, No.2, pp.189-96.

Ministry of Health and Family Welfare, 1991, *Family Welfare Programme in India: Year Book 1989-90,* Government of India, p. 113.

National Family Health Survey 1992-93, 1995, *India,* International Institute for Population Sciences, Bombay.

Pathak, K.B. 1993, "Population Challange in India". *The Sunday Times of India,* July 11, p. 12.

Pethe, V.P., 1982, "Changes in Size and Growth of Population", in United Nations (ed.), *Population of India,* United Nations, New York, p. 26.

Ramabhadran, 1982, "India: 1981 Census of India", *Asian-Pacific Population Programme News,* Vol. 11. No. 4, p. 38.

Ratcliffe, J.W., 1983, "Toward a Social Justice Theory of Demographic Transition: Lessons from India's Kerala State", *Janasamkhya,* Vol. 1, No. 1, pp.1-38.

Sadik, Nafis, 1991, "State of World Population Report," *Popline,* Vol. 13, p. 4.

Sharma, A.K., "Population of North Eastern Zone of India", in B.Datta Ray (ed.). *The Patterns and Problems of Population in North-East India,* Uppal Publishing House, New Delhi, pp. 51-62.

Sorokin, P.A., 1928, *Contemporary Sociological Theories,* Harper & Row, New York, p. 379.

4

DEMOGRAPHIC PROBLEMS, MODELS AND TECHNIQUES

Demography is one of the most developed disciplines among social sciences in India. As a matter of fact some consider demography to be a science rather than a social science. It is because demography enjoys quantitative methods more than other social sciences such as sociology, economics, psychology and anthropology. Like any other science (or social science) it has had its own paradigms; it has its own problems, programmes and biases. In this chapter an attempt is made to reflect on theories, models, techniques and problems of demographic data. The discussion presented here is, however, indicative of the broad trends in theories and models and it does not provide a comprehensive review of works done in various branches of demography, *e.g.* fertility, mortality, migration, population theory, etc.

DEMOGRAPHIC TRANSITION THEORY

Theory is a set of statements that provides an explanatory framework. Therefore, theory must relate to certain issues. Obviously, there is no theory of physics. Rather there are theories of various physical phenomena in physics. So at the outset we may say that there is no theory of demography as such. A large number of theories have been developed to explain problems in demography. Yet there are certain ideas which guide important works of research in any age in a discipline. Demographic transition theory is one such idea prevailing in the demographic community in India. In this chapter, we will use the term theory for this idea. Further, demographers have suggested certain "theories" to interpret data on specific aspects of demographic transition and systems of conceptual tools to analyse or predict various demographic phenomena. We will use the terms hypotheses and models for them. Thus a demographic hypothesis is an idea or a statment about some demographic event which is subject to empirical validation or falsification. Demographic models are isomorphic and theoretical representations built to measure, analyse, simulate or predict some specific demographic processes.

Pre-History of Demographic Transition Theory

Before independence there was no national population policy in the sense of having a deliberate intervention in the natural reproductive processes in India. Individually, however, in 1920s Dr. R.D. Karve and Shri P.K. Wattal brought the problems of family planning and population growth to the attention of masses and government. It was in the same period that first government operated birth control clinic in the world was opened in Mysore, then a princely state in the Indian Union. Subsequently, the National Planning Commitee of the Indian National Congress supported promotion of family planning as a state policy strongly (Sharma, 1985).

Mahatma Gandhi, the father of the nation, was a great supporter of the idea of population control. He felt that in his time birth control had become a religious duty. In his views, to solve political problems of India population control was necessary (Sharma, 1991). He often wrote and spoke on population control. He even hypothesised a connection between social change and fertility. He said that middle class had higher fertility than the labouring class and the reason for this was the process of Westernisation. The first Prime Minister, Pt. Jawaharlal Nehru, was also a great supporter of population control. Yet unlike Gandhi, who valued only *brahmacharya*, Nehru had accepted modern contraceptive methods also. In his direction in 1952 Government of India started world's first government sponsored family planning programme in India. In his famous work, *Discovery of India,* he observed that birth rates were falling widely in developed countries. He suggested that motivation to maintain higher standard and rise of individualism were behind the fertility transition (Nehru, 1972). Mukherjee (1930,1933), an eminent sociologist, had written widely on population trends and their implications and on the theory of optimum population.

Among the intellectuals in 1950s there existed a fierce debate on applicability of Malthusian and Marxist theories of development. Although in the Malthusian and Marxian theories speculative aspects were predominant, they paved the way for an empirical examination of population trends in different circumstances. It may be noted that initially after independence census of population was the only source of population data in India. Conducted in 1871 for the first time, and at decadal intervals uninterruptedly after that, censuses had produced data on size, growth and structure of India's population.

In post-independence India, therefore, the initial works on population concentrated on computing various rates and ratios pertaining to demographic processes from census data, with the help of analytical population models. The main theoretical problem that the early demographers faced was how could they model population processes at societal level. There was a lack of contextual thinking and due to incomplete knowledge of socio-economic determinants and consequences of population in India, they looked out for theoretical construction. In this situation Indian demographers found that demographic transition theory could give them the basic theoretical framework. Thus the theory of population development that guided Indian demographers in the beginning was the theory of demographic transition.

Demographic Transition Theory

According to demographic transition theory, as developed by Thompson, Landry, Blacker, Notestein and Berelson, there is a definite mechanism through which fertility declines from a high (natural) level to a low (controlled) level (Premi *et al.*, 1983). They believed that experience of developed countries, where fertility had already achieved low levels, could be a guide to explore this machanism. With this idea demographers and other social scientists started examining cross-national and longitudinal correlations between indicators of fertility, on the one hand, and indicators of socio-economic development on the other. The theory stated that in all primitive societies mortality was high and fluctuating (U.N., 1973). In that situation it was imperative for human society to survive that fertility should also be high, at least equal to mortality. As time passed and societies advanced technologically, their death rates started declining. This resulted in rise of population. Gradually as couples observed that (a) due to improvement in mortality family size was expanding and it was not conducive to social mobility, (b) many couples in their society had already been using birth control methods and their use had been perceived to be socially legitimate, they started using birth control methods widely. Then fertility also started declining. Consequently, societies achieved a new balance between mortality rates and fertility rates. Population size was again stabilised (Bogue, 1969). Obviously, in the primitive or high fertility phase there are no fertility differentials. Emergence of fertility

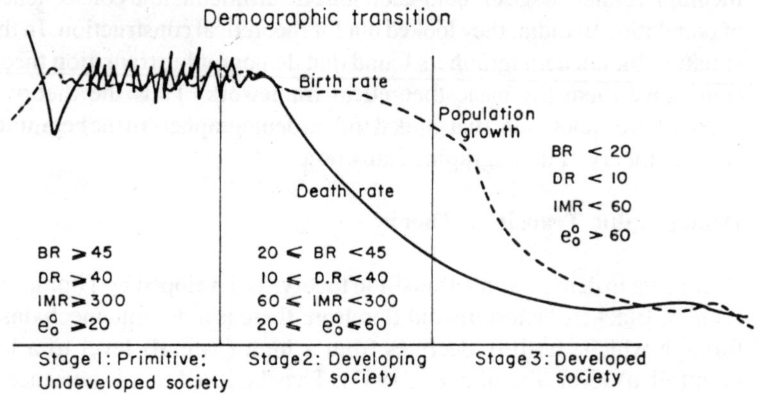

FIG. 4.1: Demographic Transition

differentials indicates the onset of demographic transition. Without a critical examination this theory was as such accepted by Indian demographers. It guided most of them up to 1970s (Sharma, 1989) and it continues to influence many even today.

The above figure shows that in primitive societies (Stage 1) both birth and death rates are high. In developing societies death rates start declining thanks to socio-economic development, improvement in medical sciences, transport and communication facilities, greater awareness of health and hygiene, changes in social organisation, etc. Birth rates ramain high or decline at a slower pace than the death rates (Stage 2) in some countries, birth rates have also been found to be increasing, followed by a greater fall. During this period population rises at the highest rate. Finally, in the developed stage (Stage 3) both birth and death rates are low leading to near zero, zero or negative growth rate. The figure also exhibits the broad range within which values of birth, death, and infant mortaliy rates and life expectancy lie in different stages.

Subsequent researches have established that demographic transition theory is not a theory at all. It does not explain anything. Developed countries have achieved low fertility not through one but through different paths (Cassen, 1978). Moreover, the pattern of social change in contemporary developing societies is not same as shown by industrialized countries. Correlations between various indicators of development in the former are much weaker than they were in the latter. Also there are some new factors affecting demographic revolution in less developed countries, *e.g.* family planning programmes, new and improved methods of contraception and new awareness about inplications of population growth, which did not exist in transitional phase in the developed countries (Rostow, 1978).

As such, demographic transition theory is silent on population distribution and internal migration but a few attempts have been made to relate rapidity of demographic transition with rate of urbanization (Friedlander, 1969; Sharma, 1979). The theory is also silent on changes in nuptiality patterns. Many studies have, however, looked at the contribution of nuptiality changes towards reduction in birth rate. Studies showed that in the developed countries fertility decline began with rise in marriage age and a reduction in proportion married. Only later when further changes in society had made contraceptives widely available, fertility continued to decline even with lowering of marriage age and reduction in celibacy.

The theory of demographic transition raised the following issues in India:

(a) estimation of vital rates at the national level;
(b) study of fertility and mortality differentials by socio-ecomomic class, region, urban-rural residence, community, caste, etc. and structural relationship between socio-economic development and demographic processes;
(c) estimation of marriage age for synthetic cohorts;
(d) measurement and estimation of migration;
(e) rates and streams of internal and international migration; and
(f) projections of national population.

Beyond the Demographic Transition

With theoretical developments in the West and examination of data from less developed countries doubts have been raised about validity of demographic transition theory in explaining demographic change in contemporary societies. The main points of cirticism of this theory are:

(a) In the period after Second World War, mortality declined much faster in less developed countries than in any Western country at corresponding levels of development.

(b) Improvement in mortality has been shared by all irrespective of socio-economic, ethnic, infrastructural and environmental levels.

(c) After the achievement of about three decades, mortality improvement has slowed down drastically. It is believed that it will be extremely difficult now to raise expectation of life further. In the future, more will depend on political will rather than economic growth.

(d) Fertility decline is not a simple function of economic growth. Perhaps social development, *i.e.,* removal of discrimination, exploitation and oppression will cause a greater reduction in fertility than mere rise in economic standards. In other words, literacy, equality, improving status of women, nutrition and low infant mortality rate are more closely associated with demographic transition than per capita income and industrialisation. In this respect examples of transition in Sri Lanka, Indonesia and Kerala State in India are commonly given.

(e) Change in social values could produce change in family building processes and reproduction, independent of structural transformation.

(f) Irrespective of socio-economic levels family planning programmes are quite effective in reducing birth rate.

Thus many new versions of demographic transition theory have been suggested with stress on Westernisation (Freedman, 1986), change in intergenerational flow of wealth (Caldwell, 1978), social justice (Ratcliffe, 1983), family planning intervention (Bongarts *et al.,* 1990) and culture (Handwerker, 1986). These modifications and availability of more reliable data have shifted attention of demographers from national level to regional and district levels. In the recent past demographers have shown more interest in examination of demographic processes in different ethnic and cultural groupings from the perspective of social development and justice.

PROBLEMS OF DEMOGRAPHIC DATA

There are four main sources of demographic data. They are population census, vital registration scheme, sample surveys (national, regional and local) and service statistics collected primarily for administrative purposes. Among them in India population census, has been the main source of population data. As a matter of fact, up to 1950s census was the only source of data. Census yielded information on size of population, age, sex and marital status of all Indians, and population distribution according to urban-rural residence, industrial and occupational categories, mother tongue, religion and literacy. Census is certainly not a source of direct data on vital rates. Therefore, in the beginning demographers resorted to use of analytical methods (models) which took inputs from age and sex composition of population and provided estimates of birth and death rates and other indices of demographic processes.

Over time several changes have been made in definitions and number of questions asked in census. For example, in 1971, two questions were added on marriage age of females and child born in the previous year. In 1981 census, questions on children ever born and children surviving were added. In 1991 additional information has been obtained on ex-servicemen. Changes have been made in definition of urban areas and workers. Regarding migration also new questions have been added. The 1981 census for the first time generated data on causes of migration.

Censuses have their own problems. To conduct census in India, the second largest country in the world, huge resources are required in terms of time, money, material and men. The actual enumeration work is done by school teachers and other grassroot workers with unattractive honorarium. Majority of Indians are still illiterate, superstitious and unaware of seriousness of this exercise. Therefore demographers have to develop various methods to evaluate quality of census data (Himes and Clogg. 1992).

Vital registration system is the oldest source of population data in India. Unfortunately, very few less-developed countries have reliable data from vital registration system. In many less developed countries, only small percentage of vital events are registered. Delayed registration is another problem. To quote Hill (1991):

> "In some countries with largely complete coverage, delayed registration may be a problem that affects the timeliness of the measures; if the births in some year are not all registered until four or five years later, a final calculation of the infant mortality rate for

the year will be delayed by those four or five years. Delayed registration may also affect completeness of registration: It is very unlikely that a birth that initially goes unregistered will later be registered if the child dies in infancy. Even in countries with complete and timely coverage, the ultimate timeliness of the measures may be reduced by delays in publication; even in the United States, detailed publication from vital registration data lags by three or four years. The detail available is also limited in most developing countries by a failure to publish information for small geographic units or by characteristics of the parents. Information on cause of death may be of limited quality because a high proportion of child deaths are not certified by a physician."

The statutory registration of births and deaths was introduced in India way back in the last quarter of the nineteenth century. In the pre-independence India, it was the only source of data on vital rates. Of late, several legal and administrative steps have been taken to ensure completeness of these data. In this regard Registration of Births and Deaths Act was passed in 1969. Yet it is still not a dependable source. Overall, registration is more complete in urban areas than in rural areas. For certain large cities it is more or less complete but in the rural areas where majority of population lives records are highly erroneous. There is a neeed to strengthen this data base more as this alone can give direct data on vital rates and their short-term changes.

In 1950 the Indian Government instituted the National Sample Survey Organisation (NSSO) under Ministry of Home Affairs with the purpose of collecting socio-economic data and providing national level estimates of various rates and ratios. In the first few rounds, NSSO emphasised the consumer expenditure and small scale household enterprises. In the eighth round, emphasis shifted to study of distribution of landholdings. Ninth round objective was study of employment and unemployment. Forty-seventh round, which was completed in December 1991, was devoted to collection of data on "disability" and "literacy and culture". NSSO covers all Sates and Union Territories except (a) Ladakh and Kargil districts of Jammu and Kashmir, and (b) rural areas of Nagaland.

NSSO data have been widely used in studying socio-economic trends in the country, particularly in studies of consumption patterns, poverty and employment. NSSO has developed very sound theoretical framework, sample design and vast network of investigators. Estimates of standard errors of NSSO figures are quite low. NSSO data are processed very quickly they are internationally known for the speed at which national level data are processed in a very large country. Also they have an additional advantage that along with required indicators they also provide data on wider socio-economic contexts.

In several rounds, NSSO has collected data on demographic processes. As early as the period 1951-61 NSS 14th round provided various demographic rates for rural India. Many subsequent rounds have also given such rates (NSSO, Report Nos. 48, 153, 175, 180 and 186) for rural and urban areas separately. In addition, other departments of the government have also conducted national surveys. For example in 1979, the International Year of the Child, the Department of Social Welfare and the UNICEF funded a Survey on Infant and Child Mortality that covered about 7,28,000 households in 2,345 rural and 1,328 urban units. This survey was carried out by the Office of the Registrar General. It collected data on deaths among children born alive during 1973-78 (five years preceding the survey) and on various characteristics of the ever married women and of the households or the villages and blocks with a reference date of 31 December 1978. Operations Research Group, an independent organisation, has conducted national surveys of fertility and family planning at the national level whose estimates have been widely quoted both in India and abroad.

In addition, a number of sample surveys of households conducted at the regional or local level have also provided very useful data on population trends. Among them some well known surveys have been done in the Mysore Population Study (United Nations, 1961), Agarwala's study of six urbanising villages (Agarwala, 1970), the Khanna Study (Wyon and Gordon, 1971), Dandekar's study of six rural communities (1959) and systems study of rural U.P. (Misra *et al.*, 1982). These studies and studies done at a smaller scale in various parts of India presented data on socio-economic and religious differentials in fertility (Badry, 1967; Majumdar, 1960; Rele, 1963; Sinha 1958; Srinivasan, 1967; Srivastava, 1979).

Special and in-depth surveys can certainly give detailed and more reliable data than censuses. Yet they too suffer from several problems. Apart from the practical and theoretical difficulties (Sharma, 1988) survey data suffer from the wellknown recall lapse which is generally greater for deaths and particularly infant deaths. Moreover, surveys facilitate multivariate analysis using household-and village-level data but generalisation on the basis of such data for larger population is always fraught with risks.

One special type of survey used in population studies is called multi-round survey. A typical format of the multi-round survey is to conduct a baseline survey to develop population profile (vital rates, family planning acceptance, etc.) and then to follow-up in rounds at required intervals (six months, a year or after making an intervention). Carefully planned and conducted, multi-round surveys can produce reliable estimates of fertility, childhood mortality, age patterns of demographic processes, and effectiveness of an intervention. Some commonly asked questions in such surveys on fertility and mortality are about: (a) aggregate number of children ever born and children dead: (b) survival of the previous birth; (c) survival of the most recent births or births in the last 12 months; (d) truncated maternity history; and (e) complete maternity history.

> "A close relative of the multi-round survey is the surveillance system, whereby a geographically defined population is kept under detailed study for an extended time period" (Hill, 1991). Sometimes to collect information on household births or deaths by age and sex during some reference period, typically 12 or 24 months, prior to the survey, retrospective survey questions are included in both censuses and household surveys. "However, this method could not provide information on trends except by repetition and would not, in a large scale enquiry, be very useful as a way of identifying deaths for cause-of-death investigation through the application of verbal autopsies."

The main advantage of surveys lies in greater scope, flexibility of design and the fact that they can provide in-depth information on study variables. They are of great help in policy making, evaluative studies and experimentation. In the area of family planning their usefulness in benchmark studies and in studies of knowledge, attitudes and practices (KAP) has been internationally established.

Realising that the achievement of a reasonably efficient system of vital registration is a slow and long-drawn-out process, the Registrar General, India, introduced the Sample Registration Scheme (SRS) in 1964-65. This scheme is based on the methodology of dual record system which is under use in many other developing countries including Pakistan, Turkey, Liberia, Columbia, Morocco, the Philippines and Kenya for collecting efficient data on vital events and their attendant characteristics. Today, it is recognised as the primary source of fairly reliable vital rates by both national and international agencies.

In the SRS, each vital event is recorded doubly though continuous enumeration as well as retrospective survey conducted every six months. From a modest start in seven States initially, the SRS now covers all parts of Indian Union. It provides estimates of vital rates at both national and

State levels, separately for urban and rural areas, males and females and by age. It has been found that the coefficient of variation of SRS estimates is quite low (Brahma, 1974). Chandrasekharan and Deming have given a formula to estimate number of events missed by both systems in a dual record scheme.

Now that there is an adequate knowledge of demographic situation at the national level, there is a need to enlarge scope of data collection mechanisms to yield demographic data at the regional level, preferably at the district level. SRS would not provide rates at lower administrative or district levels. Vital registration system has to be strengthened. As mentioned above for direct, detailed and district (or even village) level there is certainly no substitute of vital registration system. In the absence of these data, demographic researches in India would just continue to fill up the data gap and can spare little efforts for studying mechanisms of demographic transition and their socio-economic and political consequences.

Lastly, there are service statistics. In the area of population, statistics of family planning acceptance have been of immense use. One obvious use of these statistics is that one can calculate births averted from data on family planning acceptance. It is estimated that in India above 120 million births have been averted since the inception of the programme. From this figure reduction in birth rate and, thus, the present birth rate can be computed. Then one can compare birth rate obtained from census, NSS and SRS with estimate of birth rate obtained from service statistics. Likewise, many other types of data collected by different agencies for routine administrative purposes can be used in population studies.

MODELS AND TECHNIQUES

In the bakground of the demographic transition theory and problems of data during 1950s and 1960s, the primary objective of model building exercises was twofold: (a) to correct census data; and (b) to estimate various rates and ratios with the help of these data. Stable population model was used for correcting errors in census age returns (Shryock *et al.*, 1973) and establishing analytical and statistical relationships between various demographic parameters (Keyfitz *et al.*, 1967; Rele, 1967; Rele and Sinha, 1970; Bourgeois-Pichat, 1957). Some techniques developed for estimation were based on reverse survival ratios and census survival which made extensive use of model life tables. Since India did not have reliable registration data but had a long record of conducting decadal censuses, these techniques which required data on age distribution and growth rate of population proved to be of immense value in estimation of fertility and mortality rates at the national level. It could be safely assumed that population of India is closed to migration (Jain, 1974; Jain *et al.*, 1988), *i.e.*, in india the net impact of migration on population size (emigration and immigration) is negligible.

Stable Population

Lotka had shown that if constant schedules of fertility and mortality, *i.e.*, sets of age-specific fertility and mortality rates, operate in a population for sufficiently long period of time, they produce a unique stable population. In this resultant population, proportions at different ages become constant. The total population may, however, change; it may grow or decline at a fixed rate. Lotka had also established a precise mathmatical relationship among proportion of population between ages a and a + da, probability of survival from birth to age a, the birth rate (b) and growth rate (r) of the stable population. In notations, the proportion of population between ages a and a + da (c(a)) may be given as below.

$$c(a) = b\, e^{-ra}\, p(a)$$

If we know c (a) from census and can surmise p(a) from the life table of another population thought to be similar, or from a model population, then the inference of b and r is simple. One important property of the stable population is that the curves of cumulative age distributions never cross each other. It helps in unique identification of a stable population.

A stable population with zero growth rate (*i.e.*, r = 0) is a stationary population. A life table population is thus a stationary population. In this population a fixed number of children are born at initial time (t = 0). At each age, they die according to a given schedule of mortality and their population is closed to migration. Due to differences in age patterns of mortality, convention says that life tables be prepared separately for males and females.

Demographers assumed that population of developing countries including India has undergone pre-transitional constant and high fertility for a very long period of time. Therefore, their age distribution should be stable. Comparison of their census age distribution with that of stable age distribution with corresponding levels of fertility and mortality can help in determining extent of under-and-over enumeration in censuses and surveys at various ages. Similarly, their age distribution and growth rate can help in determining their birth and death rates.

United Nations Manual IV (1967) suggested various methodologies of estimating vital rates using stable population theory. United Nations and Coale and Demeny (Misra, 1980) developed several families of model life tables and model stable populations for demographic applications. Model life table showed schedules of mortality at different levels of mortality (i.e., expectations of life). Stable populations showed age distributions at different levels of mortality and growth rates. Survival ratio methods as simple techniques of estimation helped in computation of birth rates by projecting births (backward) and dividing them by projected population on the appropriate date in the past.

Soon it was recognised that stable population model was no more valid for less developed countries as in most of the less developed countries mortality had started declining. Such a stable population in which one of the two demographic factors—fertility and mortality - was changing was called a quasi-stable population. Several demographers suggested modification in estimates obtained through stable population model to make adjustment for mortality decline (Coale, 1963). Data showed that the rate of decline in mortality was quite sharp between 1931 and 1971. During this time, the crude death rate declined by 4 to 5 points in each decade. After 1971, the rate of decline slowed down. Crude death rate declined only by 24 points during 1971-81. By 1981, decline in mortality had almost come to a halt (Bhatia, 1983).

Gradually, as richer survey data became available, demographers started taking more interest in regional (Kohli, 1977) and socio-economic differentials in vital rates rather than the national level estimates. More studies now focused on levels and trends in infant mortality (Chandrasekhar, 1972; Gotpagar, 1985), its composition (neo-natal and post neo-natal mortality) (Singh *et al.*, 1983) and its social correlates (Caldwell *et al.*, 1983; Karkal, 1979; Ruzicka and Kanitkar, 1973). In an important study conducted in 1972 in 120 villages in Uttar Pradesh, infant and child mortality rates were computed for birth cohorts by age, parity, sex, cause of death and education of parents. It showed that mortality rates of males and females were quite different and that in India tetanus was the major cause of infant deaths (Simmons *et al.*, 1982; Smucker *et al.*, 1980). It was also observed that mortality decline is not a simple function of economic development as assumed by the demographic transition theory. Mortality in India, particularly among infants, is determined by health care intervention, culture and nutrition (Panikkar, 1975; Mahadevan *et al.*, 1986; Gandotra and Das, 1983). Bose (1980) suggested that mortality decline has its own political economy and state decisions affect the level and patterns of morbidity and mortality.

Marriage Studies

Estimation of marriage age and examination of nuptiality patterns began largely with analytical studies of census data. As time passed and need to explore nuptiality patterns was felt, various, national and sub-national surveys started including questions on marriage. Basically, studies of marriage in India have their history in sociological studies of family, marriage and kinship. But they got some momentum when Indian demographers felt that changes in marriage age and patterns could play a significant role in demographic revolution in India where, traditionally, age of marriage is low and marriage is almost universal.

In population studies, Davis-Blake framework of intermediate variables recognised the role of age at marriage and time spent in marital union in fertility transition. The first population policy statement issued by the Health Minister of India in 1976 suggested that in India age at marriage should be raised. After that government policy has consistently emphasised this point. Minimum legal marriage age has been raised to 18 years for females and 21 years for males. Violation of this law has been made a cognisable offence. Many studies have attempted to estimate by what per cent birth rate would decline if age at marriage for females is raised to higher levels.

In the beginning nuptiality had not been considered to be an important branch of demographic studies. Few demographers worked on nuptiality patterns in India. The lack of interest among demographers in this area was partly due to lack of data and partly due to their pre-occupation with fertility. It may be noted that direct data on marriages are obtained from marriage registration records only. In India, such data do not exist. The main indirect source of data are census data on age, sex and marital status distribution and sporadic demographic surveys. National Sample Survey and Sample Registration Scheme have occasionally provided some information on age at marriage and proportion married. As said earlier, a question on age at marriage was added in the individual slip for married females in 1971 census and tables on marriage age were prepared. The 1981 and 1991 Censuses have retained this question.

Demographers theorised that in India marriage is a religious ceremony. It is more of a sacred duty rather than a matter of personal convenience or arrangement. In Hindu mythology, marriage is conceived not so much for satisfaction of sexual and emotional needs as for obtaining a partner for fulfilment of one's religious duties. In the Hindu way of life, a male has to perform several sacred duties during the course of his life, and marriage is regarded as the most important of all these duties (Goyal,

1982). Data showed that marriage in India is universal and early. The pioneering work in this area was done by Agarwala (1962) and Kapadia (1966). Malaker (1978) and Goyal (1982) among others have further contributed in this area. National Family Health Survey in the country has generated lot of data on nuptiality and established that in many low marriage age states, significant rise in occurring.

One of the basic models developed in this area was that of John Hajnal (1953). Based on census data on proportion married for different age groups Hajnal suggested a method of computing mean age of marriage for synthetic cohorts. Agarwala has made some modifications and adjustments in this model. Goyal and Desai (1961) and Goyal (1975) have analysed the geographical and socio-economic differences in mean age at marriage by using census data on age and marital status.

There is clearly a need for registration of marriages. Apart form its sociological and legal advantages it will yield direct data on marriage patterns and trends. Census schedules are usually filled up by interviewing one member of the household (usually a male). His information on marriage age of females in the household may contain some error. Also in rural India marriage is not immediately followed by consummation of marriage. In between there is a custom of *gauna* or second marriage which makes it difficult to draw inferences from a simple single question on marriage age in census.

Migration Models

Migration is a purely sociological process. Unlike fertility and mortality it is not determined biologically. Therefore, it is more complex than the other two demographic processes. Studies of migration aim at examining (a) rate of migration; (b) streams of migration, *i.e.,* movements of people from a definite origin to a definite destination; (c) timings of migration; (d) characteristics of various migration streams; and (e) implications of migration. Migration includes international migration (between two countries) and internal migration (within country). Since the size of international migration to or from India is not significant from the point of view of its overall demographic impact, international migration has been a relatively neglected area. Most studies of migration in India have concentrated on internal migration. Yet some studies of international migration have explored the problems of labour migration to gulf countries, brain drain, illegal migration from neighbouring countries, impact of such migration on population of North-Eastern States and resettlement of refugees.

In order to answer questions regarding internal migration various models have been used in the past. Some of them are gravity model, regression model, cost-benefit model, stress and strain model, push-pull model, model of intervening opportunities, Marcov process, etc. (Sharma, 1985). Of them the gravity model is the oldest. Originally developed by Zipf, it expressed migration as a quantity directly proportional to population, of origin and destination, and inversely proportional to distance separating the two places. In some recent applications, scope of this model has been expanded and variables such as ethnicity, linguistic composition, labour market demands, education, etc. have also been included. Model specification has also changed and social scientists have regressed indicators of migration (*i.e.,* rate of migration, probability of migration, presence or absence of migration) against the said socio-economic variables.

Cost-benefit models assume that people are utilitarian rational. Their decision to migrate depends largely on balance of economic returns and cost of migration. Thus if the net present value of migration, obtained by adding discounted differences in expected income at the place of destination and that at the place of origin, is more than the cost of migration, people may decide to migrate and not otherwise. Psychologists have developed stress and strain models to account for various psychological factors which enter the decision-making process of subjects. To them strain is any stimulus present in the environment that makes subjects evaluate their position at the native place and strain is the outcome of this evaluation, *i.e.,* migration. Sociologists who concentrate more on situation rather than subjects have used the push-pull model which explains migration in terms of socio-economic, political and ecological characteristics of place of origin and destination. Thus migrants may be viewed either as pushed by adverse conditions at origin or pulled by attractiveness of destination. In some cases, the theory of intervening opportunities has also been introduced which says that greater intervening opportunities will thin the size of migration stream between two places. Lastly, some attempts have been made to use stochastic statistical models such as Marcov-chain-process to examine probabilities of migration between places and the resulting equilibrium.

Recently, Yadava *et al.* (1990) have developed a model of probability distribution of total number of migrants from a household. They have called it the "modified Polya-Aeppli distribution". The model was fitted to data collected in "Rural Development and Population Growth — A Sample Survey 1978", a survey conducted under the auspices of Centre of Population Studies, B.H.U. The model fitted satisfactorily several sets of observed distribution of total number of migrants at the household level.

Models of Population Projections

Estimation of future population is an another issue of great interest among Indian demographers and planners. For this purpose three types of models have generally been used: (a) mathematical models; (b) balancing equation model; and (c) cohort component model (Misra, 1980). Mathematical models assume that population would follow a definite mathematical growth pattern. Some patterns used for this purpose are linear, exponential, Gompertz, modified exponential, hyperbolic and logistic. Once a particular model is accepted, the mathematical procedure consists of fitting the model to the given set of data, *i.e.*, estimating the unknown constants of the model, and using these estimates for future projections.

Balancing equation can be used for inter-censal or post-censal estimates, in situations where data on births, deaths and migration for the projection period are available. In notations:

$$Pt - Po = B - D + IM - EM$$

Where P = Population in the initial year

Pt = Population at time t

B, D, IM and EM are births, deaths, inmigration and outmigration during the projection period, *i.e.*, between time o and time t.

Cohort component method is a more scientific and common method that gives projection of total population as well as its age and sex composition. To use this method one requires data on age and sex distribution of population in the initial year, some assumptions regarding changes in fertility and mortality rates during the projection period and migration. In this method, future population, by age and sex, is computed by multiplying population in the initial year by survival ratios appropriate for different cohorts. The population of children is computed by estimating number of births during the projection period and multiplying them by survival ratios for children. Age-wise estimates of migration are prepared separately and added to population estimates. Of late, micro-simulation models have also been used for projections. The main advantage of these models is that they can make use of more detailed information on various characteristics of population than the conventional methods. They can also provide us estimates of standard errors as in stochastic exercises. Yet due to high data needs and computational requirements their use has been rather limited. Moreover, in the area of projections sophisticated methods and greater data use do not necessarily guarantee greater accuracy.

As such, projections contain risk of unknown quantum. But

projections of sub-national populations are more problematic. The main reason is that the sub-national (*i.e.* regional, urban or local) population is affected by migration more than the national population (Saxena and Sharma, 1976). To project them, and also to project various characteristics of population, demographers have used some variant of the ratio method. Thus in place of projecting the size of sub-national population, ratios of sub-national population to national population (or population of a larger area) are projected and they are multiplied by projected population of the nation (or the larger area). Both errors in projections of ratios and projections of total population can cause errors in these sub-national population projections.

Some Recent Techniques of Analysis

In the recent past advanced demographic techniques have been developed both in India and abroad to analyse demographic data (obtained through surveys). The book edited by Saxena and Talwar, entitled, *Recent Advances in the Techniques for Demographic Analysis,* presents a broad spectrum of these techniques. A great majority of these contributions are in the area of fertility. While the previous techniques had used reverse survival ratio method or methods based on stable population model, the new techniques have been developed to analyse data obtained through sample surveys in which questions on current fertility and parity (children ever born) were asked. It was assumed that although these data suffer from errors of reference period and recall, by and large age-pattern of fertility exhibited by current fertility (child born last year) data is more or less correct. Attempts have also been made to develop mathematical functions for graduating age-specific fertility rates. Some demographers have analysed maternity history data through simulation experiments without any assumption regarding the patterns of fertility (Roy and Mukerjee, 1981).

Here mention may be made of Coale and Trussell (1974) two-parameter model schedule of marital fertility and the relational Gompertz model (Zaba, 1981). In the past, several mathematical demographers had analysed data on open and close birth intervals and developed models of birth intervals. They estimated fecundability, i.e., probability of conceiving during a month of exposure, from these data as part of their study. Recently, an attempt has been made to estimate general marital fertility rate from data on birth intervals.

Two significant departures in techniques of population in the recent past included in the above book are (a) use of Chernoff Faces as a multivariate method for causation and discrimination, and (b) use of Operations Research (OR) techniques for estimation of demographic rates including rates of various streams of migration and errors in demographic data. Further applications of these methods would be needed to test their potential for estimation.

ISSUES FOR THE FUTURE

As the above analysis shows, demographic models and techniques in India have so far concentrated on estimation of demographic rates from census and survey data. The main aim of construction of these models was to study the process of demographic transition and to suggest ways to fasten the transition. With time as more detailed and reliable data will become available, need for such models may no longer be felt. Instead demographers will have to struggle with developing social indicators of development with which demographic rates should be correlated. As of today, sociologists have little success in measuring develoment dimensions such as status of women, equity, social justice and empowerment of the downtrodden. It has to be appreciated that demographic processes exist in a socio-economic context; both their explanation and solution require as much understanding of their internal dynamics as of their context. There is also a need to reflect on demographic data in proper sociological framework (Sharma, 1989). To begin with demographers should equip themselves with sociological models and apply them to demographic data. This could perhaps fill up the gap that has been created by critique of demographic transition theory.

REFERENCES

Agarwala, R.D. 1975, "Influence of Infant and Child Mortality on Fertility in India," paper presented at the *Seminar on Infant Mortality in Relation to Level of Fertility*, CICRED Series, Paris.

Agarwala, S.N. 1962, *Age at Marriage in India,* Kitab Mahal Pvt. Ltd., Allahabad.

Agarwala, S.N., 1970, *A Demographic Study of Six Urbanizing Villages,* Asia Publishing House, New York.

Badry, M.A. E1., 1967, "Differential Fertility in Greater Bombay," *Contributed Papers: Sydney Conference,* International Union for Scientific Study of Population.

Bhatia, P.S. 1983, "Health for All by 2000 A.D.: Can India Achieve its Goals?" Paper presented in the *Ninth Annual Conference of the IASP,* Rajasthan University, Jaipur.

Bogue, D.J., 1969, *Principles of Demography,* John Wiley & Sons, New York, pp. 51-53.

Bongaarts, John, Mauldin, Parker W., and Phillips, James F. 1990, "The Demographic Impact of Family Planning Programms", *Studies in Family Planning,* Vol. 21, No. 6, pp.299-310.

Bose, Ashish, 1980, "Return of Malaria in India? - Political Economy of the Mosquito", paper presented in the *IASP Conference on Population Distribution and Development,* ISI, Calcutta.

Bourgeois - Pichat, Jean, 1957, " Utilisation de la notion de population stable pour measurer la mortalite *et al* ficundite despopulation des pays sonsdeveloppe's," *Bulletin de l Institute International de Statistque* Tome 36, 2 Livraison, Stockholm, pp. 94-121.

Brahma, P.B., 1974, "Registration Scheme - Birth and Death Rates", in Bose, Ashis, Mitra, Ashok, Desai, P.B., and Sharma, J.N. (eds.), *Population in India's Development, 1947 - 2000,* Vikas Publishing House Pvt. Ltd., Delhi, pp. 425-30.

Caldwell, J.C., 1978, " A Theory of Fertility: From High Plateau to Destabilization", *Population and Development Review,* Vol. 4, No. 4, pp. 553-77.

Caldwell, J.C., Reddy, P.H., and Caldwell, Pat, 1983, "The Social Component of Mortality Decline: An Investigation in South India Employing Alternative Methodologies," *Population Studies,* Vol. 37, pp 185-205.

Cassen, R.H., 1978, *India: Population, Economy, Society,* The Macmillan Press Ltd., Hong Kong.

Census of India, 1977, *Paper 2 of 1977: Fertility Tables, 1*971, Seris 1, India, Office of the Registrar-General and Census Commissioner, India.

Chandrasekhar, S., 1972, *Infant Mortality, Population Growth and Family Planning in India,* George Allen and Unwin Limited, London.

Chandrasekaran, C., and Deming, W. Edwards, "On a Method of Estimating Birth and Death Rates and the Extent of Registration," *Journal of American Statistical Association,* Vol. 44, No. 245, pp. 101-15.

Coale, Ansley J., 1963, "Estimates of Various Demographic Measures Through the Quasi-Stable Age Distribution, *Emerging Techniques in Population Analysis,* Milbank Memorial Fund, pp. 185-86.

Coale, A.J., and Trussell, J., 1974, "Model Fertility Schedules: Variations in the Age Structure of Childbearing in Human Populations," *Population Index,* Vol. 40, No. 2, pp. 185-258.

Dandekar K., 1959, *Demographic Survey of Six Rural Communities*, Gokhale Institute of Politics and Economics, Publication 37, Asia Publishing House, Bombay.

Freedman, R., 1986, "Theories of Fertility Decline", in Mahadevan, K., Reddy, P.J. and Naidu, D.A. (eds.). *Fertility and Mortality: Theory, Methodology and Empirical Issues,* Sage Publication, New Delhi.

Friedlander, S.L., 1969, "Demographic Responses and Population Change", *Demography,* Vol. 6, No. 4, pp. 359-81.

Gandotra, M.M. and Das Narayan, 1983, "Impact of Health care Intervention and Nutrition on Infant Mortality in India", Paper Presented in *Ninth Annual Conference of IASP.* Rajasthan University, Jaipur.

Gotpagar, K.B., 1985, "Recent Trends and Defferentials in Mortality in India", *National Seminar on the Utilization of Demographic Knowledge in Policy Formulation and Planning,* IIPS Bombay.

Goyal, R.P., 1975, "Shifts in Age at Marriage in India between 1961 and 1971, *Demography India,* Vol. 4 No. 2.

Goyal, R. P., 1982, "Nuptiality Trends and Differentials", in United Nations, *Population of India,* Country Monograph Series No. 10, United Nations New York, pp. 109-134.

Goyal, R.P., and Desai, P.B., 1968, *Inter-district Variation in Mean Age at Marriage* -1961,

Institute of Economic Growth, Delhi (Mimeo.)

Hajnal, John, 1953, "Age at Marriage and Proportions Marrying", *Population Studies,* Vol. 7, pp. 111-36.

Handwerker, W.P., 1986, "Culture and Reproduction", in Handworker, (ed.) *Culture and Reproduction: An Anthropological Critique of Demographic Transition Theory,* Westview Press, Boulder & London.

Hill, Kenneth, 1991, "Approaches to the Measurement of Childhood Mortality: A Comparative Review", *Population Index,* Vol. 57, No. 3, p. 369

Himes, Christine L., and Clogg, C. C., 1992, "An Overview of Demographic Analysis as a Method for Evaluating Census Coverage in the United States", *Population Index,* Vol. 58, No. 4, pp. 587-607.

Jain, Anrudh K., and Visaria, Pravin, 1988 (eds.) *Infant Mortaility in India: Differentials and Determinents,* Sage Publications, New Delhi.

Jain, S.P., 1974, "Some Aspects of Mortality", in Bose, Ashish, Desai, P. B., Mitra, Asok, and Sharma, J. N. (eds.) *Population in India's Development,* Vikas Publishing House Pvt. Ltd., Delhi, pp. 319-33.

Kapadia, K.M., 1966, *Marriage and family in India,* Oxford University Press, Bombay.

Karkal, M. 1979, *Child Mortality and Morbidity in Greater Bombay,* IIPS, Bombay (mimeo).

Keyfitz, Nathan, Nnagnaur, Dhruva, and Sharma, Divakar, 1967, "On the Interpretation of Age Distribution," *Journal of the American Statistical Association,* Vol. 62, pp. 870-71.

Kohli, K.L., 1977, *Mortality in India: A Statewise Study,* Sterling Publishers Pvt. Ltd., New Delhi.

Mahadevan, K., Reddy P.R., Murthy, M.S.R., Reddy, P.J., Gowri, V., and Raju, S. Siva, 1986, "Culture, Nutrition and Infant and Childhood Mortality", in Mahadevan, K., Reddy P.J., and Naidu, D.A. (eds.) *Fertility and Mortality: Theory Methodology and Empirical Issues,* Sage Publications, New Delhi, pp. 314-37.

Majumdar, D.N., 1960, *Social Contours of an Industrial City,* Asia Publishing House, Bombay.

Malaker, C.R. 1978, *Study of Indian Nuptiality,* Ph. D. Dissertation, ISI Calcutta, pp. 78-105.

Misra, B.D., 1980, *An Introduction to the Study of Population,* South Asian Publishers Pvt. Ltd., New Delhi.

Misra, B.D., Ashraf, A., Simmons, R. and Simmons, George, 1982, *Organization for Change: A Systems Analysis of Family Planning in Rural India,* Radiant Publishers, New Delhi.

Mukerji, S., 1987, "Applications of Operations Research Techniques in Demographic Analysis", in Saxena, P.C., and Talwar, P.P. (eds.) *Recent Advances in the Techniques for Demographic Analysis,* Himalaya Publishing House, Bombay, pp. 426-456.

Mukerjee, Radhakamal, 1930, "Optimum and Over-Population", *Indian Journal of Economics,* Vol. 10, No. 3, pp. 407-21.

Mukerjee, Radhakamal, 1933, "The Criterion of Optimum Population", *The American Journal of Sociology,* Vol. 38, No. 5, pp. 688-89.

Nehru, Jawaharlal, 1972, *The Discovery of India,* Asia Publishing House, Delhi.

Operations Research Group, 1972, *Family Planning Practice in India,* O.R.G. Baroda.

Pakrasi, Kanti B., 1970, *Female Infanticide in India,* ISI, Calcutta.

Panikkar, P.G.K., 1975, "Fall in Mortality Rates in Kerala: An Explanatory Hypothesis", *Economic and Political Weekly,* November 22, pp. 1811-18.

Premi, M.K., Ramanamma, A., and Bambawale, Usha, 1983, *An Introduction to Social Demography,* Vikas Publishing House Pvt. Ltd., New Delhi.

Ratcliffe, J.W. 1983, "Toward a Social Justice Theory of Demographic Transtition: Lessons from India's Kerala State", *Janasamkhya,* Vol. 1, No. 1, pp, 1-38.

Rele, J.R., 1963, "Fertility Differentials in India", *The Milbank Memorial fund Quarterly,* Vol. 41, pp. 183-85.

Rele, J.R., 1967, *Fertility Analysis Through Extension of Stable Population Concepts,* Institute of International Studies, University of California, Berkeley.

Rele, J.R., and Sinha, U.P. 1970, "Fertility and Mortality in India, 1951-60", in Bose, Ashish, Desai, P.B., and Jain, S.P. (eds.), *Studies in Demography,* George Allen and Unwin Ltd., London, pp. 212-26.

Rostow, W.W., 1978, *The World Economy: History and Prospect,* University of Texas Press, Austin & London.

Roy, T.K. and Mukerji, S. 1981, "Analysis of Maternity History Data: A Simulation Experiment", in Srinivasan, K., and Mukerji, S. (eds.) *Dynamics of Population and Family Welfare,* Himalaya Publishing House, Bombay, pp. 15-29.

Ruzicka, G.T. and Kanitkar, T. 1973, "Infant Mortality in Greater Bombay", *Demography India,* Vol. 2, No. 1, pp.41-55.

Saxena, P.C. and Shrama, A.K., 1976, "Population Projections for Cities of Maharashtra, *IIPS Newsletter,* No. 55, pp. 10-14.

Saxena, P.C. and Sharma, A.K., 1976, "Projections of Rural and Urban Population of Districts of Maharashtra", *IIPS Newsletter,* No. 52. pp. 1-5.

Shrarma, A.K., 1979, "Demographic Transition: A Determinant of Urbanization", *Social Change,* Vol. 9, No. 3, pp. 13-17.

Sharma, A.K., 1985, *Social Inequality and Demographic Processes,* Mittal Publications, New Delhi.

Sharma, A.K., 1988,"Fieldwork in Large Scale Surveys", in Sawhney, Nirmala, Talwar, P.P., and Misra, B.D. (eds.) *Large Scale Surveys in Health and Family Welfare Programmes in India,* Population Centre, U.P., Lucknow.

Sharma, A.K., 1989, *Issues in Social Demography,* Mittal Publication, New Delhi.

Sharma, A.K., 1991, "Gandhian Theory of Population: Revelence and Implication", *The Journal of Family Welfare,* Vol. 37, No. 4, pp. 32-45.

Shryock, Henry S. and Siegel, J.S., 1973, *The Methods and Materials of Demography,* Vol. II, U.S. Government Printing Office, Washington, pp. 188-251.

Simmons, G.B., and Bernstein, Stan. 1982, "The Educational Status of Parents and Infant and Child Mortality in Rural North India", *Health Policy and Education,* Vol. 2, pp. 349-67.

Singh, S.N., Dwivedi, S.N. and Singh, K.N. u.d. "Trends in Neo-natal and Post-natal Mortality Rates in India", Centre of Population Studies, BHU, Varanasi (mimeo).

Sinha, J.N. 1958, "Differential Fertility in Uttar Pradesh", *Population Studies,* Vol. 2, p. 162.

Smucker, C., Simmons, G.B., Bernstein, S. and Misra B.D., 1980, "Neonatal Mortality in South Asia: The Special Role of Tetanus", *Population Studies,* Vol. 34.

Srinivasan, K., 1967,"Fertility Trends and Differentials in Athoor Block", *Bulletin of Institute of Rural Health and Family Planning,* Gandhigram, Vol. 2, No. 1, pp. 67-68.

Srivastava, H.C. 1979, "A Study of Fertility Differentials among Hindu and Muslim Women in Bhiwandi", in Srinivasan, K. and Mukerji, S. (eds.) *Dynamics of Popluation and Family Welfare in India,* Popular Prakashan, Bombay, pp. 284-92.

Srivastava, J.N. and Saksen, D.N., 1980, "Infant Mortality in an Urban Setting: Study of Socio-Demographic and Health Care Differentials", paper presented in *The IASP Conference on Population Distribution and Development,* ISI, Calcutta.

United Nations, 1961, "The Mysore Population Study: A Cooperative Project of the United Nations and the Government of India," *Population Studies,* No.34, New York, p. 119.

United Nations, 1967, *Manual IV: Methods of Estimating Basic Demographic Measures from Incomplete Data,* Department of Economic and Social Affairs, New York, pp. 22-28.

Vaidyanathan, K.E. (ed.), 1972, *Studies on Mortality in India,* The Gandhigram Institute of Rural Health and Family Planning, Gandhigram.

Wyon, J.B. and Gordon, J.E., 1971, *The Khanna Study: Population Problems in Rural Punjab,* Harvard University Press, Cambridge, p. 163.

Yadava, K.N.S., and Singh, Ram B., 1991, "A Probability Model for the Distribution of the Number of Migrants at the Household Level," *Genus,* Vol. 47, Nos. 1-2, pp. 1-20.

Zaba, B., 1981, "Use of Relational Gompertz Model in Analysing Fertility Data Collected in Retrospective Surveys," *CPS Working Paper,* Series 81, No.2, London School of Hygiene and Tropical Medicine.

5

POPULATION AND SUSTAINABLE DEVELOPMENT

Population has figured prominently in the economic theories in all ages. Physiocrats, mercantalists, classical and neo-classical economists, all have reflected on the place of population in their theories of development. Yet it was only after the Second World War that it achieved perhaps the greatest place on the agenda of social scientists, when both analysts and statesmen observed the complexity of linkages between population factors and variables of economic growth. Great aspirations for development in all countries and the thinking that development planning entails a clear understanding of demographic processes and management belong to our age. Tremendous works have been done by social scientists in general and economists in particular on the relationship between population and development in the recent time.

Of late, the interest in development has been replaced by the interest in sustainable development. Thus the theories of development are being re-examined in the framework of theories of sustainable development. In this context, a need has arisen to examine relationship between population and sustainable development. This chapter attempts to conceptuallse sustainable development and its implications for population processes.

What is Sustainable Development?

Sustainability has been conceptualised in such a varying manner in studies of development that, in a way, it has become a vacuous word. The dictionary meaning of the word "sustainable" would be a thing that can be kept up, maintained or prolonged. Thus sustainable development is that process of development which lasts. Beginning with the famous work of

Meadows and others sponsored by the Club of Rome in 1972, entitled *The Limits to Growth.* A feeling grew that the developmental processes are limited by their own results, that the much valued growth cannot be sustained for long. A year before this Forrester had published his book entitled *World Dynamics*, and in 1967 Kahn and Wiener had asserted that a framework be developed for speculation on the future. Forrester had showed how factors such as crowding , pollution, food supply, and natural resources can not only bring the exponential population growth to halt but they can also lead to sudden and tragic collapse of population. This gave rise to Malthusian credence that development not accompanied by population control would cause misery (rise in death rate) in the long-run. At this point natural resources (later called natural capital) rather than capital became central to economic discourse. Studies by Mesavoric and Pestel (1974), Barney (1980), and Higgins and others (1982) established that development is neither a universal nor an irreversible process. Implicit in these studies is an idea that sustainable development is that which does not lead to shortages of "renewable" resources such as water and soil, forests and fisheries, and "non-renewable" mineral resources in the future.

The above perception of development has, however,not been free from difficulties. In the perspective of sustainable development questions are raised about the following:

— values or desired levels and structure of development
— welfare of future generations
— relationship between man and environment
— science and technology
— processes of growth in less developed countries
— market mechanisms
— equality and justice

The State of World Population 1992, the report prepared by UNFPA quotes the following definitions of sustainable development:

(a) Sustainable development is development that meets the needs of the present without compromising the ability of future generations to meet their own needs .... Living standards that go beyond the basic minimum are sustainable only if consumption standards everywhere have regard for long-term sustainability (Brundtland Commission, 1987).

(b) Sustainable development .... involves providing a bequest to the next generation which is at least equal to that inherited by the current generation (Blueprint for a Green Economy, 1989).

(c) Development that distributes the benefits of economic progress more equitably, protects both local and global environments for future generations, and truly improves the quality of life (Our Own Agenda, Inter-American Development Bank, 1990).

(d) Sustainable development means improving the quality of human life while living within the carrying capacity of supporting ecosystems. A "sustainable economy" maintains its natural resource base. It can continue to develop by adapting and through improvements in knowledge, organisation, technical efficiency, and wisdom (Caring for the Earth, IUCN and WWF, 1991).

Obviously, development has to be sustainable there are only three options before development planners: (a) a check on the scale of living; (b) changeover from manufacturing to service; and (c) new technological developments to conserve resources, raise their productivity and reduce pollution. Yet, some economists feel that the case of limits to growth is overstated and as such the possibility of extinction is remote. They believe that once a clear perception of problems is had, human intervention can always find ways and means to solve them. To quote Davis (1990):

> "Thus the grizzly truth may turn out to be that Limits are more prophetic than its detractors and even some of its defenders thought possible. In fact during the last three decades several basic developments have occurred that together amount to a revolution in environmental concerns. First, the sheer number of discoveries of environmental problems has increased precipitously; second, the long-term seriousness of the problems has been increasingly recognized as more of the consequences of growth are felt; third, many problems formerly thought to be local in character are in fact global or near-global in scope; fourth, the involvement of science in understanding the causes of environmental change has increased rapidly; and fifth, the international scope of environmental damages has led inevitably to strong demands for conservationist policies."

The fact is that an increasing number of economists are now preoccupied with environmental matters. Keyfitz (1991) stressed that now we have to recognise the ozone layer, carbon dioxide in the atmosphere, extinction of species, waste, and desertification. At high levels of income and technological development the effects of changes in economic and demographic variables on the ecosphere are great and cannot be neglected. Like Davis, Keyfitz (1990) articulates that the world is changing. "Communication, the conquest of space, computing, the new cellular biology, atomic physics, were indeed changing the world at exactly the time when economists discovered human capital". But some important changes noticed by Keyfitz due to which he differs from Davis are: (a) non-linearity and non-substitutability of resources availability; (b) capital setting limits of economic progress; (c) structural bottlenecks in employment generation; (d) greater recognition of the fact that economy is set within the ecology; and (e) awareness of warming of the bio-sphere.

The perception of less developed countries are critical. They suspect that the very talk of environmental problems is essentially an instrument of debarring them from raising their standards to the levels of developed countries. In the framework of the theory of underdevelopment, some scientists attributed environmental problems to the exploitative world system (Fradkin and Mashbits, 1975). They felt that poverty rather than over development is the cause of environmental problems in the less developed countries. To quote:

> "With the realisation that poverty and the state of underdevelopment led to many of the environmental problems that confronted the nation, came the understanding that it was more rapid development which was the best approach. This development has to benefit people (and particularly the poor) by providing for their basic human needs and rising aspirations. Thus, many of the developmental programmes and ...., could indeed be termed as environmental management programmes" (Govt. of India, 1985).

Despite this rising environmental consciousness among masses, effects of large development projects and ecological movements are facing national governments to attach significance to sustainability.

It may be noted that sustainable development is not a strategy of development. It is a goal or a vision. To be of practical utility it has to be operationalised in specific contexts. Yet it sensitises us to the fact that the rich and the poor, the present and the future, cities and countryside, industry and agriculture, and man and nature are inseparable and they are linked with each other through complex socio-economic, cultural, biological and political chains. It stresses that the long-run welfare of "ego" depends heavily on the welfare of "alter". "The immediate objective of sustainable development is to "economize ecology" by improving energy efficiency, conserving resources, restoring habitat, monitoring the ecosystem and improving social health (U.N., 1991).

The World Bank (1992) has suggested a threefold strategy for meeting the challenge of sustainable development. They are:

(a) *Build on the Positive Links.* Growth of income promotes efficient use of resources, technology transfer, market and investment in environment improvement. Poverty removal reduces population growth and provides resources and knowledge to enable the poor to take a long range view of development.
(b) *Break the negative links.* Incentives, environment policies and institutions building are necessary to guarantee sustainability. Mere improvement in income and capacity to solve environment problems are not sufficient.
(c) *Clarify and manage the uncertain links.* Knowledge generation is important to know new relationships between man and environment and effective management of resources.

Role of Population in Models of Sustainable Development

For several decades economists thought that population growth greatly affects the growth rate of economy through its impact on saving and investment dicisions. Sociologists and others too believed that rapid growth of numbers can lead to crisis. So when the paradigm of sustainable development came, it was natural that theorists started looking upon population size and demographic processes as important determinants of sustainable development. However, quite often the results of their exercises revealed that population is not the source of environmental crisis. It is rather the mode of social organisation and technological development which affects a society's potential to develop in a sustainable manner (Flank, 1961; Duncan, 1961; Repetto and Holmes, 1983; Preston and Donaldson, 1986; Stonich, 1989; Misra, 1990; Shiva, 1991; GBIHED, 1992; Srivastava, 1992). In a recent study of relationship between population growth and environment, Commoner concludes "that the rate of increase in pollution is largely determined by the technology factor, which governs the amount of pollution generated per unit of goods produced or consumed .... and the results of efforts to reduce them support the view that the decisive factor determining environmental quality is the nature of the technology of production, rather than the size of population" (Commoner,1991).

Broadly, regarding the relationship between population growth and environmental problems there have been the following three major approaches:

(a) A new-Malthusian approach which says that unrestrained population growth cannot be sustained. Inevitably it will lead to ecological and economic problems and cause misery.

(b) An anti-Malthusian approach which says that the present day environmental crisis has resulted mainly from faults of capitalist or old economic thinking, modern institutions, and industrialisation. It stresses that in both the developed and the developing countries the rate of environmental degradation far exceeds the rate of population growth.

(c) A modified neo-Malthusian approach which says that even though industrialisation and economic growth are the more important factors behind environmental damage, slowdown in population growth would help greatly in finding solution to the environmental problems, and the high population growth will worsen the already bad condition of environment (Ananta, 1990).

At the same time the role of population in sustainable development cannot be ignored. High rate of growth of population not only raises the demand for natural resources, it also affects most of those proximate variables which hamper the sustainability of development, *e.g.* organisation of production, innovations, technological developments, politics, values and market. Population processes also affect the indicators of sustainability such as equality, justice, absence of abject poverty, and greater participation of people in development.

In the less developed countries where population growth rates are high, and particularly in those countries where densities are also high, the possibilities of raising carrying capacities of scarce land resources (*i.e.* the maximum numbers that resources can support) are low, and alternative employment opportunities are limited, the people have responded in ways which are not conducive to sustainable development (Thapa and Weber, 1989). They have adopted "strategies of expanding of agricultural lands into marginally suited areas, of enlarging the size of their herds of livestock, and of outmigrating." This is to cope with their rising demand for food, clothing, shelter and medicine.

As such population growth would lead to fragmentation of land, and cause low productivity, unemployment and reduced on farm supply of fodder. People would either migrate to cities or be compelled to expand agriculture. Some of them may respond to low farm productivity by increasing the number of livestock. The agricultural expansion, and growth of livestock are two major factors behind destruction of forests and pastures. They also cause soil erosion and thus ecological imbalance. As a matter of fact population growth, poor economic conditions, deforestation, soil desiccation and ecological imbalance tend to reinforce each other through dynamic multicycle structures.

In the light of the above, let us look at the Indian data. Table 5.1 shows data on availability of land in India, for the period 1950-88. The table shows it clearly that over the years per capita availability of forest land has declined. It has declined from 0.127 hectare in 1965-66 to 0.083 hectare in 1987-88, due to population growth, and modernisation induced deforestation and agricultural expansion. At the same time per capita availability of agricultural land in rural areas has also been declining constantly since 1950-51. While it was 0.638 hectare in 1950-51 it was only 0.325 hectare in 1987-88. It may be noted that the implications of these figures are larger than figures themselves. With fragmentation of land, small farms being unviable in capitalist agriculture, and ground

TABLE 5.1: Availability of Land in India

Year	Forest land availability per person (hectare)	Per capita availability of agricultural land in rural area (hectare)
1950-51	0.113	0.638
1955-56	0.131	0.557
1960-61	0.124	0.503
1965-66	0.127	0.455
1970-71	0.115	0.410
1975-76	0.110	0.388
1979-80	0.102	0.360
1980-81	0.099	0.356
1981-82	0.097	0.349
1982-83	0.095	0.343
1983-84	0.093	0.336
1984-85	0.090	0.332
1985-86	0.088	0.327
1986-87	0.085	0.327
1987-88	0.083	0.325

Source: *C.S.O., Selected Socio-Economic Statistics of India 1991*, Department of Statistics, Ministry of Planning, Government of India, p. 23.

water level going down, small farmers start selling off their land, causing greater inequality in rural areas, and migration towards cities.

Table 5.2 shows percentage distribution of area by land use. The data may contain some errors of unknown quantum and should be used with caution. Yet certain trends are clear: (a) per cent area under forests, fallow land, permanent pastures and other grazing land and net area sown show an erratic trend; (b) per cent area under miscellaneous tree crops and culturable waste land has declined; (c) per cent net area sown and per cent area sown more than once have risen. After 1983-84 there has been little progress in multiple cropping. It appears that at the prevailing levels of technology all that could be done to raise agricultural production through intensive and extensive cultivation has been done and future population growth will only cause deforestation and pressure.

TABLE 5.2: Percentage Distribution of Area by Land Use

	Percentage of total area under							
Year	Forests	Not available for cultivation	Permanent pastures & other grazing land	Land under misc. tree crops not included in net area sown	Culturable waste land	Fallow land	Net area sown	Area sown more than once as percentage of net area sown
1950-51	14.2	16.7	2.3	7.0	8.1	9.9	41.8	11.3
1955-56	17.6	16.6	3.9	2.0	7.4	8.3	44.2	14.1
1960-61	18.1	17.0	4.7	1.5	6.4	7.7	44.6	14.7
1965-66	20.1	16.2	4.9	1.3	5.6	7.3	44.6	14.0
1970-71	21.0	14.7	4.4	1.4	5.8	6.4	46.3	18.2
1975-76	22.0	13.0	4.1	1.3	5.7	7.2	46.7	20.2
1980-81	22.2	13.0	4.0	1.2	5.5	8.2	46.0	23.3
1982-83	22.1	13.1	3.9	1.2	5.4	7.8	46.6	21.8
1983-84	22.1	13.3	3.9	1.1	5.1	7.5	46.9	26.2
1984-85	21.8	13.4	3.9	1.2	5.2	8.2	46.3	25.7
1985-86	22.1	13.4	3.9	1.1	5.1	8.2	46.2	26.9
1986-87	21.8	13.5	3.9	1.2	5.1	8.6	45.9	26.2
1987-88	21.9	13.5	3.9	1.2	5.1	9.7	44.7	26.9

Source: C.S.O., Secected Socio-Economic Statistics of India 1991, Department of Statistics, Ministry of Planning, Government of India, p. 24.

The direct impact on the environment is determined by interaction of three factors: size of population, consumption standards, and wastages of resources for each unit of consumption (UNFPA, 1992),

Impact = Population x consumption per person x technology effect

According to findings of Commoner (1972) in the United States between 1949 and 1968, population growth accounted for 14 per cent of the combined increase. Consumption accounted for only 5 per cent and change in technology was responsible for as much as 81 per cent of the increase. However, the three factors are not independent. Changes in population size and consumption (or income) per capita may be partly compensating as there is usually a negative correlation between the two but their intreraction with technology effect is far from clear (Demeny, 1990). According to Demeny, a significant change in the demographic parameters is found to cause shifts in relationships between population, income and resource-use-intensity, sometimes compensating and sometimes reinforcing the environmental impact. To quote:

> "In particular, over time non-linearities to scale may appear. Quantitative increases can generate qualitative changes; thresholds separating, for example, tolerable levels of pollution from levels that generate unacceptable risks for human health may be crossed. Up to a certain level, damage to a renewable resource such as a forest ecosystem, may be corrected by a spontaneous and relatively rapid biological process; beyond that level the damage may be irreparable, or the natural recovery or the human-engineered repair of the ecosystem in question may require a very long time or entail exorbitant cost."

Developmental and environmental conservation plans have generally recognised demographic factors as critical factors which influence consumption patterns, production, life styles and long-term sustainability. It has become clearer than ever before that population induced demand for natural resources, employment, education and social services will make attempts to protect natural resources and improve standards of living more and more difficult (UNCED,1992).

Population Consequences of Sustainable Development

The complex relationship between population, environment and development has often been called the development paradox: while population pressure can slow the process of development, development can act as a contraceptive (U.N., 1992). Although in the literature on population role of demographic factors in development has been greatly explored, not much work has been done to establish the other side of the equation, *i.e.*, the role of sustainable development in population management. Only in 1987 the World Commission on Environment and Development—the Brundtland Commission—urged that "all should keep in mind that sustainable economic growth and equitable access to resources are two of the most certain routes towards lower fertility rates." *The State of World Population 1993* has now clearly demonstrated that more often than not international migration, the emerging problem of demographics, has been caused by environmental disruption; control of migration requires sustainable development and environmental planning.

Part of the difficulty in treating sustainable development as a determinant of demographic processes arises from the fact that there is no single blueprint of sustainability. Economic and social systems differ widely among countries. Thus although sustainable development has become a global objective, each nation will have to work out its own concrete policy (World Commission on Environment and Development, 1987). Also in the different regions of the world the nature of population problems is different. The developed countries are in general characterised by low birth and death rates, low infant mortality rate, below replacement fertility, near zero or negative growth rate, high percentage urban and the problem of population implosion. The less developed countries are in general characterised by high but falling birth rate, falling death rate, falling infant mortality rate, high growth rate, high maternal mortality rate, low percentage urban and the problem of population explosion. It should be noted that several countries in both developed and less developed categories have unique demographic situation and they do not conform to the generalised pattern. Generalised solution will not be of any use there. Thus the same constituents of sustainable devleopment which may solve "population problems" (as perceived by society or by planners) in one country or one region may simply not work in the other countries or regions. They may rather aggravate the existing problems. Despite this there can be certainly broad agreement on certain aspects of development such as health, income generation, employment, productivity, poverty removal, environmental cleanliness, improvement in status of women, adult literacy, equity, and access to quality family planning services. They are all well established determinants of demographic processes. They are also important goals in themselves.

In the context of less developed countries in particular, some of the recent works in the area of population studies have clearly established that improved health services, family planning programmes, raising status of women, rise in adult literacy and promotion of equality are some factors which cause reduction in birth rate (Caldwell, 1991; Jain, 1989; Phillips *et al.*, 1988; World Fertility Survey, 1984, Rodgers, 1989; Ratcliffe, 1983). One may definitely ask a very important question: Given the paucity of resources where should one concentrate? Examination of this question is, however, beyond the scope of this paper. Moreover, given the complexity of socio-economic and demographic situation this question can never be answered to the satisfaction of demographers and planners. Perhaps it would always be a better option to use two or more strategies in combination, or develop an optimal mix of several strategies based on operations research, rather than to depend on a single strategy to reduce birth rate. Besides this, the population planners have not one objective function. For example, population explosion, caused by low death rate and persisting high birth rate, is not the only issue to be tackled in the less developed countries. There are many others: urban explosion caused by population pressure in rural areas as well as natural growth of urban areas, issues pertaining to regional demography, high infant mortality, unfavourable nuptiality patterns, rigid social stratification, illegal international migration, etc. In some situations planners will select some of them to be dealt with on a priority basis and in some other situation they will all be taken at the same time. Accordingly, practical decisions will have to be made.

Beyond the Causality of Population and Sustainable Development

Although there may be strong theoretical linkages between sustainable development and population, sustainable development is neither a necessary nor a sufficient condition for effective population management. The reverse is equally true. Falling birth rates have also not been associated with better environmental management. It may be emphasised that both the developed and the less developed countries will have to work on sustainable development and population simultaneously. Let us look at data on development and population for some selected countries which may be taken as representative of countries at various levels of economic development. Table 5.3 presents data on population and development indicators and Table 5.4 presents data on status of women and environment.

Table 5.3 shows that there is tremendous disparity in per capita income. Among the countries included in the table per capita income varies from 110 (in dollars) to 32,680, giving a ratio of 1 to 297. The table also shows that the disparity has been widening as a result of the fact that while many low income countries have experienced a negative growth rate

TABLE 5.3: Population and Development Indicators for Selected Countries, 1990.

Country	Population (millions)	GNP per capita (dollars)	Aveage annual growth rates of GNP per Capita 1965-90 (per cent)	Share of agriculture in GDP (per cent)	Life expectancy (females)	Infant mortality rate	Total fertility rate	Average index of food production per capita (1879-81=100) 1988-90	Energy consumption (kilogram) of oil equivalent)
	1	2	3	4	5	6	7	8	9
Tanzania	24.5	110	-0.2	59	49	115	6.6	88	38
Ethiopia	51.2	120	-0.2	41	50	132	7.5	84	20
Zaire	37.3	220	-2.2	30	54	94	6.2	97	71
Nigeria	115.5	290	0.1	36	54	98	6.0	106	138
India	**849.5**	**350**	**1.9**	**31**	**58**	**92**	**4.0**	**119**	**231**
Pakistan	112.4	380	2.5	26	55	103	5.8	101	233
Indonesia	178.2	570	4.5	22	64	61	3.1	123	272
Bolivia	7.2	630	-0.7	24	62	92	4.8	109	257
Turkey	56.1	1,630	2.6	18	69	60	3.5	97	857
Agrentina	32.3	2,370	-0.3	13	75	29	2.8	93	1,801
Brazil	150.4	2,680	3.3	10	69	57	3.2	115	915
New Zealand	3.4	12,680	1.1	9	79	10	2.0	102	4,971
United States	250.0	21,790	1.7	3 (1965)	80	9	1.9	92	7,822
Sweden	8.6	23,660	1.9	3	81	6	1.9	99	6,347
Japan	123.5	25,430	4.1	3	82	5	1.6	101	3,563
Switzerland	6.7	32,680	1.4	—	82	7	1.7	101	3,902
Kuwait	2.1	—	-4.0	1	76	14	3.4	—	6,414

of per capita GNP during 1965-90, many rich countries have experienced a positive growth during this period. One common characteristic of the high income countries is that in most of them share of agriculture in the GDP is less than 10 per cent.

The gaps between the rich and the poor countries in life expectancy (e^o_o) and infant mortality rate (MIR) are also great. While in the high income countries e^o_o for females is above or in the vicinity of 80 and IMR is less than 10, the same for the poor countries are around 50 and 100, respectively. Total fertility rates in the poor countries are usually above 5 and those in the rich countries are less than 2 (*i.e.*, below the replacement level). The table also shows that in the high income countries consumption of energy per capita is also very high as compared to low income countries. Regarding food production it is difficult to discern a pattern. Yet it may be said that in many poor as well as rich countries index of food production has been declining. For the poor countries in which 30-50 per cent people are below the poverty line and in which food demand remains highly unmet, consequences of this fall can be disastrous.

In terms of indicators of social development all the low income countries suffer from low school enrolment rates (specifically among females) and high maternal mortality. The relationship between income and urbanisation is not much strong but low income countries also have low levels of urbanisation. And due to high population pressure in rural areas, dwindling resources, desplacement caused by new development projects and social conflict cities in developing countries are filled with larger streams of rural-urban migrants than they can actually absorb (U.N., 1993). Many of the less developed countries have large forest area. Due to rapid population growth, modernisation, and "dependent industrialisation" they are undergoing high deforestation is evident from Table 5.4. For some countries such as Indonesia and Brazil, the annual rate of deforestation during 1981-85 has been above 10 per cent which implies that the half-life of their forests is less than 7 years.

Needless to say deforestation occurring in low income agricultural countries is a serious environmental hazard. It relates to or interacts with expansion of deserts, floods and famines, extinction of species, green house effect, pollution, atmospheric changes, etc. Surprisingly in many poor countries despite low levels of urbanisation and industrialisation annual withdrawal of water per capita is very high. This is due to demands of modern agriculture and industrialisation. *World Development Report 1992* and enormously growing literature on environment have described how bad is the development scenario in high income as well as low income countries. One has to make a pause here and ponder: is there a way out?

TABLE 5.4: Status of Women and Environment Indicators for Selected Countries, 1990

Country	Primary school enrolment females 1989	Maternal mortality rate (per 100,000 live births)	Percentage urban	Forest area (thousands of square kilometers	Annual defores-tation 1981-85	Annual withdrawal of water (1970-87) as per-centage of total water resources	Annual withdrawal per capita 1970-87 (cubic meters)
	1	2	3	4	5	6	7
Tanzania	63	370	33	420	3.0	1	36
Ethiopia	30	2,000	13	272	0.9	2	48
Zaire	67	800	40	1776	3.7	0	22
Nigeria	63	1,500	35	148	4.0	1	44
India	**82**	**500**	**27**	**640**	**0.5**	**18**	**612**
Pakistan	27	600	32	25	0.1	33	2,053
Indonisia	115	800	31	1169	10.0	3	452
Bolivia	77	480	51	668	1.2	0	148
Turkey	108	207	61	202	-	12	1,144
Argentina	114	85	86	445	1.8	3	1,059
Brazil	108 (1965)	150	75	5,145	13.8	1	212
NewZealand	105	-	84	92	-	0	379
United States	-	9	75	2,960	1.6	19	2,162
Sweden	104	4	84	278	-	2	479
Japan	102	15	77	53	-	20	923
Switzerland	87 (1965)	5	60	11	-	6	502
Kuwait	91	18	96	0	-	-	234

Source: The World Bank, *World Development Report* 1992, pp. 218-283.

Yes there is a way. That way is the Gandhian way. The way is for all those who realise: (a) that the resources of earth may be great but are finite; (b) that they can neither support infinite human population nor can they satisfy infinite demands of finite population; (c) that to intervene in the ecological processes is not only possible but it has also become a religious duty in our times; (d) that the processes of development need to be regulated by the higher law of species; and (e) that we require local solutions keeping in view the satiability of earth, flora and fauna, local needs and global systems. We live in an age in which we have to prepare ourselves to face global problems and work out local solutions. These local solutions should be built in our approach to agricultural development, energy generation, industrial progress, demographic pressure, peace, gender relations and justice. A feeling has to grow that development is defined not by statistics of per capita income etc. but by society's power to last. Today this all may appear ideal or theoretical or dream, the will to survive will make it real tomorrow.

REFERENCES

Ananta, Aris, 1990, "The Impact of Demographic Variables on the Quality of the Environment", *Indonesian Journal of Demography,* Vol. 17, No. 33, pp. 1-16.

Barney, G.O., 1980, *Global 2000: The Report to the President Entering the 21st Century,* U.S. Government Printing Office, Washington D.C.

Caldwell, J.C., 1991, "The Soft Underbelly of Development, Demographic Transition in Conditions of Limited Economic Change", in Fischer, Stanley, Tray, Dennis de, and Shah, Shekhar (eds.), *Proceedings of the World Bank Annual Conference on Development Economics, 1990,* World Bank, Washington D.C., pp. 207-254.

Commoner, Barry, 1991, "Rapid Population Growth and Environmental Stress", *International Journal of Health Services,* Vol. 21, No. 2, pp. 199-227.

Dasgupta, Sugata, 1985, *Towards a Post-Development Era: Essays in Poverty, Welfare and Development,* Mittal Publications, New Delhi.

Davis, Kingsley, 1990, "Population and Resources: Fact and Interpretation, in Davis, Kingsley, and Bernstam, Mikhail, S. (eds.), *Resources, Environment and Population: Present Knowledge, Future Option,* Population Council, New York, pp. 1-24.

Demeny, Paul, 1990, "Tradeoffs between Human Numbers and Material Standards of Living", in Davis, Kingsley and Bernstam, Mikhail, S. (eds.), *Resources, Environment and Population: Present Knowledge, Future Option,* Population Council, New York, pp. 408-21.

Duncan, O.D., 1961, "Human Ecology and Population Studies", in Hauser, P.M. and Duncan, O.D. (eds.), *The Study of Population,* Asia Publishing House, Bombay, pp. 678-716.

Flank, P.W., 1961, "Ecology and Demography", in Hauser, P.M., and Duncan, O.D. (eds.), *The Study of Population,* Asia Publishing House, Bombay, pp. 652-76.

Forrester, J.W., 1971, *World Dynamics,* Wright - Allen Press, Canbridge, England.

Fradkin, N.G., and Mashbits, Y.G., 1975, "Capitalist Society" in Gerasimov, I.P. *et al., Man, Society and the Environment,* Progress Publishers, Moscow, pp. 45-55.

G.B. Pant Institute of Himalayan Environment and Development, 1992, *Himalayan Environment and Development: Problems and Perspectives,* Gyanodaya Prakashan, Nainital.

Government of India, 1985, *Seventh Five Year Plan 1985-90, Vol. II,* Planning Commission, New Delhi, p.385.

Higgins, G.M., *et al.,* 1982, *Potential Population Supporting Capacities of Lands in the Developing World,* Food and Agricultural Organization, Rome.

Jain, Anrudh, K., 1989, "Fertility Reduction and the Quality of Family Planning Services", *Studies in Family Planning,* Vol. 20, No. 1, pp. 1-16.

Kahn, Herman, and Wiener, A.J., 1967, *The Year 2000: A Framework for Speculation on the Next Thirty-Three Years,* Macmillan, New York.

Keyfitz, Nathan, 1990, "Toward a Theory of Population-Development Interaction", in Davis, Kingsley, and Ernstam, Mikhail, S., (eds.), *Resources, Environment and Population: Present Knowldege, Future Option,* Population Council, New York, pp. 295-314.

Keyfitz, Mathan, 1991. "Population and Development within the Ecosphere: One View of the Literature", *Population Index,* Vol. 57, No.1, 1991, pp. 5-22.

Meadows, D.H., Meadows, J.R. and Behrens, W.W. III, 1972, *The Limits to Growth,* Universe Books, New York.

Measavoric, M., and Pestel, E., 1974, *Mankind at the Turning Point,* E.P. Dutton, New York.

Misra, B.D., 1990, "Population, Eco-System and the Environment: An Indian Scenario", *Demography India,* Vol. 19, No. 1, pp. 59-64.

Nagchaudhuri, B.D., and Bhatt, S., 1987, *The Global Environment Movement: A New Hope for Mankind,* Sterling Publishers Private Ltd, New Delhi.

Ness, G.D., 1991, "Population, Development and Global Change", *Populi,* Vol. 18, No.1 pp. 24-33.

Phillips, J.F., Ruth, Simmons, Koenig, M.A., and Chakraborty, J., 1988. "Determinants of Reproductive Change in a Traditional Society: Evidence from Matlab, Bangladesh, *Studies in Family Planning,* Vol. 19, No. 6, pp. 335-53.

Preston, S.H., and Donaldson, Peter, 1986, "Population Growth and Economic Development", *Asia-Pacific Population Journal,* Vol. 1, No. 2, pp. 3-12.

Ratcliffe, J.W., 1983, " Toward a Social Justice Theory of Demographic Transition: Lessons from India's Kerala State", *Janasamkhya,* Vol. 1, No.1, pp.1-38.

Repetto, Robert, and Holmes, Thomas, 1983, "The Role of Population in Resource Depletion in Developing Countries", *Population and Development Review,* Vol. 9, No. 4, pp. 609-32.

Rodgers, G., 1989, "An Overview", in Rodgers, G. (ed.), *Population Growth and Poverty in Rural South Asia,* Sage Publications, New Delhi.

Shiva, Vandana, 1991, *Ecology and the Politics of Survival: Conflicts over Natural Resources in India,* Sage Publications, New Delhi.

Srivastava, Aseem, 1992, "Overpopulation: The Great Red Herring", *Economic and Political Weekly,* Vol. 27, No. 38, Sep. 19, pp. 2033-38.

Stonich, S.C., 1989, "The Dynamics of Social Processes and Environmental Destruction: A Central American Case Study", *Population and Development Review,* Vol. 15, No. 2, pp. 269-96.

Thapa, G.B., and Weber, K.E., 1989,"Population and Environment in the Hills of Nepal", *Asia-Pacific Population Journal,* Vol. 4, No. 2, pp. 49-70.

The World Bank, 1992, *World Development Report 1992: Development and the Environment,* Oxford University Press, New York.

United Nations, 1991, *Notes for Speakers: Earth Summit 92: The United Nations Conference on Environment and Development,* United Nations, p. 14.

United Nations, 1992, *Earth Summit in Focus,* No. 6, United Nations Department of Public Information.

United Nations Conference on Environment and Development, 1992, *The Global Partnership: for Environment and Development: A Guide for Agenda 21,* UNCED, Geneva.

United, Nations Population Fund, 1992, *The State of World Population, UNFPA,* New York, p. iii.

World Commission on Environment and Development, 1987, *Our Common Future,* Oxford University Press, Oxford, p. 40.

World fertility Survey, 1984, *World Fertility Survey: Major Findings and Implications,* pp. 23-24.

SECTION-B

AN OUTLINE OF GANDHIAN THEORY OF POPULATION

6

GANDHIAN SOCIOLOGY
An Alternative Philosophy Of Social Sciences

Social sciences are well developed disciplines among sciences in India today. Most of the universities have independent departments of various social science disciplines catering to needs of teaching at graduate and post-graduate levels and research. There are also university departments and professional institutions offering courses in general or applied social sciences to students of sciences, technology, medicine, agriculture, etc. Some of them bring out good number of journals which publish articles/ research papers in social sciences. ICSSR, different ministries, and many international organisations are providing funds for social research. Many-a-social scientist of India have achieved high status at international level in the community of social scientists. It is natural that at this juncture social scientists are reflecting and looking back at the state of art in their subject. Questions are often asked: What is Indian in Indian social sciences? Do we need an Indian social science for India? What will be the nature of that ? Many important social scientists have dealt with these questions at length. However, a really indigenous concept in the light of which Indian facts can be examined has not yet emerged.

On the face of it, there are two distinct traditions in Indian social sciences. They may be called theoretical and empirical traditions. The theoretical social scientists have looked at structure and processes of Indian society, and social problems in definite western theoretical frameworks. The theoretical frameworks provide the methodology and quite often the problems also for investigation. Indian social scientists have made use of all existing theoretical frameworks for this purpose, *e.g.* functional, Marxian, social action and phenomenological perspectives. Thus one finds that there are several distinct lines of thinking in Indian social sciences. The theoretical sociologists and anthropologists have concentrated on the following:

(a) assertion of adequacy or legitimation of the western theoretical framework to explain patterns and changes in Indian society;
(b) explanation and prediction of social phenomena; and
(c) required modifications in the western framework in the light of Indian data.

Functionalists have looked at various institutions and processes and related them to wider context, either as causes or as consequences of the social structure, dynamics or social movements. Marxists have, by and large, characterised Indian society as a semi-feudal and semi-capitalist society. They stress that conflict in relations of production is the main basis of social conflicts and that legal, educational, political and cultural patterns in contemporary India reflect the exploitative character of Indian economy. Weberian theorists have emphasised multidimensional and complex nature of social stratification in India in studies of social tension and political changes. Existentialism and phenomenology have not been much used. However, these perspectives have indirectly influenced works of many Indian social scientists, especially in understanding meanings and their relationships in the field of socialisation.

Empirical social scientists, on the other hand, have paid greater attention to data, methods, measurements and statistical inference. Often they hold grand theories of society and culture in contempt. Their guiding belief is that data speak for themselves. They say that in place of debating over adequacy of theoretical frameworks, social scientists must sharpen their tools of research so that reliable data can be obtained on various aspects of society. They would normally shun a theoretical debate. They prefer fieldwork and surveys more than speculation data more than theory. Many of them have accepted theoretical and methodological triangulation covertly or overtly.

Of late, many social scientists in India have expressed dissatisfaction with prevailing strands of thoughts in social sciences. They are looking for alternatives both in theory and methods. In the West itself, new methodological experiments are being performed to suit the conditions of the "post-industrial" or "post-modern" world. In this context, the present chapter offers an interpretative Gandhian theory as an alternative philosophy of social sciences for India.

India has its own unique life world. According to Singh (1973) traditional India was characterised by political fragmentation, linguistic and regional insulation, hierarchical social division and institutionalised inequality, cultural-ethnic diversity and social tolerance, primacy of group over individual and transcendence of mundane concerns. The cardinal values of traditional Indian society were hierarchy, pluralism and holism. Gandhi was one of those thinkers who recognised these characteristics of India's life world and felt that only that epistemological or metaphysical worldview which has relationship with this life world could adequately handle India's problems. Unfortunately, in the post-independence period, uncritical import of the Western theory and neglect of India's life world have caused some new trends and movements which in place of solving India's problems have themselve contributed to national crisis.

GANDHI: HIS LIFE AND THOUGHT

It is not an easy task to interpret the work of a great leader of masses who worked in very different situations for various purposes and among different people. He was subject to contradictory influences. Hence he grew with time. His struggle began with the demand for a full citizenship in British Empire and ended with protest against Indian elite who replaced the British after India's independence. His movement corresponds to neo-social movement which aimed at value transformation rather than at the capture of state power. It involved all classes of people (Nargolkar, 1975; Chandra, 1992).

Gandhian theory has been interpreted by different theorists in different ways. It is interesting to note that different people have assigned very different meanings to Gandhian theory to suit their interest. Also while Western interpreters have generally admired and appreciated Gandhi, modern Indian intelligentsia has been highly critical of his values and programmes. According to E.M.S. Namboodiripad, Gandhi was an idealist leader who helped the cause of bourgeoisie during national liberation struggle but his idealism became an obstacle in it after independence (Namboodiripad, 1959). As a result of this he became more and more isolated from bourgeoisie in the later days of his life. Disillusioned by moral degradation and factional squables in Congress circle, he did not even participate in any rejoicing on 15 August 1947, nor did he give any message on 26 January 1948.

Benudhar Pradhan (1980) says that Gandhi's sources of inspiration are Ruskin's concept of moral society, Tolstoy's concept of bread labour, Thoureau's concept of living by labour, *Gita* and *Bible.* Gandhi believed that accumulation is inconceivable without exploitation and violence, and, therefore, it is unethical, immoral and sinful. Like Fanon, Marcuse, Sartre and other New left thinkers, he wanted to have individual at the centre of the stage, restoring man to his proper place. Gandhi is known to have said that while the machine age aims at converting men into machines, he was aiming at reinstating man-turned-machine to his original state (Government of India, 1975). E.H. Erikson finds in him a *religious actualist.* Gandhi attempted to make truth actual in all compartments of life (Erikson, 1975). He was a religious innovator for his very passion and power will make him want to make actual for others what actualises him.

Mira Behn stressed that his emphasis on spinning-wheel and its use as the emblem of his ideals was a stumbling block to clear comprehension of his message as a whole and it lessens people's faith in the practicableness of his theories. His self-sufficiency objective for villages must be achieved in the light of "50 years" of science and technology development.

Gunnar Myrdal expressed that Gandhi was a *radical liberal,* who stood on the side of the downtrodden and who attempted to elevate dignity of labour to its proper level. His concept of trusteeship was a practical compromise. His purpose of throwing out the foreign rule was to bring about radical changes in social and economic order.

Indira Gandhi said that in our times it was Nehru who translated Gandhian thought into contemporary terms, to make it more comprehensible and to extend its influence to young people and intellectuals. "Gandhi did not shun the railways, and he was a punctilious user of watches. And if we use railways and watches, does it not make sense to manufacture them ourselves?" He was intensely concerned with poverty. Regarding machines his outlook was broader and more humanely practical than some literalist interpreters would have us believe. He identified with common man but was receptive to the best thought from other parts of the world. He paid equal positive respect to all religions. Gandhi and Nehru complemented each other (Radhakrishnan, 1968).

On the other hand, Ambedkar (1982) wrote:

> "The Mahatma appears not to believe in thinking. He prefers to follow the saints. Like a conservative with his reverence for consecrated notions he is afraid that if he once starts thinking many ideals and institutions to which he clings will be doomed. One must sympathise with him. For every act of independent thinking puts some portion of apparently stable world in peril. But it is equally true that dependence on saints cannot lead us to draw the truth. The saints are after all only human beings...."

Martin Luther King of the US proclaimed indebtedness of American Negroes to Gandhi in their struggle for racial equality. Some Christian Missionaries coming to India found in him living Christ. Romain Rolland, Rene Fillop-Miller, Arnold Toyanbee, etc. declared that he was prophet of their generation. USSR revised assessment of Gandhi several times. T.K. Oommen, an Indian sociologist, wrote that Gandhi established *Swaraj* though he could not build *sarvodaya* (Oommen, 1979). To him Gandhi failed to build *sarvodaya* because Gandhi and Gandhians kept away from authority. If they want to succeed they should achieve authority and use it for *sarvodaya.*

According to Pyarelal:

> "Man, the individual, is the centre of Gandhi's spiritual development of man. Man is primarily his consciousness, his capacity to be self-conscious and his built-in potentiality to judge between good and evil, between what will help him in evolution to higher levels of being and what will obstruct his path. This gives him a leverage, not only to aspire after higher levels but to endeavour to attain the same. Gandhi believed in self-effort and the path he outlined lay through ethical, moral and spiritual disciplines. The key-note of his ethics is love. The core of Gandhi's theory relates to truth and it belongs within the mainstream of India's ethical and philosophical tradition."
> Pyarelal (1956) has written that Gandhi refused to have anything (even salvation) which could not be shared with others. Freedom of Gandhi's conception has not come. "—we must retrace our steps and restart from the point where we took the wrong turning or else the farther we travel the worse shall we fare."

The above are varied conceptions of Gandhi and Gandhian theory. R.T. Templin, Professor of sociology and community development and missionary of Methodist Church, once wrote that Gandhi belonged to the coming age of hope. The lesson is that if life survives, in the new age the human spirit will be master over earth's forces, beginning with its own soul force (Templin, 1969). The present age is not of economic or industrial man as is commonly believed but of political power, robot, workmanship, inequality, manipulations and fraud. Prabhu and Rao expressed that the deep study of various sciences related to spinning wheel will lead to Gandhian sociology. To them spinning wheel stands for service, simplicity, indentification with the poor, an instrument of relationship with God, non-violence, improvement of *Harijans,* freedom, unity and equality (Prabhu and Rao, 1967). Contrary to this , Vidyarthi and Unnithan assess that Gandhian theory is against human nature, political realities and historical perspectives.

In order to examine the distinguishing characteristics of Gandhian approach we may divide approaches to study of human society into two categories: Western perspectives and Indian traditional perspectives. Commonly, all Western sociological perspectives, *i.e.*, functionalism, Marxim and phenomenology, etc. may be put in the same category for the purpose of finding out their common theoretical bases. Buddhism, *Sankhya,* Vedanta, Sikhism, Jainism, etc. are put in the category of Indian tradition. Here one may ask why do we not include Christianity in the Western perspective. It may be noted that the term Western does not imply a geographical concept. Gandhi said in 1908 that Westernization as a concept refers to the process of change that occured in the Western countries during the past 100 years or so. In other words, pre-modern West is not the model of Westernisation. In a letter to his son Gandhi referred to Emerson as a Western Guru of Hinduism. Thus many forms of Christian thinking are close to Indian rather than "Western" perspective. The Western sociologists tend to use the utilitarian rational model of man to unearth the logic of social structure. An attempt is made to abstract this model from social contexts. In other words, the Western perspective combines normative sociologistic model of society and the utility rationality model of man. Since the two perspectives are largely autonomous various seemingly different perspectives have emerged from the combination of the two. They present several dialectical relationships as between man and nature, nation and world, class and economy, individual and society, ethnic group and plural society, etc. Consequently, in the Western framework, there is an individual, formed partly by himself and partly by his cultural milieu who is constantly attempting to rationalise his interaction with the outside world. Perhaps the distinguishing characteristic of the Western theory, its recognition that consciousness of man is determined by social environment, is itself the product of historically situated interaction between biological and social forces.

As opposed to the above, Gandhi offers a critical traditional metaphysics. He wanted to build a society based on pluralism and holism but free from inequality. He showed that in his times Indian tradition had developed many inconsistencies. One of them was juxtaposition of inequality and pluralistic holism. To him pluralistic holism is essentially the negation of inequality and thus creative use of pluralistic holism can greatly help in countering inequality in India. In this respect he did not stand alone. Tolstoy, Aurobindo, Ambedkar, Guru Nanak, Dayananda, all attempted precisely this. The unique contribution of Gandhi lies in evolving a practical shape of modern political institutions in the light of this perspective. To quote Saran (1979):

> "The true aim of furthering the Gandhian ideas is to effect Metanoia, that is, to bring about a state of affairs in which more and more people are in their right minds."

It may be noted that as such the concepts of pluaralism and holism are amorphous. Used in the Gandhian framework, they reflect a certain religious metaphysics unique to interface of Indian philosophies and common thought categories of Indians. Needless to say, both macro level philosophies and micro level thought categories are inseparably linked with the life world. To Gandhi, Western thinking is part of the Western culture. It is a materialistic culture which has industrialisation at the centre. It is growth oriented, open and immoral. In his opinion, many of the present day civilisational problems of India such as poverty, illiteracy, unemployment, exploitation, marginalisation of villages have been created by modernisation. Perhaps the pre-modern society managed itself much better. Here pre-modern society is a concept which includes large number of pre-modern societies as well as certain contemporary thought patterns. Sorokin's ideas can throw light on this understanding of Gandhi.

In his cyclical theory of change, Sorokin says that society oscillates between ideational and sensate phases. The difference between Western and non-Western societies of today lies in the fact that they have entered the sensate phase at different times (Sorokin, 1947). This sensate culture will die a natural death and will be replaced by an ideational culture. Both in Gandhi's *Ramrajya* and Sorokin's ideational phase the reality is supersensory and superrational; it cannot be deduced simply from biological and social materiality. A *satyagrahi* or an ideational presonality, therefore, looks for the transcendental truth. On the other hand, a Western theorist explains human behaviour in ecological and historical terms at the macro level and utilitarian, cognitive and situational terms at the micro-livel.

At this juncture it may again be stated that Gandhi recognised the problematique of classification as Western or Indian because of the interplay of several factors. He was opposed to rationalisation of tradition. To him everything in the Western culture was not wrong. As early as 1908, he condemned that modern Western civilisation only which had emerged during the preceding 100 years and had produced cultural anarchy in the West (Government of India, 1962). As the Western paradigm emerged from the actual life world of the West, he believed that Indian paradigm should emerge from the actual life world of India. And above all how he mingled a world of thought into a world of action is one of the most important aspects of his life and thought.

CONCEPTUAL FRAMEWORK OF GANDHIAN INTERVENTION

The central philosophy of Gandhi may be mentioned in relation to theories of development and change. Certainly, the views (i) interpretation of Indian institutions requires use of indigenous—esoteric or exoteric - cultural perspectives and (ii) rules of social intervention require that solutions to political-economic problems of present day India are consistent with the Indian cultural perspectives are well articulated today both by Western and Indian sociologists. Yet because of the biographical and theoretical reasons their interpretation of Indian perspectives is biased by their own belief systems. Thus it is not rare that many Westerners have looked at India in the thought categories of the West. For them the structure of Indian tradition is not a methodological concept but it is an object of analysis that they have analysed in the Western framework. Therfore, it is important to distinguish traditional theory from theory of Indian tradition. This leads to a need to identify key concepts of Indian tradition in the light of which modern problems of India can be examined. Gandhi had done precisely this. Gandhian sociology offers the conceptual scheme of revolutionary tradition, consistent with Indian philosophy as the scheme of understanding and action.

In India, as in many less developed countries, social scientists used the theory of modernisation and development in 1950s and 1960s to analyse social change. According to this theory, development is the universal characteristic of all societies. Every society starts with the same baseline conditions, *i.e.,* the conditions of zero-development, and moves towards higher and higher levels of development. But the process of development in less advanced countries shows a time lag. Some countries have started early and some late. India as a less developed country is a late starter. In the 1970s social scientists began criticising this theory of development on three main grounds: (a) changes in levels of economic growth hide the variations in income inequality: (b) development is a broader concept than economic development; and (c) less developed countries of today are underdeveloped countries and not undeveloped, and further development of the developed countries and underdevelopment of the less developed countries are two sides of the same coin. Moreover, not all problems are due to tradition. Modernisation itself has presented several new problems which are, izonically, attributed to tradition. Modernisation along capitalist line is not desirable to solve contemporary social problems and that as such modernisation will bring greater crisis in its train. This perception led to the following alternative approaches to development and modernisation:

(a) to examine ways in which Western societies themselves are solving both of their problems, those caused by vestiges of the past and those caused by modernisation itself;
(b) to recognise that many problems of India are unique but still amenable to solution in the Western framework;
(c) to combine Western and traditional technologies and institutions to solve contemporary problems;
(d) to use traditional institutions of today's modern civilisations to solve civilisational problems:
(e) to revive a traditional society in alll aspects and total rejection of modernisation; and
(f) to look for new framework of solutions with help of all traditional, modern, cognitive, historical, economic and political solutions, *i.e.*, to define man and his environment newly which may imply revolutionising tradition in some situations, traditionalising modernity in others, and looking for solutions beyond tradition-modernity in other situations.

Majority of planners and scientists in India have preferred solutions in the Western framework. Weberian combinatorial rationality also has the same substratum. Scholars such as Coomaraswamy and Saran have opted for revival of tradition. Among many social reformists of 19th and 20th century is such as Bankim Chandra, Tagore, Vivekananda, Dayananda and many varieties of Gandhies also this tendency can be seen. Schumacher wanted to return to good society (Schumacher, 1979). Problems with those approaches have increasingly become clear. Catching-up with the West is not really feasible. Combinatorial ideas are not ingenious and total return to traditional society is only romantic and impossible. The real choice is to go beyond tradition-modernity debate. Although it is at present not very clear what shape would it take but its roots are present in the works of Sri Aurobindo, Gandhi, Binova, Rifkin and many modern scientists and ecologists. It would be a non-dualist perspective which does not differentiate between cultures, generations, classes, castes, nations ideas and practice. It is neither individualistic nor sociologistic. It is a non-violent scheme of simultaneous tranformation of man and his social order. It enjoys both subjective and objective knowledge which Bankim Chandra wanted Indians to have.

Thus a new perspective is needed which recognises that we are morally related to a non-human physical world, that our relations are not only physical but moral as well. Here we require a wider conception of the moral self. To quote Shirk (1988):

> "The moral was once understood to be creature of a specific time and place, responsible to itself reflexively and to other humans interactively. But with the new awareness of the self's moral relations with a physical world, the self gains an extended life. The moral self and its obligation thus extends across time. It becomes related to a succession of selves which its action affects. The biological continuum becomes a moral one as wel. While this may be old hat to biologist, it is surely new to the ethical enquirer."

Aurobindo, who declared that we are in the age of individualism and are moving towards age of subjectivity and world unity, had the similar conception of man and self (Iyengar, 1972). This offers a new concept of society and bridges the gap between micro and macro realities. Gandhi's *Ramrajya* exhibits it. To quote: "The sense of the word *Ramrajya* is that under such a rule the poor will be fully protected, everything will be done with justice, and the voice of the poeple will be respected". Gandhi says: "No one can predict when we shall attain *Ramrajya*. But it is the duty of every one of us to contemplate it day and night. And true contemplation is that in which proper methods have also been used for the establishment of *Ramrajya*. Looking at Gandhian thought from the micro perspective a man whose soul controls his sense organs lives in *Ramrajya* irrespective of external circumstances (Government of India 1971, Pyarelal, 1956).

Gandhi presents a model of the *samatvayoga* or the *samyayoga* (the non-dualist tradition), mentioned earlier. As suggested by Madan and Unnithan, his ideas are influenced by Islam and Christianity but rooted in Hinduism. His political and social ideas reflect the creative and critical component of Indian tradition (Hinduism, Buddhism and Jainism) (Madan, 1987; Unnithan, 1979). To quote Madan:

> "Mahatma Gandhi genuinly respected all religions and his outlook on life was influenced by Jainism and Christianity and Islam. Though he considered all religions to be equally true, and equally imperfect, the 'centre of his being' in words of his admiring Christian friend Charles Andrews, ever remained firmly fixed in Hinduism."

To understand his sociological ideas one can examine his reflections on socialism. During his last detention at Poona he read Marxist writings intensively. He found that "all for each and each for all" or "from each according to his capacity and to each according to his need" were the quintessence of the teaching of Marx. However, Marxism is not the only way or even the best way of achieving this goal. There are many significant differences between Gandhi and Marx on this account:

1. According to Marxism our ideologies, ethical standards and values are altogether a product of our material environment without any outside basis but according to Gandhi as we are, so our environment becomes.
2. Gandhi had very great faith in non-violence. To him neither democracy nor socialism are possible in an environment of violence.
3. While Marxists have favoured an urban-industrial culture and stressed the emancipatory role of machine, Gandhi favoured autonomous villages and limited use of machine.
4. Marxist theory says that sometime some individuals may transcend their material environment but as such human behaviour is class behaviour and is determined by material conditions. To Gandhi what an individual can do or achieve, the whole class of people can also do or achieve. Non-violent non-cooperation movement is a technique for transcending the material environment.
5. Marxist theory lays greatest emphasis on economic forces but Gandhian theory says that in different circumstances some unseen power determines history and people's mind. Here lies the major difference in the two approaches to social conflicts and wars. To Marx to abolish war we have to abolish private property. To Gandhi to abolish war we have to abolish possessiveness, greed, lust and egotism.

In July 1947, Gandhi published two articales on socialism in *Harijan*. In those articles he stressed that non-violence and truth are twins and that only truthful, non-violent, pure hearted socialists will be able to establish a socialistic society. Socialism begins with first convert, said Gandhi. Very much like Marx, he accepted the role of revolutionary consciousness. To quote (Government of India, 1975): "When labour is intelligent enough to organize itself and learns to act as one man, it will have the same weight as money if not much greater. The conflict is really between intelligence and unintelligence. Surely it will be folly to keep up such a conflict. Unintelligence must be removed."

Gandhi was against industrialisation. He was particularly against the indiscriminate use of modern machinery (Raghavan, 1986). He believed that industrialisation inevitably leads to imperialism, colonisation and violence. We cannot build non-violence on a factory civilisation. If India becomes industrialised, we shall need a Nadirshah to find out other worlds to exploit, said Gandhi (Government of India, 1975). Also to make the dumb millions of our land happy, healthy and spiritually developed we do not require machine. At the same time he accepted machine that helps all men. If expropriation of surplus and exploitation have transformed feudal society into an industrial society, the natural tendency in a non-exploitative non-profit making society would be to substitute handicrafts for machinery for whatever can be done better by hand, and to give the worker a healthy and satisfying form of an occupation. Achievement of this society will not be production of statistics of per capita income but its power to last, *i.e.*, its capacity to have sustainable development. It suffices to say that Gandhian model is:

(a) a model of post-industrial society;
(b) a model of *samyayoga;*
(c) a model of simultaneous transformation of man and his institutions; and;
(d) a model that draws freely from all economic, political and religious systems and welds them into a single system of simultaneous and sustaining development.

It must be said that Gandhi laid great emphasis on that social intervention which links present with the desired future as much as the micro with the macro. Therefore, the strategies and goals of interventions reflect the final goal as much as the present milieu. In each age, Gandhian theorists must innovate new ways which will help society move in the right direction. In our times we cannot always accept what Gandhi himself did or say. As a matter of fact Gandhi did not favour developing any ism. He would often contradict himself and say that if ever contradicts himself his new ideas should be accorded importance. He felt that adherence to isms may cause many problems.

METHODOLOGICAL ISSUES

It is difficult for a modern Westernised man to fully comprehend meaning behind thoughts of Gandhi through his writings, not only because many-a-time Gandhi's writings appear to be inconsistent and polemical but also because he is likely to look at Gandhian thoughts in the framework of modernisation. Gandhi derived inspirations from several sources many of whom have also been interpreted in different ways. Our understanding is that on the relationship between man and society Gandhian framework would provide a two-fold classification of theories. We may call them socio-centric theory and self centric theories. According to the socio-centric theory examination and evaluation of action require a sociological space. It implies that improvement in degree of happiness or freedom lies in social transformation. On the other hand, the self-centric theory focuses on action, abstracting it from limited social context and relating it to rules of self. It, therefore, does not accept institutional change as an end in itself. It assumes that if man follows rules of self, good society will emerge. Gandhi's *Ramrajya* must be seen in this perspective because Gandhi's *Ramrajya* must essentially be defined in terms of properties of living individuals and not in terms of social structure (Government of India 1971).

Gandhian thought contains both view points. Socio-centric theory, consistent and seemingly true, is presented in the discussion of social institutions but the self-centric theory forms the substratum of this theory. Fundamentally, the socio-centric theory appears as *vishadyoga* (a theory of confused mind). Contrary to this the self-centric theory leads to *samyayoga*. To Gandhi the great majority of Indians were held by common ancient culture, and self rule implied mutual maximisation of greater and higher unity among them (Erikson, 1975).

For the construction of self-centric theory Gandhi's writings offer the following:

(a) an ontological and metaphysical basis in the theory of birth and rebirth (Patel, 1981);
(b) classification of action as freedom yielding and bondage yielding action and classification of determinants of action into natural (self) inclinations, bodily properties, etc.;
(c) a method of classification of men into divine and satanic (Saran, 1987) according to their properties;
(d) imitation of leaders as a source of change;
(e) laws of productive work *(yagya)* and consumption *(paap);*
(f) purposes of action as *lokasangraha* (social welfare) and *sthitapragya* (self-realisation) (Iyer, 1973);
(g) reflection on chain of causes of destruction—bondage, attachment, sex, anger, destruction of intellect and meterial destruction (Chacko, 1986); and

(h) deep structure of typology of action—in terms of constructs of wisdom, political action and inertia.

Accordingly, in the Gandhian framework, we can talk of two minds: objective (images of truth) and subjective (feelings of truth). It may be said that both Truth and Untruth have their own logic and thus a set of internally consistent arguments. It may appear that in some situations following rule of self may even lead to anomie. But it constantly reminds us that we are in the midst of an unreal world. It has no past or present. Length of life or reduction in mortality rate etc. may be considered as objective indices of quality of life. The subjective aim of life is to gain an exhaustion of its existing mental impressions. In this context, a man should prepare himself to participate in society and remove its contraditions for improvement of self. Such a man may have to fight not only rivals but also his own kinsmen. A good society must prepare man and provide him opportunities to act according to his capabilities, qualities and aptitude for self-experience and to fight even his own people if ever needed. Gandhi, who said that even the nation can be sacrificed for truth, follows the subjective theory (Government of India, 1975).

Some of the differences between present orientations and Gandhian orientation are indicated in Table 6.1.

TABLE 6.1: Differences in Present Sociological Orientation and Gandhian Orientation

	Present orientation	Gandhian orientation
1.	Social cost-benefit analysis as a decision rule.	Freedom-bondage categories for decisions.
2.	Based on pleasure-pain principle of action.	Has a transcendental perspective that goes beyond pleasure-pain principle
3.	Accepts objective indices of quality of life	Accepts experience of self as an index of quality of life
4.	Counter-force as source of destruction of regimes	Attachment as source of destruction
5.	Stresses wants and distribution of produce	Stresses needs and not beyond
6.	Indentifies others against whom struggle/movement must be directed and rates strategies on the basis of effectiveness	Identifies issues and creates readiness to fight both "other" and "us" during the movement (Iyer, 1986) and judges movement itself in the moral terms; success is not important.

Further, methodological problems may be discussed at two levels, *i.e.*, at the level of philosophy and at the level of procedures. At the level of philosophy Gandhian sociology would say that the hallmark of the development of knowledge is commitment to Truth. Thus academic work is directed to exploration and conceptualisation of Truth. On the other hand, in the Western framework scholars emphasise originality. It is said that a good researcher is one who makes an original contribution. The assumption behind this is that knowledge progresses in a linear evolutionary manner and originality is an index of accumulation of new knowledge. In the recent past, this thinking has been replaced by multilinear and paradigmatic theories. On the other hand a Gandhian scholar would emphasise truth. He would divide ideas and practices on the basis of whether they reflect or promote truth or untruth. It may be noted that in the Indian tradition those who have known truth are called *drashta* or observers and not philosophers. In one sense, originality may even be suspected. Originality means that something is new and it did not exist in the past. Truth always exists. Truth and absence are contradictory. At no time truth can be absent. Originality may be falsehood and a myth. Originality may also lead to such truth-claims that even though true in a given socio-political context, may cause violence, hatred, destruction and harm, and promote unhappiness in other contexts. Gandhi did not claim originality for his work. For him ideas that he presented were part of the tradition. They were common property of the whole mankind. Ruskin, Blount, Nordau, Maine, Binova, Tolstoy, etc. are custodians of this tradition. Moreover, Western scholars have attempted to capture Truth through untrue apparatuses of mind and perceptions. For Gandhi, the categories and qualities of mind themselves are objects of analysis and intervention.

Gandhi felt that to know truth one has to be a *satyagrahi, i.e.*, one who lives according to rules of Truth. A *satyagrahi* is *sthitapragya* and has balanced mind or the steadfast intellect. Instruments of *satyagraha* are spiritual disciplines, *e.g.* truth, non-violence, non-stealing, non-possession, fearlessness, control of palate and *brahmacharya.* One whose approach towards truth is not freed from his material interests cannot know truth. In other words, *darshan* of truth can only be had by a man of pure detachment. Anger, greed, pride, fear, all these things draw a veil across the seekers' eyes. Sociologists have often talked about investigator's bias and attributed that to biographic situation of the researcher. Gandhi goes a step forward and says that not only life but also properties of embodied self affect approaches to truth. In this context, it may be noted that while Gandhi used all available methods to know facts—experiments (mostly on his own self), non-reactive research or participant observation method, survey, as well as secondary material—his main method was interview. At every stage in every campaign that he conducted throughout his long life of political involvement scrupulous records were kept. To Gandhi fact finding was an indispensable preliminary to embarking on any action. Any volunteer who ever distorted the facts was severely taken to task (Chatterjee, 1983). Gandhi would not comment on politics if he does not have first hand or true knowledge (Government of India, 1971). Whether in Champaran, in Noakhali, in Bihar or in Punjab (after Jalianwala's massacre) he would interview all concerned. He would approach people with love and sympathy and try to know others' point of view, particularly the opponent's point of view. Dialogue with the rival parties, conducted with full sincerity and warmth gave him tremendous insight into problems. He believed that we must apply laws of natural science to spiritual questions and laws of spiritual world to science.

In truth-centred theories, history occupies a back seat. History is important only to the extent that one has to work in a given space, time and condition. Interventions are needed always to correct distortions of space and time and establish truth. Gandhi knew that norms are relative and he did not insist on continuity of laws and other norms. As a matter of fact insistence on values rather than institutions made him a most creative religious man. This factor has often been responsible for his defeat, withdrawal and hypnotism. History did not make him cleverer. Long cheated by a rival he would still not lose faith in his essential goodness.

Max Weber said that Indian religion produced economic traditionalism (Weber, 1958). Many people said that Gandhi was also traditional (in economic and social spheres). It may, however, be said that his traditionalism led to what Weber calls the inner-worldly asceticism rather than the world rejecting asceticism. For him man was an instrument of God. He should not intellectually bother about "ultimate meaning" and in his vocation and rational action should simply carry out the will of God. We believe that tradition in India could not have survived for thousands of years without being constantly revolutionised. Gandhi understood this relationship between tradition and revolution. Gandhi was traditional with respect to ends of Indian civilisation and his socio-economic and political thought exhibited his commitment to revolution in social structure.

The problem with Indian social theorists today is that since India lacks a tradition of having historical perspective on change, Indian mind in the modern times has depended too heavily on non-Indian historical frameworks of social construction. In the pre-independence period, Islamic, British, Marxist and reactionary Hinduism were four main frameworks. After independence they have continued to exert their influence directly as well as indirectly through aggressive *dalit* ideology and theories of development and modernisation. These theories and frameworks are the main biases or distortions in understanding contemporary problems of India. They also are the main causes of fragmentations of India. Muslims, Westerners, Marxists, Hindu fanatics and *dalits,* all are writing histories newly to suit their political interests. But in the process of knowing itself historically Indian consciousness has negated its very character.

Similar is the tragedy with Gandhian theory. Gandhi always believed in practice. He would not theorise beyond the space of practice. But now a charge is labelled that although Gandhian utopia is based on sound theoretical principles and is worth pursuing on its own right, it is against human nature and material conditions. Unnithan who makes this charge assumes that human beings have a need for possession. If this is true should we assume that Christ, Shankar, Buddha, Guru Nanak and Mahavir lived an artificial life? Were only capitalist exploiters, political foxes, and corrupted priests true to themselves? Is a businessman happier than a saint? Is a politician less alienated than a *jeevanmukta*? Actually, some of these problems arise when sociologists assume that Gandhian goal is individual and social reform; non-violence and truth are its means (Unnithan, 1979). For Gandhi truth is the end and non-violence is the instrument.

In the end, it must be said that due to its peculiar circumstances and a distinctive metaphysics Indian people's thought system has truly been a universal system and Gandhi in our times presented its ture essence. Even those who say that Gandhi has harmed Indian interests would agree that Gandhi stood for humanity and for the depressed and not siding with national parochial interests he served the Indian interests best. Gandhi's religion is ethical religion. When he was in South Africa, his writings were more on Biblical side and after his return to India he often made use of Hindu discourse. Moreover, for Gandhi, Hinduism was a conceptual structure and not a dogma. He used to say that the quintessence of Hindu dharma is to be found in that verse of *Ishopanished* which says that the whole universe is abode of God, man must use this universe always remembering God but he should never get attached to it. He believed that even if all works of Hindu religions are thrown away, Hinduism can be saved by saving this one verse.

However, when we look at world around us in the light of the Gandhian perspective following points must be kept in mind:

1. Gandhi was a human being. He must have made errors and may have departed at times from his own philosophy in practice possibly for some practical reason. We must understand his basic approach and without defending each and every position of Gandhi evolve new solutions.
2. Truth-centric (or self-centric) theory that he propounds attmpts to bridge the gap between the distortions of the present and the ideals of the future. If this is so, changes in the baseline circumstances will naturally cause variations in approaches, and moods and expression.
3. Gandhian vision is holistic and plural. His notions of holism and plurality are traditional.
4. The goal of Gandhian intervention in society and polity is improvement (or realisation) of self. Thus Gandhian approach presents a self-centric concept of revolutionary tradition to look at society and to change it. There is a need to analyse present day empirical situation in the light of this concept.

REFERENCES

Ambedkar, B.R., 1982, *Annihilation of Caste.* Bhim Patrika Publications, Jalandhar, p. 159.

Chacko, K.C., 1986, *Metaphysical Implications of Gandhian Thought,* Mittal Publications, New Delhi, p. 63.

Chandra, Bipan, 1992, *The Epic Struggle,* Orient Longman, New Delhi, pp. 15-28.

Chatterjee, Margaret, 1983, Gandhi's Religious Thought, The Macmillan Press Ltd., New Delhi, p. 61.

Diwakar, R.R., 1967 "The Relevance of Gandhi", in Ramachandran, G. and Mahadevan, T.K. (eds.) *Gandhi: His Relevance for Our Times.* Gandhi Peace Foundation, New Delhi.

Dubey, B.R., 1969, "Gandhi's Views on Status of Women", in Biswas, S.C. (ed.), *Gandhi: Theory and Practice, Social Impact and Contemporary Relevance,* Indian Institute of Advanced Study, Simla, pp. 113-21.

Erikson, E.H., 1975, *Dimensions of a New Identity,* Light & Life Publishers, New Delhi.

Fisher, Louis, 1963, *The Essential Gandhi,* George Allen & Unwin Ltd, London.

Government of India (ed.), 1962, *The Collected Wroks of Mahatma Gandhi,* The Publication Division, Ministry of Information and Broadcasting, Vol. 8, p. 211.

Government of India (ed.), 1971, *The Collected Works of Mahatma Gandhi,* The Publication Division, Ministry of Informtion and Broadcasting, New Delhi, Vol. 44, p. 138.

Government of India (ed.), 1975, *The Collected Works of Mahatma Gandhi,* The Publication Divison, Ministry of Information and Broadcsting, Vol. 62, p. 223.

Iyenger, K.R., 1972, *Sri Aurobindo: A Biography and a History,* Vol 1-2. Sri Aurobindo Ashram Trust, Pondicherry, pp. 837-875.

Iyer, Raghavan N. 1973, *The Moral and Political Thought of Mahatma Gandhi,* Oxford University Press, New Delhi.

Iyer, Raghavan N. (ed.), 1986, *The Moral and Political Writings of Mahatma Gandhi,* Vol. 1-3., Clarendon Press, Oxford.

Madan, T.N., 1987, *Non-Renunciation: Themes and Interpretations of Hindu Culture,* Oxford University Press, New Delhi.

Namboodiripad, E.M.S., 1959, *The Mahatma and the Ism.,* People's Publishing House, New Delhi.

Nargolkar, Vasant, 1957, *JP's Crusade for Revolution,* Ram Nagar, New Delhi, pp. 40-67.

Oommen, T.K., 1979, "Rethinking Gandhian Approach", *Gandhi Marg,* Vol. 1, No. 7, pp. 416-23

Patel, C. N., 1981, *Mahatma Gandhi in His Gujrati Writings,* Sahitya Akadami, Delhi, pp. 8-9

Prabhu, R.K. and Rao, U.R., 1967, *The Mind of Mahatma Gandhi,* Navajivan Publications, Ahmedabad.

Pradhan, Benudhar, 1980, *The Socialist Thought of Mahatma Gandhi,* G.D.K. Publishers, Delhi.

Pyarelal, 1956, *Mahatma Gandhi: The Last Phase,* Navajivan Publishing House, Ahmedabad, Vols 1 & 2.

Radhakrishanan, S. (ed.), 1968, *Mahatma Gandhi-100 Years,* Gandhi Peace Foundation, New Delhi.

Raghavan, V. R., 1986, "Reflections on Gandhian Economics", *Gandhi Marg:* Vol. 7, No. 1, pp. 107-10.

Saran, A.K., 1978, "On the Promotion of Gandhian Studies at the University Level", *Gandhi Marg,* Vol. 7, No. 1, pp. 363-81.

Saran, A. K., 1987, "Traditionalism and Transcendantalism in Indian Society", in Hellen, G. C. (ed.) *Sociology in India,* Vol. 1, Rohini Publications, Meerut, pp. 336-44.

Schumacher, E.F., 1979, *Good Work,* Harper and Row, New York.

Shirk, Evelyn, 1988, "New Dimensions in Ethics: Ethics and the Environment", *The Journal of Value Inquiry,* Vol. 22, pp. 77-85.

Singh, Yogendra, 1973, *Modernization of Indian Tradition,* Thompson Press, Delhi.

Sorokin, P.A., 1947, *Society, Culture and Personality: Their Structure and Dynamics,* Harper & Brothers Publishers, New York.

Templin, R.T., 1969, "Gandhi Belongs to Tomorrow" in Cousins, Norman (ed.). *Profiles of Gandhi: America Remembers a World Leader,* Indian Book Company, pp. 114-16.

Unnithan, T.K.N., 1979, *Gandhi and Social Change,* Rawat Publishers, Jaipur.

Weber, Max, 1958, *The Protestant Ethic and the Spirit of Capitalism,* Charles Scribner's Sons, New York.

Weber, Max, 1964, *The Sociology of Religion,* Beacon Press, Boston.

7

POPULATION THEORIES
Malthus, Marx and Gandhi

This chapter presents three speculative theories of population: Malthusian theory, Marxian theory and Gandhian theory. Population changes have wide ramifications and, therefore, philosophers, social reformers, clergymen, administrators, social scientists and politicians, all have expressed their views on population. It is a difficult task to collate and analyse critically all theories of population here. We have chosen the three—Malthusian, Marxian and Gandhian—theories for the simple reason that they have had the greatest impact on social scientists working in the area of population studies. Among them also since Malthusian and Marxian theories have been widely discussed and debated in population literature, they will be summarised. It may be said that at present there is, no such thing as Gandhian theory; and what we present here is therefore, our interpretative understanding of thoughts of Gandhi on population. More space is given to this.

MALTHUSIAN THEORY

During the whole of the eighteenth century, it was an accepted theory in England that human population was decreasing. Although reliable data on population did not exist before 1801 when the first official census was conducted, some indirect estimates were made on the basis of parish registers, and statistics of taxation and burials. People believed that depopulation was an empirical fact that arose due to excessive increase in armed forces, wars, emigration, overtaxation, price rise and engrossing of farms. Only towards the end of the eighteenth century, Arthur Young proposed that the growth rates of population and wealth are positively correlated (Charm, 1984) and the relationship between the two is reciprocal. A serious crisis, however, developed in 1795 and 1796 when bad harvests caused widespread destitution and poverty. Two years later in 1798, Malthus, a clergyman and professor of political economy, published his essay on the principles of population anonymously. Against the prevailing progressive theories of society, Malthus argued that institutional changes alone could not really solve the problem of human destitution. To him a constant tendency to increase beyond nourishment present in all animated life is the most important and universal cause of misery. Thus, the institutional reforms as suggested by many other philosophers were of limited and short-term value only.

He made two postulates. First, that food is necessary for the existence of man. Second, that the passion between sexes is necessary and will remain nearly in its present state. Assuming these postulates to be true, he said that the power of population is indefinitely greater than the power of the earth to produce subsistence for man. Unchecked population increases in a geometric ratio, but subsistence increases in only an arithmetical ratio (Malthus, 1965). Regarding the growth of population, he observed that in the United States of America, "where the means of subsistence have been more ample, the manners of the people more pure, and consequently the checks to early marriages fewer than in any of the modern states of Europe", the population had been found to double itself in twenty-five years. This ratio to him, " though short of the utmost power of population yet as the result of actual experience", could be taken as the general rule. He stressed that by the best possible policy, breaking up more land, and great encouragement to agriculture, the most optimistic conception regarding food production could have been that it would equal the present produce in any future twenty-five years period.

In simple terms human species would always increase in a ratio of — 1, 2, 4, 8, 16 ..... and subsistence in the ratio of — 1, 2, 3, 4, 5 ..... This would result in a rapidly growing imbalance between the size of population and the availability of the means of subsistence. According to Malthus, this principle of population applies not only to human beings but to animals and plants also. All of them are impelled by powerful instinct to reproduce and afterwards their growth is checked by want of room and nourishment. To quote:

> "This natural inequality of the two powers of population and of production in the earth, and that great law of our nature which must constantly keep their effects equal form the great difficulty that to

me appears insurmountable in the way to the perfectability of society. All other arguments are of slight and subordinate consideration in comparison to this. I see no way by which man can escape from the weight of this law which pervades all animated nature. No fancied equality, no agrarian regulations in their utmost extent, could remove the pressure of it even for a single century" (Malthus, 1965).

Malthus accepts that temporarily a number of factors do affect the conditions of labourers, e.g. introduction or failure of certain manufacturers, greater or less prevalent spirit of agricultural enterprise, years of good and bad harvests, wars and pestilence, poor law, invention of processes for shortening labour without a proportional extension of the market, the difference between nominal and real wages, and the conspiracy of the rich class, but in his opinion the action of misery is constant.

> "Human institutions appear to be the obvious and obtrusive causes of much mischief to mankind; yet in reality, they are light and superficial, they are mere feathers that float on the surface, in comparison with those deeper seated causes of impurity that corrupt the springs, and render turbid the whole stream of human life" (Malthus, 1965).

Since the imbalance between population and food cannot go on increasing indefinitely, Malthus suggested that beyond a point this imbalance is removed by positive and natural checks. Positive checks are those checks on population which raise the death rate. In general, population may be checked by preventive checks (raising age at marriage and celibacy), rise in death rate (misery) and vice (sexual practices which do not result in child birth including use of contraceptives). If preventive checks are absent, positive check and vice operate. In an unequal society, the positive checks may be confined to the lowest stratum of society.

Severely attacked by his opponents, Malthus revised his essay several times and published its six editions in 1798, 1803, 1806, 1807, 1817 and 1826. A seventh edition was published posthumously in 1872. Though he did not change his basic position regarding universality of the principle of population growth, in the second revised edition he did admit the role of moral restraints in human society. There he intended to prove the following propositions:

"1. Population is necessarily limited by the means of subsistence.
2. Population invariably increases when the means of subsistence

increase, unless prevented by some powerful and obvious checks.

3. These checks, and the checks which repress the superior power of population, and keep its effects on a level with the means of subsistence, are all resolvable into moral restraint, vice and misery".

Malthus states that although moral restraint also causes unhappiness, it is a lesser evil than vice, *e.g.* promiscuous marriage, prostitution, homosexuality, use of contraceptive methods, etc., and misery, *e.g.* unwholesome occupations, severe labour, exposure to the seasons, extreme poverty, bad nursing of children, great towns, excesses of all kinds, and the whole train of common diseases and epidemics, wars, plague and famine. In the first edition of his essay he had expressed that voluntary restraints such as celibacy and postponement of marriage were believed to be of oscillatory nature. Their oscillations depend on the cycles of material conditions. For example, when excessive population produces hardships the labourers have to work harder, wages decrease, marriages are discouraged, freedom is lost, many poor persons are reduced to severe distress and the population becomes constant. When the food-population balance is re-established the labourers can again live comfortably and the restraints to population are weakened. In the second edition, he accorded greater importance to reasoning and education. Also he allowed for the possibility of sustained decline in population growth rate due to education and development. The third and later editions were mostly unchanged (Morris, 1969). It may be noted that being a clergyman Malthus himself did not approve use of artificial contraceptive methods. Therefore, those who later pleaded for family planning programmes due to the fear of population explosion were called neo-Malthusians.

Critique of Malthusian Theory and Later Developments

The population theory of Malthus came under severe attack in his life time and later. Apart from Marx, whose theory is discussed below, Sorokin, Sadler, Doubleday, Spencer, Gini and Dumont criticised him on various grounds (Premi, 1983). Sorokin stressed that population cannot indefinitely increase in a geometric fashion. In his opinion, logistic curve had a more sound theoretical basis than the geometric model because at a given level of technology and economic efficiency rise in population density is associated with rise in mortality and outmigration and fall in the birth rate. Sadler also said that as number of human beings rises their fecundity (physiological capacity to increase) declines and human society would cease to grow at the exact point where the people would enjoy the greatest happiness. This idea was same as that expressed by the theory of optimum population developed independently (Robbins, 1927). Doubleday envisaged the same future of population trends but related that not to rise in population density so much as to food supply. According to Doubleday, there is a negative correlation between the threats to survival and fecundity. He said that the poor who suffered from shortage of food most had higher population growth as compared to the affluent people who were decreasing, and the medium class had stationary population. Josne do Castro suggested the same theory later but related fecundity directly to protein content rather than food. As an interventionist he suggested that to control fertility in the less developed countries, protein intake would have to be raised substantially. Similarly, Spencer, a social evolutionary sociologist, believed that with social evolution/development there will be greater individuation of people, human organism will become more complex, people will have to make more strenuous effort for personal advancement and even girls will develop career orientation. As a result of this fecundity as well as people's interest in reproduction will decline. Thus Sorokin, Sadler, Doubleday and Spencer contradicted the Malthusian position that development would induce population growth and the real level of happiness would not improve. They observed that with development population growth will start diminishing and at a certain point human society will have to face negative growth.

Unlike Malthus and his critics mentioned above Gini attached more importance to biological factors in determining rate of population growth. He said:

(a) Population cycle starts with cross breeding between different groups caused by migration and other social movements;
(b) There is a positive selectivity in reproduction, *i.e.,* each generation is product of the relatively more fecund social groups; and
(c) Beyond a point physical exhaustion, a process of deterioration of germinal cells, caused largely by mobility of highly fecund groups into low fecundity upper social classes, leads to decline in natural increase (Thompson and Lewis, 1965).

The above issue of social mobility was more vital to "social capillarity" theory of Dumont (Keyfitz, 1972). He observed that the process of social mobility was analogous to the physical capillarity principle. In the 19th century Europe, the main cause of fertility decline was that people started realising that as level to which water can rise in a tube under the force of capillarity depends on how thin is the tube, they and their children can rise on social ladder depending on how small is their family size. For Dumont, the relationship between social mobility and family size was reciprocal. So, not only small family was found to be conducive to mobility, upward social mobility in turn made people more self-conscious. With social mobility people were isolated from their context they lost interest in collective welfare and developed more of personal orientation in life. Sociologists have widely used this theory to explain causes of reduction in birth rate in developed as well as less developed countries.

Despite criticisms Malthusian theory of population has survived in the discourse on development. To quote:

> "Malthus's ideas of the dynamism of population change were elementary and his suggestions for checking multiplication of people were naive. Yet the continuing controversy which has centred around his name has highlighted a problem which is central in world affairs today, and for which a solution has not yet been found" (Morris, 1969).

Morris suggests that the main point of Malthus's theory is that availability of sustenance determines the upper bound of population below which relation between available and prospective employment determines population. Different scholars have looked at different aspects of Malthusian theory (Peterson, 1965) including the law of diminishing return. It has been suggested that in place of asking whether Malthus was wrong or right attempt should be made to examine complex relationships between population, social organisation and power (Chamberlin, 1970).

MARXIAN THEORY

In his famous work *Capital,* Marx who said that the "Essay on Population" by Malthus was nothing more than a school boyish superficial plagiary of De Foe, Sir James Stuart, Townsend, Franklin, Wallace, etc. and the great sensation caused by that was solely due to party interest, maintained that an abstract law of population did not exist for man. According to his dialectical materialism, all historical modes of production have their own special laws of population which are valid only within their limits.

Marx said: "The correlation between accumulation of capital and the rate of wages is nothing else than the correlation between the unpaid labour transformed into capital and the additional paid labour necessary for setting in motion of this additional capital. It is therefore, in no way a relation between two magnitudes, independent of the other: on the one hand, the magnitude of the capital; on the other the number of labouring population; it is rather, at bottom, only the same labouring population" (Marx, 1974).

Contrary to Malthus, Marx attributed poverty, unemployment and misery of the working class to exploitative capitalist institutions. He wanted workers to realise that in capitalist society their condition cannot improve. Of course temporarily if the quantity of unpaid labour supplied by the working class, and accumulated by the capitalist class, increases so rapidly that its conversion into capital requires an extraordinary addition of paid labour, wages rise. But soon they reach their limit. At the point at which adequate surplus labour is not available to nourish capital, a reaction sets in. Then a smaller part of revenue is capitalised, accumulation lags, and the rising tendency of wages stops.

"The General Law of Capitalist Accumulation", discovered by Marx says that in a capitalist society the labouring population produces, alongwith the accumulation of capital, the means by which it is rendered superfluous and surplus to an increasing extent, creating the myth of overpopulation. Marx divided capital into two parts: constant capital and variable capital. The part of the capital which is represented by the means of production, raw and auxiliary material and instruments of labour was called the constant capital. Part of the capital represented by labour-power was called the variable capital. Marx noted that while the constant capital does not undergo any change of the quantitative value, the variable capital produces itself and a surplus. Therefore, with development and accumulation of capital the composition of capital is simultaneously changed. Growth of capital implies a rise in ratio of constant capital and a corresponding decline in variable capital. In other words, variable part of the capital rises only in diminishing proportion despite a constant increase in productivity of labour. Consequently, the demand for labour that depends on the variable part of the capital falls progressively and working population by creating more wealth in society makes itself surplus. Not only this, with the advancement of the capitalist mode of production labourers are set free more rapidly than a reduction in the variable part of the capital because with this the capitalists can increasingly exploit the individual labour power. Ultimately, the overwork of the employed class, reduction in the variable constituent of capital, and greater exploitation expand the ranks of industrial reserve army and force the workers to subjugate themselves under the dictates of the capital, independent of the natural increase of population.

For greater understanding of surplus population under capitalism, Marx divided surplus population into three categories: floating surplus, latent surplus and stagnant surplus. Any member of the working class who is unemployed or only partially employed belongs to this pool. In modern industries where modern division of labour exists, only a small number of workers continue to find employment in them. The majority of them are regularly discharged. They constitute the floating surplus. Actually, the modern sector exhibits a contradiction. In this sector, a complaint of the want of hands and unemployment exist side by side. Capitalist development of agriculture causes another type of surplus in rural areas, *viz.* latent surplus which results from pauperisation of agricultural workers and their constant movement towards industrial towns. Also, as some branches of industry decay, handicraft leads to manufacturing and manufacturing to mechanisation, it creates a long reservoir of stagnant surplus to capital, consisting of workers with extremely irregular employment, low wages, and longer working hours. Surplus in domestic industry is an example of this type of surplus.

Marx held that "an abstract law of population exists for plants and animals only, and only in so far as man has not interfered with them" (United Nations, 1973). In his view, each socio-economic formation has its own law of population growth. Since he concentrated on capitalist society, he showed primarily how does a capitalist society produce population surplus. Later socialists have undertaken the task of developing theories for other types of societies more systematically. Some important contributions to Marxist theory have been made by Engels and Lenin. Engels rejected the law of diminishing return implicit in Malthus's theory. Also he said that even if Malthus were right with respect to the reproductive behaviour of workers, social reorganisation was necessary, for only this reorganisation and the enlightenment of masses could make moral restraints possible. Propounding a similar theory, Lenin saw birth control as part of human rights.

Marxist writers have paid little attention to population question. Yet some of them have examined the role of population growth in crisis of feudalism and the transition to capitalism. It may, however, be noted that population policies in socialist countries have been guided largely by practical considerations rather than ideology. To quote:

> "Lenin (1913) took a very hostile attitude to what he called reactionary and impoverished neo-Malthusianism, and Marxist-Leninist demographers in general have been strongly anti-Malthusian. But actual population policies in the USSR and Eastern

Europe seem to have been influenced mainly by practical considerations, including the demand for labour and concern about declining fertility. In China, on the other hand, rapid population growth has led to very active measures to reduce fertility, again mainly for economic reasons" (Bottomore and Himmelweit, 1983).

In an interesting paper published in *Population Studies* in 1971, Daly (1971) has tried to synthesise Malthusian and Marxian views of population and development. His synthesis is quite close to the theory of demographic transition. He says that in the views of Malthus, development leads to growth of population but the empirical correlation between income and population growth at the global level is negative. This empirical relationship does not necessarily contradict the theoretical because this relationship is mediated by a number of factors such as traditions and customs, norms, ethics, material standards and law. Regarding Marxian theory he says that the Marxian theory is based on the experience of the nineteenth century when population was growing rapidly; if the rate of population growth is less than the rate at which workers are displaced by machines, there cannot be any surplus population or reserve army. Daly divided society into four major classes as follows:

1. *Upper class*—the class of those who earn from property and control births. The people of this class are Protestant capitalists, rational in business, and observe a rational barrier between sex and procreation.
2. *Middle class*—the class of those who earn from property and do not control births. They may be called unstable or transitional bourgeoisie. They are Catholic capitalists and they face downward mobility in the next generation.
3. *Neo-Malthusian labourers*—the class of those wage earners who control births. They are unstable or transitional proletariat and testify the class mobility theory developed by Dumont.
4. *Lower class*—the class of those wage earners who do not control births. They are stable proletariats.

According to Daly, in primitive society all belong to the lower class and in future classless society all will belong to the upper class. Dual societies have upper and lower classes and the pre-demographic transitional societies have only middle and lower classes. He has imposed on the demographic transition theory, the idea that in primitive society no man owns property, transitional societies are marked by development and unequal distribution of property, and in developed classless society all are property owners and there is no class of labourers as such. He does not explain the manner in which the future developed society would emerge from the present day dualist society (Sharma, 1984).

GANDHIAN THEORY

Earlier Views on Population in India

It is believed that Indian tradition as any other tradition in the world favoured high fertility. It is also believed that in old days polygamy was practised. Family and kinship ties were strong. Sons were source of power and couples had natural fertility. To support this position, verses from ancient religious and secular texts are quoted. It is shown that many mythodological characters had many wives and many sons. Moreover, analysis of beliefs of tribal communities, peasants and traditional people also shows that they wanted to maximise children. Blessings at the time of marriage commonly preached high fertility value. Premi *et al.* (1983) say that "Hinduism encouraged large families due to the agrarian economy of the country. Procreation was considered as *Dharma* and newly married couples were always blessed by the elders to have eight sons and five daughters". Yet *Balmiki Ramayana* which aims at presenting a solution to problems of *Kaliyuga* describes *Kaliyuga* right in the beginning of the epic—as showing high mortality, large population and social interdependence, implying that in *satayuga,* the ideal society population is less . In the secular works, Kautilya in his famous *Arthashastra* has mentioned about population census methodology, optimum size of villages and responses to population growth. A study by United Nations comments about sex being restricted in India during large number of days in a year on religious grounds (United Nations, 1973). These sources show that in the ancient India large family could not always have been part of the normative structure.

However, in the Muslim and the British periods when India was in feudal or semi-feudal stages, like any other settled village feudal society, India may have experienced some rise in mortality and fertility. At this stage due to demands of peasant economy, social conflicts, religious factor, social security consideration and patriarchal system, large family had become a strong value. Most Westerners including Karl Marx, by assuming that India has remained unchanged for millenia have attempted to discover India through study of this feudal society in their own thought categories. Therefore, there is a need to re-examine theories of traditional demographic patterns in India.

Indian civilisation is one of the oldest living civilisations. In response to environmental changes and its own inner needs it has passed through several phases. It is unlikely that these changes did not affect demographic regimes or thought of ancient Indians. There are reasons to believe that the Hindu India had a plural society with lot of regional and structural variations and the various sections of society must be having different conceptions of population emanating from differences in their condition and worldviews. As conditions changed, invasions and assimilation affected Indian thought, and new patterns evolved. At that time the mainstream spiritual tradition provided the framework of moral discourse. According to this framework, happiness could not be attained through worldly possessions including sons; it could be achieved through control of desires only. This framework should have been a deterrent to high fertility value in society.

Rigveda is supposed to be the oldest book of knowledge. In *Rigveda* there is a prayer about progeny:

> "May a brave, strong and wise son be born in the house of the worshipper. May be, with a golden halo around him, be well nourished and healthy, and favourite of the learned. May our Sculptor, the creator, give progeny to continue our line of succession. May we have ample food to tread along with path of divine wisdom" (Saraswati and Vidyalankar, 1977).

Indian religious literature make several indirect references to merit small family. In *Mahabharat* when Pandu wanted a fifth child, Kunti said that only donkeys have more than four children. Mythological books show that a hundred sons of Dhratarashtra could not save him against five Pandavas. Sagar had 60,000 sons who all perished due to a curse of a seer on them and only later Bhagirath a single descendant of theirs saved them all by bringing the river Ganges to the place where their ashes were lying. Books also show that when the father of the great Shankaracharya was asked to choose by God between a long living but stupid son and a short living wise son he chose the latter. As a matter of fact the meaning of son in Sanskrit is that son is one who saves the father from the hazards of hell. This clearly implies that male child not capable of helping the father in the attainment of liberation should not really be called a son.

More popular among religious works among masses, Tulsidas's *Rama Charit Manas* says that large family is a cause of despair. *Srimad Bhagavata Mahatmya* says that in Bharatvarsha, only where a man can shape his destiny through actions, wives conceive merely once toward the closing year of life. *Manusmriti* says that thousands achieved heaven without producing a progeny, while *Chanakyaniti* maintains that one good son is better than thousand bad sons (Sharma, 1991). All of them show that contrary to beliefs today Indian tradition valued small family. Gandhi recognized it clearly.

There is an abundance of academic material on Gandhian thought. Both in India and abroad, particularly in North America and England, a large number of publications on thought and critical appraisal have been brought out during the last five decades. Recent years have seen a renewal of interest in Gandhian theory, possibly due to ecological thinking, economic problems, terrorism and the 'crisis' of civilisation. However, in keeping with Gandhian tradition, most of the published work has concentrated on metaphysical questions or on particular aspects of social movements and transformation. Social scientists have not paid heed to the Gandhian framework by raising issues or analysing empirical data. Social demography, that is, the sociological theory of population, is no exception. Social demographers have used Malthusian, Marxian and Weberian theories of demographic change. There is also a feeling that the Western perspective has been applied to no avail. In such a situation, when social scientists in general, and demographers in particular, are looking for a non-Western alternative and a more apposite paradigm to look at Indian reality, there appears to be a great need to examine the Gandhian thought on population.

In the study of the Gandhian thought on population, the following questions may be raised:

(a) What is the Gandhian theory of population? How did Gandhi himself view the growth and control of population?

(b) What, in general, are the metaphysical and political implications of the Gandhian paradigm for population control? In other words, what are the covert functions of Gandhian social transformation for population control?

(c) What are the pitfalls of the Western theory of population?

(d) What charges are usually levelled against the Gandhian theory and how does it counter them?

(e) How can the Gandhian theory of population be applied today and what would its implications be?

This section attempts to examine the above question. Here, it may again be noted that Gandhi was not a social scientist. He was a practical idealist who had neither the time nor the aptitude for constructing systematic philosophy (Iyer, 1986). Therefore, when one examines his ideas in the context of social scientific tradition one may find that they are open to several interpretations. To the author certain observations are salient in analysing Gandhian theory: (a) Gandhian theory of society is rooted in Gandhian metaphysics which is strongly influenced by the Indian mystical tradition common to different schools of Indian philosophy; (b) It needs to be constructed partly from his own writings, speeches, notes, etc. and partly from his social experiments; and (c) It has evolved with time, sometimes contradicting the earlier position in some respects, but without ever negating its metaphysical substratum.

Gandhian Theory of Population

Gandhi had expressed a deep concern for population control on several occasions. The main source of his ideas on population are his autobiography and the report of the summit meeting on birth control in 1935, in which he had held lengthy discussion with Margaret Sanger, the American proponent of birth control. It may be noted that at that time there were not many buyers of the population theory. Margaret Sanger had just undergone a jail term for 30 days (in her own country) for holding views favourable to birth control.

Gandhi had favoured population control. Yet his argument in favour of population control was not the usual Malthusian fear of over-population. In 1925, in *Young India* he wrote that if suitable improvements could be made in the laws relating to land and the state of agriculture, and an allied occupation could be provided, India could support twice its population (Suman, 1969). The population of India at that time was about 262 million. Now it is going to touch 1 billion mark soon. Therefore, today, there is all the more reason to control the population, particularly since the perception of the ecological crisis is more vivid than it was in Gandhi's time. His support for birth control was related to the political situation of the country. He said that there could be no two opinions on the necessity for limiting births (Suman, 1969). But, like Marx, he rejected the idea of a universal theory of population. In some circumstances it may be considered quite rational to encourage reproduction but in many others birth control becomes a rational act. According to Gandhi, in his days, religion favoured a small family and birth control had become a political duty. Some of his committed supporters found his involvement with birth control a little embarrassing, but for Gandhi the political situation at that time demanded that people avoid any kind of wastage of the vital force

(Desai, 1973), and take up the task of ending colonisation and poverty more seriously. Thus, politics had become a religious activity.

Gandhi made two observations (Sanger, 1969):

(a) The burden of large families falls on the middle class; as far as fertility is concerned, it is greater among the middle than the lower classes. If that were not true one would not have the low average of five children per family in India.

(b) Women do not want many children but they cannot resist their husbands. If they could do so without causing bitterness, birth control would be possible in 99 per cent of the cases.

Gandhi was the first person in India to make an observation on the correlation between family size and class. Later, empirical data collected through research studies have confirmed the theoretical validity of his observations. In the pre-transitional stage, fertility in India was certainly nowhere near the biological maxima. A common standard of pre-transitional fertility is taken from the Hutterites, a religious group living in the north-western United States and Canada. They have been a very prosperous group and followed a pronatalist policy (Cassen, 1978). India family size in the 1950s was a little more than half their family size in the 1920s. Researches have also shown that in India development and modernisation caused a rise in fertility in the early years of the post-independence period (Srinivasan, 1986).

In observation (a) above, the term "middle class" requires some clarification. In the Gandhian framework, middle class is not an income category. It is a class of people who have begun to Westernise their life style and serve as go-betweens. They imitate the modern imperialists and control the consciousness of traditional colonial people. Behavioural changes among the members of this class have ensued as a result of modernisation. As such, modernisation leads to a rise in fertility. In the West, this rise was arrested by a simultaneous change in aspirations of social mobility which motivated couples to control family size. This fertility-depressing effect of modernisation did not operate among the middle classes during the early phases of development.

The main aspect of the Gandhian theory of population is its rejection of artificial birth control methods. In this respect, he is closer to Malthus than to Marx. Except for a brief period during his stay abroad as a student, Gandhi was always against using external family planning methods. His commitment to *brahmacharya* (celibacy) was basic. Initially, he used it for the limited purpose of restricting family size but as his thoughts matured, he advocated it essentially for Truth realisation: to follow *brahmacharya* completely, is truth realisation, said Gandhi. According to him, he had found it experientially and continuously step-by-step (Gandhi, 1957) and subsequently confirmed it with statements enshrined in religious literature. It may be said that for Gandhi *brahmacharya* in itself was not a means but a value. According to him, the purpose of the reproductive organs was to produce offspring (of high quality); it was wrong to use them for gratification. From this it also follows that householders can also lead a life of *brahmacharya.* To quote: "If a man controls his semen, except on the occasion of such purposeful cohabitation, he is as good as an avowed *brahmachari*. Just imagine, how many occasions for such cohabitation can there be in a lifetime? In the life of a healthy and virile man or woman, there may be only one such occasion. Why should such persons not be looked upon as avowed *brahmacharis* (Gandhi, 1971)."

Observation (b) shows that in contemporary society women have lost the force (of soul) to resist their husbands. Population workers should, therefore, concentrate on ways to improve soul-force among women and propagate the value of *brahmacharya* both among men and women.

It may be startling to some and a revelation to others that Gandhi approved sterilisation under certain circumstances. He was of the view that persons suffering from incurable or sexually transmitted diseases and wanting a sterilisation may be permitted (Suman, 1969). Since he believed that men had generally used women as object of sex and women were more suited for practising non-violence and *brahmacharya*, he favoured the idea of voluntary (but not compulsory) acceptance of the male operation. Obviously, it again shows Gandhi was not a traditionalist. He saw that modernisation could not deliver the goods in this country, nor could tradition—only a revolutionised tradition adapted creatively to changing conditions could solve India's problems (Maitra, 1986).

This analysis contradicts the position of Gunnar Myrdal that Gandhi's authority in his times was a strong psychological barrier to the adherence to the view of India's overpopulation. To Myrdal, Gandhi was a radical liberal who denied that India was overpopulated. He derives his position from Gandhi's statement that if all laboured for their bread, there would be no cry of overpopulation, no disease and misery (Myrdal, 1968). Myrdal seems to have committed the mistake of looking at Gandhian literature in the thought categories of neo-Malthusianism and modernisation. Gandhi's support to population control was unequivocal and unflinching. His theory of man was, however, a holistic one and not one of a "one-dimensional" man.

Implications of the Gandhian Theory of Social Reconstruction for Population Control

The above points are taken directly from Gandhi's views on population control. Now, let us look at the indirect consequences of the Gandhian programme of social reconstruction for population control. Gandhi wanted India to develop as a world nation, a nation that stands for universal human values, and not one that simply aims to catch-up with powerful countries. He wanted to build a new society based on truth and non-violence. He wanted India to move towards the Kingdom of God, and for Indians, *Ramrajya* portrays this concept. *Ramrajya* (as defined in various religious works on Rama such as *Rama Charit Manas* of Tulsidas) signifies a state of perfect equality, love, order, happiness, truth, non-violence, and control of senses. He felt that the establishment of *Ramrajya* would lead to the true welfare of not only the Indian people but of the entire world. He felt that India should be protected to save the world from the vices associated with Western civilisation. *Ramrajya* means gaining control over the horses, symbolising the senses, by the human soul, the charioteer, said Gandhi (Gandhi, 1971). The soul that gets carried away by the horses is defeated, and the one that controls the senses lives in *Ramrajya* no matter what the outward circumstances are.

In *Ramrajya* a commitment to truth is the most cherished value and non-violence provides the framework of the normative order. While a modern man uses his creative energies for selfish aims, and to use the Dostoevaskian term, suffers from isolation, a man in *Ramrajya* acts largely for the purpose of truth realisation. But *Ramrajya* was the first order social ideal. The second order ideal or the short run goal for India was to attain political freedom (Bandopadhyay, 1969). Political freedom must gradually pave the way for self-rule or *Ramrajya*. Here, the meaning of attaining political freedom was the capability of a population to declare itself free at its own will. At a more practical level, for India, it depended on the implementation of the constructive programme in areas such as elimination of untouchability; development of Khadi and other village industries; village sanitation; new or basic education; adult education; working for economic equality (which attacks poverty directly); uplift of women (which reduces the preference for sons); education in hygiene and health (which together with sanitation, women's welfare, prohibition, removal of untouchability, and economic equality is relevant to improvement in infant and child mortality); basic and adult education (which leads to reduction in fertility through the spread of education); Hindu-Muslim unity; propagation of *Rashtrabhasha* (national language);

and cultivating love for one's own language. Our question is: Had India taken this constructive programme seriously what would its implications have been for population trends?

The constructive programme has obvious links with an effectively implemented fertility control programme. It can help in reducing or eliminating such barriers to fertility reduction as poverty, son preference, old age security, high infant and child mortality, poor status of women, low levels of literacy/education, low age at marriage, and resistance to family planning programme for religious and other reasons (Sharma, 1989). Moreover, the actions indicated in the programme are mutually reinforcing, and success achieved with respect to one area would facilitate success in others. In other words, the application of the Gandhian theory of social transformation would be very conducive to the progress of the family welfare programme in the Indian context.

Regarding nuptiality, as early as 1925, Gandhi spoke in favour of raising the age at marriage in India. When the Sarda Act was under formulation, Gandhi opted through *Young India* (August 27, 1925): "Any sensible legislation in the direction of raising the age of consent will certainly have my approval". He believed that ordinarily a girl under 18 years should never be given in marriage. Two years later in 1827, he said, "If I could do so, I would lay down 20 as the minimum. Twenty years is early enough even in India" (Dubey, 1969). Had India taken Gandhi seriously on this matter, a statistically significant part of the left tail of the fertility distribution curve would have been truncated.

Gandhi took a keen interest in women's issues too. He tried to change public opinion about the age of marriage, widow remarriage, education of women and equality of status between men and women. But his approach to women's problems was different. There are two aspects of women's status—absolute and relative. The absolute status concerns such measures as literacy and educational achievements, work participation rate, longevity, political awareness and consciousness of rights in general, while the relative status measures women's achievements in relation to those of men. In present day India, we face a contradiction: while objective indices indicate a rise in women's status, atrocities on women, rape, cases of bride burning, etc. are also on the rise. Gandhi laid great importance on developing inner (soul) strength among women than on social engineering.

Even in the pre-colonisation days, girls attended schools and participated in cultural and economic activities. Some were educated at home and they in turn educated their children (Dharampal, 1983). Gandhi did not believe that women in rural India were helpless creatures. He felt that they were the real heads of the household and could protect themselves. He wanted women to practice *brahmacharya* and gain strength to say "no" to their husbands. It would do them no harm. He was convinced that it is only in a society practising *brahmacharya* that women will not and cannot be treated as objects of sexual gratification. They would also not seek fulfilment in sex and reproduction alone, and would rather participate in the political, social and cultural life of the nation along with men, and realise truth. Only such a society could be demographically balanced.

Gandhian Critique of the Western Theory

In his first major book, *Hind Swaraj,* Gandhi attacked Western civilisation. He attempted to show that Western values and not the British rule were responsible for India's problems. He observed that Western civilisation is based on greed and materialism, has no purpose, and is unable to solve problems which it has itself created in traditional societies. Only truth and non-violence can redeem contemporary society from the sin of Westernisation. It was his conviction that beyond a limit, material progress kills moral concerns and thus civilisation itself. Supporters of birth control programmes claim that population growth in present-day developing countries slows down the pace of development and, therefore, population control is conducive to development. For them, modernisation of developing societies is the goal. But for Gandhi, modernisation and the present processes of development were in themselves faults which developing societies must check.

In 1936, Gandhi said that family planning through artificial methods of birth control may certainly limit population growth to an extent and eliminate the problem of starvation faced by the average man, but the moral harm it does to practising individuals and society is great. In the Gandhian framework one may think of the following major dysfunctions of using contraception:

1. it may increase coital frequency among married couples, leading to ill-health, loss of vitality, greater incidence of foetal wastage and depression of spirit;
2. it may encourage pre-marital sexual activities leading to the problem of teenage pregnancy;
3. it may cause loss of sacredness and sanctity of marriage;
4. it may lower the image of women in society;
5. it may strengthen the legitimacy of sex as a source of pleasure,

leading in the long-run to a questioning of incest taboos, unnatural sex, and sexual abuse; and

6. it may increase the incidence of unwanted births among those who do not have knowledge of or access to such methods.

The Western societies have already undergone the above consequences of contraception and that is clearly shown by their family and demographic statistics. Although we lack reliable data at the national level, it is felt that in India also traditional and religious restrictions on sex are weakening and coital frequency may be rising. A trend towards the liberalisation of sexual norms can also be noticed. Pornographic material is easily available in cities and the female figure is increasingly being used for advertising various products. Interestingly, several women's groups in India and other less developed countries are strongly protesting against new developments in contraceptive technology on the grounds of freedom of choice, health and social status.

Around 1946, Gandhi wrote that the use of artificial birth control methods is an insult to women. To him, the only difference between a prostitute and a woman using artificial birth control methods was that while a prostitute sells her body to many men the latter does so to only one man. A woman should have such a strong will power that she is not controlled by man; unless the wife wants a baby, the husband should have no right to touch her (Suman, 1969). He, thus, saw self-control as a question of the dignity of women, sublimation and self-actualisation.

It may be noted that *brahmacharya* is a eugenic method. According to the well-known Indian medical expert, Susruta, diet and physical and mental condition of a woman during *Samagama, i.e.*, one month after conception, determine child psychology. Gandhi also emphasised that intercourse during pregnancy is particularly dangerous for the future of mankind.

On "Problems" with the Gandhian theory

Critics have labelled various charges against the Gandhian theory in general and the Gandhian theory of population in particular. One charge against his theory is that Gandhi was a bourgeois leader and his theory is an idealist theory. During the freedom struggle he emerged as a great leader of Indian bourgeoisie when his political work helped their economic interest. But after independence his theory became an obstacle to their industrial interests and was, therefore, abandoned (Namboodiripad, 1959). So, Gandhian theory has no political significance now. Another criticism is that while the goals of Gandhian intervention are very well defined, the approaches to relative consummation of the values are not so clear.

The neo-Malthusianists have appreciated Gandhian theory for the support is lends to the concept of population control but they have criticised it for its rejection of artificial birth control methods. Few people in India know that Malthus himself was a clergyman and consistent with the Christian viewpoint he himself had not accepted artificial birth control methods. Only the followers of (Malthus and Nehru in India) fearful of the perception of the population bomb exploding in less developed countries, became ardent supporters of all means of birth control. To quote Nehru:

> "In the interest of social economy, family happiness and national planning, family planning and a limited number of children are essential and the state should establish a policy to encourage this. It is desirable to stress the need and to spread knowledge about cheap and safe methods of birth control" (Lala, 1989).

It is commonly said that *brahmacharya,* as a method of population planning, is not practicable. In his convocation speech delivered at the International Institute for Population Sciences, Bombay, Dr. P.N. Srivastava, Member, Planning Commission of Government of India, enunciated that Pandit Nehru is reported to have said that "to limit consideration of birth control on the lines suggested by the first Health Minister, Rajkumari Amrit Kaur was absurd" (Srivastava, 1989). Rajkumari Amrit Kaur was a devout disciple of Gandhi. She believed in the Gandhian theory and tried to implement it.

Defence of the Gandhian framework in general is beyond the scope of this essay. Here, we are concerned with the appositeness of the Gandhian theory of population. Yet, it may be said that Gandhian theory is like Kuhnian paradigm which can be applied only in totality. It is impossible to envisage an otherwise modern society controlling its size through *brahmacharya*. Gandhi himself saw that man and his environment are dependent on each other, and a man who wishes to change himself must simultaneously attempt to change his environment. For this purpose, he developed the institution of *ashram* (settlement). Gandhi founded several such settlements in his lifetime and each came as a response to a particular practical situation (Chatterjee, 1983).

Gandhi wanted to build a system in which human relationships are based on truth and equality, and which are conducive to the realisation of intersubjective freedom. That should be the ultimate goal even of a partial implementation of the Gandhian theory. Brahmacharya is difficult to practise but not impossible. In a proper environment it may become a highly satisfying activity. As indicated above, Gandhi was not a traditional fundamentalist, and in certain situations he approved of even the most controversial methods such as sterilisation. Gandhi wanted to say that the concept of birth control is not new to Indian *Dharmic* tradition but in the *Dharmic* tradition, *brahmacharya, vanprastha* and *adhilavana* (withdrawal) are the methods of population control. only those who have failed to train themselves to follow *Dharma* need artificial methods. They may be allowed to do so but the use of artificial methods must be treated as an index of failure on the part of their users. Upadhyaya said that "those who follow the rules of healthy living and do not easily fall ill, need not go to the hospital, though the state sees to it that hospitals are provided as a matter of course" (Upadhyay, 1969). This is the Gandhian way. Thus in some situations and for some people artificial methods may be allowed but the users must be made to feel that they are not to be enjoyed as methods of gratification without reproductive consequences but to be taken as medicine (for consequences of not following the right path).

Further, history shows that the widespread use of artificial birth control methods is not essential for demographic transition. In a large number of countries in the West, fertility started declining even when artificial methods of birth control were either not available or were legally banned. Natural methods were used by married couples to limit family size. Nineteenth century optimism and high social-mobility aspirations were behind the motivation. So, if the natural methods theory worked in Europe under compulsion because artificial methods were not allowed, it could certainly work in India in a voluntary manner if Westernisation, modern education and media did not distort people's perceptions.

Relevance of Gandhian Theory to Solving India's Population Problems

Let us first look at the way in which the birth control programme has developed in India. The family planning programme, which is another name for the birth control programme, has always stressed that the country is facing a population explosion of crisis dimension and, therefore, people must refrain from producing many children. Thus family planning is a question of responsible parenthood. The matter of the fact is that in the process Indians have neither known statistics and economic equations nor have they been made to show any great concern for social responsibility. Then at the micro level a small family is often subjectively found to be conducive to material prosperity of the parents themselves and also of their children. In a rigidly stratified system where the masses lack the basic facilities to develop skills, people see little logic in the fertility-mobility argument. It is basically social-mobility aspirations among the better-off sections of society and the Malthusian fear among others which have produced some results. Yet in the process, the programme has caused a loss of people's traditional concept of family planning.

In general, the following factors may be identified which are at the root of the population problem:

1. In India, the health programme has been quite successful in achieving a rapid reduction in mortality though not to the standard of developed countries. No attempt was made to combine health and birth control values, so the health programme worked faster. People were not made to realise that unrestrained longevity may under certain conditions cause more problems than a short lifespan. It has not been said that birth control is a moral duty of both providers and takers of health services. Rules of health, hygiene and sanitation were not given due importance in mortality improvement and birth control programmes. Consequently, we are faced with three problems: inequality with respect to health facilities, mortality improvement without morbidity improvement, and population explosion.
2. Excessive faith in the power of science and technology to improve the material conditions of the nation has led to an undermining of local resources, local skills and local initiative. This situation has killed efficacy. In this situation, men have developed an external locus of control. To quote:

"Modern science and technology is not always used as a brutish tool by the rich and powerful to dispossess the poor. It has also been used subtly to undermine the confidence of the poor in their own resources and resource use patterns. Particularly if a natural resource used traditionally by people is so widely available that it just cannot be monopolised, every effort is made in the name of scientific progress to discredit that natural resource as archaic and useless. This drive to discredit a resource is undertaken to the extent that even the poor who often have no alternative except to use that resource, look forward to the day when they can do without it" (Agarwal, 1986).

Although the above was said basically in regard to physical resources, the same can be said about cultural resources also. As a matter of fact cultural alienation is both antecedent and consequence of changes in physical resource use patterns.

3. Modernisation has brought about major changes in women's position. Among the urban educated, it has improved the objective indices of women's status, *e.g.* education, legal rights, and participation in socio-economic and cultural life. Even in rural areas, it has weakened restrictions on their schooling and mobility and raised the age at marriage and social participation. But the woman's body is increasingly projected as an instrument of man's pleasure. Also, due to changes in technology women's traditional economic position has been marginalised. So, in a very large segment of the population, women's authority has declined. A large number of surveys have shown that women want a smaller family size than men and report a high incidence of unwanted births. Women in certain communities themselves want to do something to control family size but are so afraid of their husbands' disapproval that they are reluctant even to accept this fact before their husband and parents. Ignorance of various non-terminal contraceptive methods and non-accessibility of suitable methods are other problems.
4. Gandhi had mentioned about villages being reduced to dungheaps but the problem of hygiene and sanitation in villages was never so acute as it is today. Similar is the situation in urban slums. This has hindered the reduction of infant and child mortality, and in several regions parents still feel that since child survival involves a risk they should produce more children than desired. Simultaneously, it has become increasingly difficult to reduce child mortality further. The per capita expenditure on what is ultimately delivered to villagers in the name of health facilities is dismal. Quite often the medicines are fake and injurious. The health delivery system in many States of India is very deceptive and inadequate. Nutritional levels are also poor. Thus, the lack of cleanliness exposes villagers to various infectious diseases. It is unfortunate that simple rules of healthy living which could give them better resistance to diseases are not followed, not so much because of lack of money as because of lack of education and co-operation.
5. Development in the country has been associated with such processes that the poor have become pauperised and marginalised

leading to deprivation, confusion, chaos and crisis. It has not made them rational and self-conscious. This has harmed the family planning programme in several ways. It has lowered the credibility of government communication, and killed local initiatives and aspirations. It has contributed to people's stresses, fears and anxieties. The author has observed that in villages of Uttar Pradesh, when "cases" are brought for "family planning" (sterilisation) to urban centres they are operated and given pain killers and antibiotics for five days. After that nobody cares—if the couple need any medical help after that, they must find their own way.

6. The state has shown no willingness to enter into a dialogue with the religious elite on family planning. It must be realised that the role of the religious elite in some communities is important. The political elite are aware of the importance of the religious factor; they have even used it to promote their political interests but they have not used it to promote progressive and positive values for social reconstruction.

The list of the causes of population problem may be extended further. The crux of the problem is that economic development in the post-colonial India has benefited people at the top more than others. It has expanded the middle class and raised their aspirations, at the same time, marginalising the poor. To sustain (its exploitative character) it has divided society into smaller groups which are encouraged to organise along ethnic lines. The media are projecting woman as a repository of love and sex. The poor lack in self-initiative. They expect the Government to do everything for them. If they have anywhere organised (as in Kerala), and shown a readiness to change life, they have controlled family size also. Wherever they are made to enjoy dole (as under the IRDP) family planning work suffers. The middle classes still show son preference. The modern elite have used contraception but their function to population control is far less than the dysfunction arising from their support to an industrial economic system which has weakened the cultural props of productivity and creativity among the poor. In some communities, the modern elite, accepting family planning for themselves, have no motivation to diffuse the family planning message among the masses. Finally, due to lack of proper educational work, health and hygiene have suffered and morbidity and mortality levels have shown resistance to change. This again is a major obstacle in achieving demographic transition.

In sum, the following are the lessons which emerge from an

examination of the Gandhian theory of population:

1. In the present-day circumstances, Indians should control population.
2. The main purpose of population control is political, that is to end poverty, starvation, isolation, exploitation and unequal social relations and promote equity and justice.
3. The method of population control should be such that it prepares man to fight for political equality and takes him toward truth realisation. *Brahmacharya* is this method. Universal love and non-exploitation require practice of *Brahmacharya*.
4. Those (males or females) who cannot control themselves may accept sterilisation or other contraceptive methods. *Brahmacharya* is the goal that people must gradually approach according to their limitations.
5. The present unacceptable situation has come about due to post-colonial industrial modernisation. We should revolutionise tradition to save us from the perils of modern civilisation.
6. Experiments must be conducted in *Brahmacharya.* It should change public opinion in favour of population control, and may help build ashrams for the successful practice of *Brahmaacharya* and for preparing some to propagate it.

Many spacing (non-terminal) methods are new. They were not used in those days. It may be said that if Gandhi had approved of sterilization in some situation he would have approved of spacing methods also. At the same time it must be kept in mind, as mentioned earlier, that not Niroth (condom) but *nirodh* (control) of desires is the path to ending political inequality at the societal level, and truth realisation at the personal level. Contraception seems to help society in solving the population crisis but its abuse damages those moral and spiritual qualities which are necessary to establish an ideational society. The *nirodh* (control) of desires is the way to it.

In conclusion, it may be said that while Malthusian theory focuses on the consequences of population growth and Marxian theory focuses on the causes of surplus population (Sharma, 1984), Gandhian theory stresses the relationship between the method of population control and the correct political action. Population growth may be checked in several ways but only one of them is conducive to the construction of a good society, and that is *Brahmacharya.*

REFERENCES

Agarwal, A., 1986, "Politics of Environment", *Gandhi Marg,* Vol. 87.

Bandopadhyay, J., 1969, *Social and Political Thought of Gandhi,* Allied Publishers, New Delhi.

Blacker, C.P., 1947, "States in Population Growth", *Eugenics Review,* Vol. 39, pp. 81-101.

Bottomore, Tom, and Himmelweit, Susan, 1983, "Population", in Bottomore, Tom (ed.), *A Dictionary of Marxist Thought,* Oxford University Press, Delhi, pp. 378-80.

Cassen, R.H., 1978, *India: Population, Economy, Society,* The Macmillan Press, Hong Hong.

Chamberlin, N.W., 1970, *Beyond Malthus: Population and Power,* Basic Books, New York.

Chartterjee, Margaret, 1983, *Gandhi's Religious Thought,* The Macmillan Press Ltd., New Delhi.

Daly, H.E., 1971, "A Marxian - Malthusian View of Poverty and Development", *Population Studies,* Vol. 25, No. 1, pp. 25-30.

Desai, M., 1973, *Day-to-day with Gandhi,* Sarva Seva Sangh, Varanasi.

Dharampal, 1983, *The Beautiful Tree: Indigenous Indian Education in Eighteenth Century,* Biblia Impex Private Limited, New Delhi.

Dhawan, G., 1963, *Sarvodaya Tatva Darshan,* Nav Jivan Prakashan Mandir, Ahmedabad.

Dubey, B.R., 1969, "Gandhi's Views on Status of Women", in Biswas, S.C. (ed.), *Gandhi: Theory and Practice, Social Impact and Contemporary Relevance,* Indian Institute of Advanced Study, Shimla.

Gandhi, M.K., 1957, *Satya Ke Prayoga,* Nav Jivan Mandir, Ahmedabad.

Gandhi, M.K., 1971, *Collected Works of Mahatma Gandhi,* Ministry of Information and Broadcasting, New Delhi, Vol. 44, p. 68.

Goswami, C.L., and Sastri, M.A., 1982, *Srimad Bhagavata Mahapurana,* Gita Press, Gorakhpur.

Iyer, R., 1986, *The Moral and Political Writings of Mahatma Gandhi,* Vol. 2, Clarendon Press, Oxford.

Keyfitz, Nathan, 1972, "Population Theory and Doctrine: A Historical Survey", in Peterson, William (ed.), *Readings in Population,* The Macmillan Company, New York, pp. 41-69.

Lala, E.S., 1989, "Nehru's Vision of Women, Development and Family Planning", *The Journal of Family Welfare,* Vol. 35, No. 6.

Landry, A., 1935, *Las Revolution Demographique,* Sirey, Paris.

Maitra, P., 1986, *Population, Technology and Development: A Critical Analysis,* Gower Publishing House.

Malthus, T.R., 1965, *First Essay on Population 1798,* M. Kelley, New York.

Margaret, Sanger, 1969, "A Summit Meeting on Birth Control", in Cousins, Norman (ed.), *Pofiles of Gandhi: America Remembers a World Leader,* Indian Book Company, New Delhi.

Marx, Karl, 1973. quoted in United Nations, *The Determinants and Consequences of Population Trends,* United Nations Publications, New York, pp. 47-50.

Marx, Karl, 1974, *Capital Vol. 1,* Progress Publishers, Moscow, pp. 574-600.

Morris, J.K., 1969, "Professor Malthus and his Essay", in Kammeyer, K.C.W. (ed.), *Population Studies: Selected Essays and Research,* Rand Mc Nally and Company, Chicago, pp. 54-75.

Myrdal, G., 1968, *Asian Drama: An Enquiry into the Poverty of Nations,* Vol. 3, Penguin Books.

Namboodiripad, E.M.S., 1959, *The Mahatma and the Ism,* People's Publishing House, New Delhi.

Notestein, F., 1953, "Economic Problems of Population Change", *in Proceedings of the Eighth International Conference of Agricultural Economists,* London.

Ojha, S.D., 1987, "Prachin Bhartiya Parampara Our Janasankhya Shiksha". in Misra, B.D. *et al.* (eds.), *Janasnkhya Siksha,* Population Centre, Lucknow.

Petersen, William, 1965, *Population,* The Macmillan Company, New York, pp. 307-35.

Premi, M.K., Ramanamma, A., and Bambawale, Usha, 1983, *An Introduction to Social Demography,* Vikas Publishing House, New Delhi.

Robbins, Lionel, 1927, "The Optimum Theory of Population", in Gregory, T.E. and Dalton, Hugh (eds.), *London Essays in Honour of Edwin Cannan,* Routledge, London, pp. 103-34.

Saraswati, Swami Satya Prakash, and Vidyalankar, Satya Ram, 1977, *Rigveda Samhita,* Vol IV, Veda Pratisthana, New Delhi, P. 915.

Sharma, A.K., 1984, "Aspects of Population Debate and Stratification", *The Journal of Family Welfare,* Vol. 31, No. 1, pp. 37-50.

Sharma, A.K., 1989, *Issues in Social Demography,* Mittal Publications, New Delhi, pp. 23-40

Sharma, A.K., 1989, "Growth of Muslim Population in India: Some Policy Issues", *The Eastern Anthropologist,* Vol. 42, No. 4.

Sharma, A.K., 1991, " Gandhian Theory of Population ", *The Journal of Family Welfare,* Vol. 37, No.4, pp.32-43.

Srinivasan, K., 1986, " Has Modernisation Increased Fertility in Karnataka India", *Demography India,* Vol. 15, No. 2, p. 281.

Srivastava, P.N., 1989, "Convocation Address", *IIPS Newsletter,* Vol. 30, No.3, p.2.

Suman, Ramnath, 1969, *Samaj Sudhar: Samasyayen aur Samadhan,* Gandhi Sahitya Prakashan, Allahabad.

Thompson, W.S., 1929, "Population", *American Journal of Sociology,* Vol. 34, pp. 959-75.

Thompson, W. S. and Lewis, D.T., 1965, *Population Problems,* McGraw-Hill Book Company, New York, pp. 37-54.

United Nations, 1973, *The Determinants and Consequences of Population Trends,* Vol. 1, United Nations Publications, New York.

Upadhyay, D. 1969, "The Family Planning Policy", in Daswani, P.R. (ed.), *Issues of National Policy,* Jaico Publishing Company, Bombay.

SECTION-C

ISSUES IN DEVELOPMENT

8

SOME ISSUES IN DEVELOPMENT

Man is essentially creative. Since the beginning of human civilization he has been making continuous efforts to make his life better and more meaningful. Everywhere and in all epochs in human society this urge can easily be evinced to have been present. Man is gifted with the quality of co-operation with fellow beings to achieve aims of better living. As a result of this human society has developed from primitive nomadic stage to the modern and post-modern stages. This change in material conditions in lives of people and groups from primitive agrarian stage to post-modern stage may be called development. Development has essentially an economic connotation and it should be conceptually distinguished from cultural modernisation or positively evaluated progress. It has been observed that the pace of development has, however, not been uniform in different societies and different periods. Rapidity, direction and characteristics of development have been influenced greatly by the other properties of society such as culture, political institutions, religion, etc. and therefore, sociologists have looked upon development with great interest. In this chapter some sociological aspects of development are discussed.

Development is both a status and a process. As a status it refers to level of material advancement, particularly income, and as a process it refers to the process through which the developed countries of the West have achieved high levels of material advancement. When used in the former sense, it refers not to income in a particular year but society's capacity to generate high income on a more permanent basis. In other words, it implies strength of techno-ecoomic institutions and structures that makes generation of high income possible.

Parameters of Development

For thousands of years Indians lived in self-sufficient villages with little structural differentiation. Karl Marx used the term "Asiatic mode of production" for this state of affairs. There were of course differences in power, privileges and life styles of kings and masses but masses were more or less homogeneous. They were not divided into economic classes of exploiters and exploited. With foreign invasions and coming of aggressive rulers from outside began a process of planning for structural change by the rulers. They started interfering in Indian social processes to achieve their own political ends. This interference became more destructive with the advent of industry and the British rule. Consequently, during the British period people of India remained undeveloped. On the one hand, the British rule caused emergence of class differentiation among the people who had earlier organised their life systems largely on the principle of caste (co-operative occupational groups with a strong sense of moral obligation), and on the other, it took away work from the people. We might say that during the British period development and industries in India suffered a setback. Non-agricultural employment declined and the per capita welfare reduced considerably.

The national liberation struggle, the umbrella under which people of India waged their war against exploitation made them think about national development. Most Indian perspectives on development in India present today can be traced back to people's intellectual initiatives in those days. Gandhian theory of automnomous village republics, socialist reconstruction of society, liberal theory of development, the concept of welfare state are some of them. Finally, when India became free, due to prevailing socio-political conditions at that time and charisma that Pandit Nehru had enjoyed Indian state opted for the mixed economy model which would have both a competitive efficient private sector and a strong socialist government sector. Nehru himself had a great bias for industrial socialistic model of society. It was observed that while there were tremendous differences in models of political economy between capitalist market economies and developed socialist countries, they had achieved development through a similar path, the path of industrialisation.

Looking at development from this angle, following parameters of development can be identified:

— National income
— Growth rate of income
— Share of national income coming from the industrial sector

— Equality
— Investment and savings
— Urbanisation
— Literacy and education
— Transport and communication
— Energy
— Application of science and technology
— Infrastructure

During the First Five-year Plan period (1951-56) a large number of studies were conducted to obtain data on the above and to suggest ways to remove bottlenecks. Attempts were made to raise the level of investment by generating more domestic savings and borrowings. In the Second Five-year Plan (1956-61) the fate of Indian development got decided when the national plan took a decision to invest greater resources in heavy industry, big dams, power generation, production of capital goods and in building scientific and technological institutions in the country. Attempts were made to improve transport and communication systems, infrastructure in rural and urban areas, literacy and education standards and to promote urbanisation. The main academic architect of this model was Prof. Mahalanobis in whose name the Second Plan model was called the Mahalanobis model.

Economists suggested that everywhere in the developed countries, it is the investment that has caused all round development in society. Thus to reach a higher stage of development in a predominantly agricultural country that India was at the time of independence, consumption should be curtailed to the extent possible and money could be freely borrowed from rich countries and international monetary agencies. To achieve higher levels of savings and investment, the idea of population control was also mooted. As time passed the attention of planners started shifting more towards equality, social justice, removal of poverty, maximum possible use of science and technology, and attainment of self-reliance. To quote (Government of India, 1985):

> "The government has to play a major role in the development process in order to promote the interests of the poor, reduce disparities in income and wealth, curb regional inequalities in the level of development, protect the environment, strengthen the scientific-technological base for long-term growth and safeguard the interests of future generations. These are matters which cannot be left to the free play of market forces. Purposive Government Intervention in these crucial areas is central to our growth strategy."

Interrelationship between Social, Economic and Scientific Factors

Socio-economic and scientific factors are intricately and reciprocally related with each other. Socio-economic conditions are both causes and consequences of scientific and technological levels. As a cause, economic factors determine the level and type of technological requirements, ability of society to produce them, resources availability for research and development (R&D) efforts, and capacity to build scientific and technological institutions. Obviously, the poor countries can ill-afford to buy new capital-intensive technology even when its efficiency is quite proven. They lack an adequate size of scientific and technical manpower. They do not have good science and technology colleges. They do not have enough resources for building industries and certainly not for research and development. Similarly, social conditions determine those values, attitudes and motivations which are necessary for the promotion of science. The package of psychological traits which are conducive to promotion of science is called scientific temperament. Traditional societies lack this scientific temperament. Social conditions also shape the nature of hierarchy within scientific organisations and among scientists, communication among scientists and between scentists and society, social responsibility, efficiency, creativity, commitment and work culture. Sociologists of science have shown how even the goals of science are determined by the properties of social structure. In India, political leaders, intellectuals and practising scientists have often stressed the need to develop scientific temperament among the people which they are found to be lacking due to various historical, ethnic and ethical forces active in society for centuries.

The consequences of application of science and technology for socio-economic conditions are many. Some are obvious, intended and manifest. Some are hidden, unintended and latent. Among the manifest consequences are improvement in skills, efficiency of manpower, productivity rise, quality gains, competitive advantages in the international market, energy generation, etc. And urbanisation, cultural change, widening of communication networks, diffusion of modern ideas, homogenisation and globalisation of values, rationalisation, secularisation, etc. are the latent consequences which may also have bearing on socio-economic transformation. In other words, science and technology lead to socio-economic transformation directly as well as indirectly through changes in values and consciousness.

Role of Science and Technology in Development

As mentioned above, science and technology play very crucial role in development of a country. The successive Five-Year Plans have stressed that for sustaining the thrust towards emergence of an industrialising economy with rising levels of scientific and technological maturity and self-reliance, a major effort in science and technology is clearly called for (Planning Commission, 1985). Per capita income and standard of living depend heavily on technology. Some significant contributions of science and technology towards development are as follows:

- — Productivity and quality gains in agricultural and industrial sectors
- — Upgrading of existing industries to make them domestically attractive as well as export competitive
- — Energy generation
- — Improvement in defence capabilities
- — Exploration and extraction of new natural resources
- — Conservation of resources
- — Development of human resources—food, health, sanitation and hygiene, nutrition, water supply, immunisation
- — Reduction in regional imbalance
- — Employment generation and removal of poverty

Normally, the income contribution of science and technology is considered to be more important than its contribution towards abatement of class and regional inequalities. The reason for this is that the political, educational and social elite are first to take advantage of new knowledge and new understanding. The fruits of science and technology do not reach the bulk of the population and, therefore, do not contribute in sufficient measure to their economic and social growth. Yet it is necessary to develop, borrow and apply technology for strengthening income generating capacity of the whole economy. Without income welfare of the poor is inconceivable. "For science and technology to be effectively applied, there is a need to complete the total innovation chain consisting of basic research, applied reearch, design and development, prototype fabrication, upscaling, extension, awareness building, production engineering, design and consultancy, and production and services."

In India, the importance of science and technology to economic development was recognised quite early. Pandit Nehru, the first Prime Minister of independent India had a very strong commitment to utilising science and technology in all national efforts. National Committee on Science and Technology was entrusted with planning for various sectors. Recently, the Science Advisory Council to the Prime Minister submitted "an Approach Paper to a Perspective Plan for 2000 AD: Role of Science and Technology" (1988) in which six issues were identified as major issues of relevance to perspective planning: They are: (a) control of population, (b) need for increased food production, (c) protection of the environment, (d) improving human health, (e) control of hyper-urbanisation and (f) reducing unemployment. The Government of India has also created Technology Information Assessment and Forecasting Council (TIFAC) and the Technology Development fund (TDF) for technology assessment and resource generation.

The West would not have developed without industry, and industrialisation would not occur without innovations in science. It is by acquiring technological excellence that the developed Western countries emerged as major imperialistic force during the 19th century and are able to maintain techno-economic imperialism in the present-day world system. Western hegemony would perpetuate till the countries of the South, *i.e.*, the Asian, African and Latin American countries have developed an alternative technology that suits their own political and economic interests.

Measurement of Development

For a long-time, development was measured primarily by statistics of Gross National Product (GNP). To take into account variation between size of population of countries for cross-country comparisons, GNP was divided by population size and thus per capita net national product, *i.e.*, per capita income was used to measure development. To capture the rapidity of the pace of development, one can use growth rate of national income. It should be kept in mind that during the period for which we compute growth rate of income prices may change and in view of this income change should be shown both at the current level of prices and at the level on a fixed prior date.

Data showed that the less developed countries not only had low per capita income but were also more rigidly stratified. The share of bottom 20 per cent (or 40%) in the national income in less developed countries was very much lower than that in the developed market economies or the socialist countries. The reason was that when the less developed countries started developing, the elite were the first to take advangage of this and consequently they had the lion's share in small income gains these countries made. In this context indices of income inequality were constructed to examine whether less developed countries are moving towards a more equitable development also. To quote:

> "The questions to ask about a country's development are therefore: What has been happening to poverty? What has been happening to unemployment? What has been happening to inequality? If all three of these have declined from high levels, then beyond doubt this has been a period of development for the country concerned. If one or two of these central problems have been growing worse, especially if all three have, it would be strange to call the result 'development' even if per capita income doubled" (Seers, 1969).

Table 8.1 shows the available estimates of income inequality for some selected countries. These estimates have been prepared by the United Nations' International Comparison Programme and published in The *World Development Report 1993*. The data clearly show that some of the low income countries are also the countries with greatest disparity in income. For example, in Sri Lanka, the highest 10 per cent households receive as much as 43.0 per cent income, and the highest 20 per cent households receive 56.1 per cent income. In Pakistan, the highest 20 per cent households receive 45.6 per cent income while the lowest 20 per cent households receive only 7.8 per cent income. On the other hand, some of the rich countries, such as Sweden and Japan are also the countries where levels of income inequality are lowest.

Another difficulty in measuring development in the context of less developed countries arises from inconsistency of different parameters of development. In the West, development occurred over a long period of more than two centuries. It was slow, multi-dimensional and spontaneous. Slow and sustained changes in economic field were closely linked with gains in education, civil liberties, urbanisation, skills, health and longevity, and changes in psychological and cultural variables. Contrary to this in the less developed countries, development in post-World War II period was confined only to certain economic areas; it did not produce cultural or structural transformation. A question is often asked: Are the oil rich countries of the Middle East developed? If development is measured simply by per capita income they are of course developed; some of them are more developed than advanced market economies. However, if data on literacy and education, unemloyment, population growth rate, infant mortality rate, maternal mortality rate, inequality, etc. are collected, they are found to be as less developed as other unerdeveloped countries of Asia and Africa. To resolve this problem of inconsistency between the data, sociologists suggest that development be viewed as a multidimensional process and index of development be shown as a vector rather than a scalar quantity.

Development for Whom?

Of late, commentators on development have shown that the development, as it is occurring in various parts of the world, has caused a new colonialism. The present-day forces are such that they help the rich and harm the poor. At the international level, 30 per cent rich countries are exploiting 70 per cent poor countries. Within the poor countries also the top 30 per cent are exploiting the remaining 70 per cent. The former include people who call the shots at various levels, such as politicians, industrialists, businessmen, officials, policemen, planners, professionals like lawyers, engineers, management experts and chartered accountants, the rural rich and rural and urban mafias. The victims, constituting the overwhelming majority, are the poor, uneducated, frequently unorganised and vulnerable members of certain ethnic or minority groups, tribes, women, landless labourers and small and marginal farmers, marginal urban elements like pavement dwellers, etc. (Karlekar, 1992). The driving force of this type of development is the satisfaction of consumer desires of the rich and the burgeoning and increasingly prosperous middle class. The economy is run for the benefit of the elite and the subsistence needs of the common people are ignored. For example, when multipurpose dams and large industrial complexes are developed, the elite themselves benefit most from the job opportunities that they create. The local inhabitants do not have necessary skills to take advantage of new opportunities. Rather, the local people are deprived of their natural resources and traditional rights; they are not only denied adequate resettlement, they are also not even compensated properly for loss of land that they had been using for generations. This type of development has led to widening of gaps of all kinds, between urban and rural areas, industrial and agricultural sectors, regions, the rich and the poor, men and women, social groups and communities. Success of green revolution in some selected parts of India has, therefore, been associated with rising inequality in the countryside, unemployment, marginalisation of the landless labourers, and ethnic tension. No wonder that people are protesting against this exploitative development and asking: Whom is this development for? Where are the old ideas of *sarvodaya* and *swaraj*?

Egalitarianism was a principal component of the Nehruvian vision

TABLE 8.1 : Income Distribution

Country	Year	Percentage share of household income by percentile group of households					
		Lowest 20 per cent	Second quint-ile.	Third quint-ile	Fourth quint-ile	Highest 20 per cent	Highest 10 per cent
Bangladesh	1985-86	10.0	13.7	17.2	21.9	37.2	23.2
India	**1983**	**8.1**	**12.3**	**16.3**	**22.0**	**41.4**	**26.7**
Pakistan	1984-85	7.8	11.2	15.0	20.6	45.6	31.3
Ghana	1988-89	7.1	11.5	15.9	21.8	43.7	28.5
Sri Lanka	1985-86	4.8	8.5	12.1	18.4	56.1	43.0
Indonesia	1987	8.8	12.4	16.0	21.5	41.3	26.5
Colombia	1988	4.0	8.7	13.5	20.8	53.0	37.1
Poland	1987	9.7	14.2	18.0	22.9	35.2	21.0
Malaysia	1987	4.6	9.3	13.9	21.2	51.2	34.8
Hongkong	1980	5.4	10.8	15.2	21.6	47.0	31.3
Belgium	1978-79	7.9	13.7	18.6	23.8	36.0	21.5
United Kingdom	1979	5.8	11.5	18.2	25.0	39.5	23.3
Canada	1987	5.7	11.8	17.7	24.6	40.2	24.1
Sweden	1981	8.0	13.2	17.4	24.5	36.9	20.8
Japan	1979	8.7	13.2	17.5	23.1	37.5	22.4

Source: The World Bank, 1993, *World Development Report 1993*, Oxford University Press.

of industrial socialism and the Gandhian vision of *sarvodaya* and *gram swaraj* during freedom struggle in India. At some stage in the process of development after attaining freedom, the state became an agent of international techno-economic corporate imperialism and the poor were thrown out at the periphery of development. They were just forgotten. Gandhi had feared precisely this when he asked questions about *swaraj* as early as 1908. No wonder that these forgotten people have been mobilised by neo-social movements and they are protesting against development policies of the state either as a socio-economic group, or as an ascriptive group fighting on behalf of socio-economic groups.

In the beginning, it was argued that development travels from the centre to the periphery, *i.e.,* the material and cultural advantages of development are diffused to wider sections of society as time passes. Data show that capitalist development creates dualism both at the international and national levels. Contrary to the diffusionist assumption, underdevelopment of the periphery is the result of the development of the

centre. International aid or schemes for the poor are mere an eye-wash. Expansion of the core sectors/areas creates and perpetuates underdevelopment of the peripheral sectors/areas. Underdevelopment is, therefore, not absence of development but a condition created by the evolutionary process of development itself.
Naik (1982) describes this situation as follows:

> "The two main forces of modernization, education and science and technology, have allied themselves with the elite and helped them to improve their standards of living but have not done (or were not to do) a corresponding service to the masses of people. The elite themeselves had a brief honeymoon with the people in the pre-independence period to present a united front against the British and to drive them out. But once this goal was achieved, they returned to their original position of a ruling and exploiting group, notwithstanding the many populist slogans they had learnt in the meanwhile to mouth. In fact, this new society of modernized elite ruling over a still traditional people is far worse than that of the past when both the eite and the people were traditional, when neither of them had any access to modern science, when the gap between their standards of living were not so wide nor felt so keenly, and when the elite did not have access to all the modern means of tyranny and suppression".

Development of the poor requires an alternative conceptualisation. Social scientists have shown that this new conceptualisation will attach greater importance to needs over consumerism, equality over competition and ecologically sustainable models over capitalist model which is highly wasteful of natural resources.

Gandhi's image of *sarvodaya* is one such ideal image. To quote:

> "In the Gandhian model of *sarvodaya* society, mass production, at least where the vital necessities were concerned, would disappear. When production and consumption both become localized, the temptation to speed up production indefinitely and at any price would also disappear. There could be no accumulation in the pockets of the few and want in the midst of plenty in regard to the rest. There would be decentralization of power through a combination of state ownership in a few public utility works and village ownership and trusteeship in the rest of the economy. The heavy machinery for work of public utility would be owned by the state. If the rich failed to behave as trustees, society would have deprived them of their

possession through the state with the minimum exercise of violence. The labour-intensive, small scale, and cottage industries in the small towns and rural areas will use less equipments" (Chowdhuri, 1993).

Quality of Life (QOL)

Models of quality of life are new conceptual tools which raise questions about goal of development. These take into account individual gratification as well as social needs (Dube, 1988). As early as 1977, UNESCO report defined quality of life as follows:

> "QOL is an inclusive concept which covers all aspects of living including material satisfaction of vital needs as well as more transcendental aspects of life such as personal development, self-realization and a healthy eco-system".

Physical quality of life (PQOL) was operationalised by the Overseas Development Council as the degree of progress made towards achieving maximum levels of literacy, expectation of life at birth and reduction in infant mortality rate (Morris, 1979). Literacy enables people to participate in the process of development and take full advantage of cultural progress. Expectation of life at birth measures the degree of achievements made in the field of health. Reduction in infant mortality relates to environmental cleanliness and availability of clean drinking water. Data on PQOL show that GNP per capita is not always a good predictor of PQOL. In this respect, examples of Sri Lanka and Kerala State of India are commonly cited. Both of them are poor in terms of per capita income but they have achieved high levels of literacy, life expectancy and reduction in infant mortality rate. Transition in fertility in Sri Lanka and Kerala is attributed to their high PQOL.

According to Dube (1988), quality of life may be defined as a balance of satisfaction of the biological, derived and integrative needs of people in their social settings. To him some of the more important requirements of a preferred quality of life on the individual and societal levels are as follows:

- Survival
- Community
- Cultural and psychic
- Welfare
- Adaptive
- Progressive

All the above needs/requirements are further elaborated. To Dube the basic question in conceptualising quality of life for the world's poor generally, and for the majority in the Third World particularly, is that of survival needs. These needs are given below:

Survival needs/requirements

At individual level	At societal level
(a) Adequate nutrition, including ready access to uncontaminated water supply	(a) Organisation of food/ security/production and distribution systems supply of clean water
(b) Adequate housing	(b) Housing schemes for low income groups
(c) Adequate clothing	(c) Organisation of production/ distribution system for clothing
(d) Access to preventive and curative medicine	(d) Organisation of network of medical facilities
(e) Security of life and property	(e) Security and police
(f) Gainful employment	(f) Employment schemes
	(g) Mass education ; covering areas of nutrition, water use, child care and health care
	(h) Management of environment

In 1990, UNDP proposed a new measure of development called Human Development Index (HDI). It attempts to capture multidimensional nature of development and includes both economic and social aspects of development. It may be defined as absence of average deprivation with respect to income, adult literacy and expectation of life at birth. To compute deprivation, difference between actual and desired (maximum) values of the indicator is divided by the difference between maximum and minimum values.

Table 8.2 exhibits the values of Human Development Index computed for different States of India. The table shows that the State of Kerala has the highest value of Human Development Index followed by Punjab and Maharashtra. Punjab of course has the highest per capita state domestic product also, but Kerala has achieved highest value of the Human Development Index despite a rather low level of income thanks to Kerala's low deprivation with respect to life expectancy and adult literacy. The two worst States exhibiting lowest values of Human Development Index are Uttar Pradesh and Bihar. These two States are most deprived in all aspects of development. Three other deprived States are Madhya Pradesh, Rajasthan and Orissa. They are also deprived in all respects except that Rajasthan has done somewhat better in the economic field than other less developed States.

Sociologists use the term social devlopment for quality of life. In the social development framework, one looks upon development as achievement in provisions of social services of life, health, education and housing for all, social justice for the socially disadvantaged and deprived sections, and normative and integrative upgrading of social order (Sharma, 1989). It identifies asymmetry in social relationships (discrimination), economic exchanges (exploitation) and power relationships (oppression).

Recently, the United Nations (1990) has identified 10 major concerns of quality of life which are covered in official publications on social indicators and social statistics. They are: (1) health, (2) education, (3) culture and time use, (4) housing, (5) environment, (6) public safety, (7) employment and working life, (8) income, consumption and wealth, (9) social welfare and (10) popular participation.

Role of Planning

Planning is a way of making better decisions for the future. Planning is an important component of development activities. Individual firms, professional bodies, governments, corporate sector, all take decisions for the future. Their decisions influence economic growth, inter-sectoral co-ordination, social welfare and social relations. Yet the concept of planning has been identified more with extensive government control over the economy. That is why socialist countries became known as "centrally planned" economies.

Planning plays an important role in a mixed economy also. A plan declares a perspective on planning covering periods of fifteen to twenty years. It lays down broad targets of national economic growth and specific sectors such as agriculture, energy and transport, industry, health and family welfare, science and technology, etc. Specifically in the context of mixed economy, a plan acts as a means of co-ordinating actions within the public sector and between the public and the private sectors. Since 1951, successive Five-Year Plans prepared by the Planning Commission of the Government of India have specified targets to be achieved and provisions of financial resources to achieve them in different sectors of the economy.

TABLE 8.2: Human Development Index for 17 Indian States, 1987

	Life expectancy at birth	Adult literacy rate (per cent)	Real SDP per capita (PPPS)		Deprivation				Human development index	SDP per capita rank 1987	HDI rank minus SDP rank
			Actual	Log	Life expectancy	Adult literacy	Minimum purchasing power	Average of the three			
Uttar Pradesh	49.1	35.3	787	2.90	0.80	0.74	0.59	0.708	0.292	5	4
Bihar	54.1	33.6	625	2.80	0.66	0.76	0.66	0.694	0.306	1	-1
Madhya Pradesh	52.1	42.4	756	2.88	0.71	0.66	0.60	0.656	0.344	3	0
Rajasthan	55.1	32.7	864	2.94	0.64	0.77	0.56	0.653	0.347	7	3
Orissa	53.0	44.2	694	2.84	0.69	0.64	0.63	0.652	0.348	2	-3
Assam	52.4	48.5	785	2.89	0.71	0.59	0.59	0.628	0.372	4	-2
Jammu and Kashmir	56.8	36.9	887	2.95	0.59	0.72	0.55	0.619	0.381	8	1
Andhra Pradesh	58.0	35.3	983	2.99	0.56	0.74	0.51	0.603	0.397	9	1
Himachal Pradesh	56.6	52.2	1,109	3.05	0.60	0.55	0.47	0.538	0.462	12	3
Gujarat	56.8	52.5	1,116	3.05	0.59	0.54	0.47	0.535	0.465	13	3
West Bengal	56.6	53.3	1,116	3.05	0.59	0.53	0.47	0.533	0.467	13	2
Karnataka	60.6	48.0	1,037	3.02	0.49	0.59	0.50	0.525	0.475	10	-2
Tamil Nadu	58.1	55.4	1,074	3.03	0.56	0.51	0.49	0.517	0.483	11	-2
Haryana	60.6	46.2	1,600	3.20	0.49	0.61	0.36	0.486	0.514	16	2
Maharashtra	60.2	56.5	1,348	3.13	0.50	0.50	0.41	0.468	0.532	15	0
Punjab	64.3	47.7	2,143	3.33	0.38	0.60	0.26	0.414	0.586	17	1
Kerala	67.6	84.1	829	2.92	0.30	0.18	0.57	0.349	0.651	6	-11

Source: Shiv Kumar, A.K., "UNDP's Human Development Index: A computation for Indian States, *EPW*, Vol. 26 No. 41, 1991, p. 2344.

These plans require approval of the National Development Council, which includes Chief Ministers of all the States.

Planning in India is highly centralised. To some extent this is unavoidable. But this centralisation of plans has some weaknesses too. The planners at the Centre do not have adequate information about conditions in the local areas related to the local problems. Secondly, the States are so heavily dependent on the Centre for financial resources that they do not know until a fairly advanced stage what resources will be available to them. Thirdly, it leaves little room for local initiative.

Sundrum (1987) suggested that in India we have to choose between planning from above and planning from below. We should go in for an iterative method of planning in a number of steps. The first step would be for the Centre to formulate a broad strategy of development, dealing with measures to be adopted for education, infrastucture, new technology, the balance between sectors, the distribution of income and the alleviation of poverty. The second step would consist in translating broad principles into specific projects at the lower levels, *i.e.,* at the level of particular areas. It would deal with such measures as irrigation, soil conservation, seed multiplication, market improvement, credit supply, education, etc. It has to be an elaborate technical exercise in which all sections of the community should be involved. Fanally, once a national perspective formulated, the third step would be to lay down priorities for the various measures that have to be undertaken.

Indian economy has made progress through the planning process. However, our plans have only occasionally reached their growth tragets. Lack of firm commitment for action, lack of area specific approach to interventions and vagaries of international system are the main reasons for this. To make the planning process more effective, the following would have to be accorded greater importance than done in the past:

— Decentralisation of the planning process
— Firm political commitment for action
— Participation of all sections of the community
— Self-reliance
— Greater co-ordination between the public and the private sectors
— Involvement of non-government organisations (NGOs)
— Emphasis on implementing the plan as a package of co-ordinated activities
— Evaluation and monitoring of the programmes

Lastly, it may be noted that in the recent past national economies including economies of socialist countries have been opening up more and more. Role of market forces has increased and systems have become more liberal. In this situation, planners have an extremely complex task before them to find the optimum combination of public and private efforts to achieve the best results. Various international donors and Government of India are planning strategies to involve non-governmental organisations (NGOs) and Voluntary Organisations (VOs) not only in plans to raise income but also in social and human development efforts. Planning is needed to make small improvements in income and social levels of the vast masses rather than great improvements in income and social levels of a tiny section of the elite. Thus there is a great challenge ahead. This is the challenge of our times. We will have to look afresh at the Gandhian theory, keeping in view the demands of the time and the constraints of globalisation.

REFERENCES

Chowdhury, Kunal Roy, 1993, "Gandhi's Theory of Sarvodaya Socilalism, *Gandhi Marg,* Vol. 15, No.1, pp. 62-77.

Dube, S.C., 1988. *Modernization and Development*, Vistaar Publications, New Delhi.

Government of India, 1985, *Seventh Five Year Plan* 1985-90, Vol.1, Planning Commission, Government of India, New Delhi, p.5.

Karlekar, Hiranmay, 1992. *Colonialism Redivivus: The Implications of Exploitative Development from Above.* Indian Express, November 28, New Delhi, p.8.

Morris, M.D., 1979. *Measuring the Condition of the Worlds' Poor: The Physical Quality of Life Index.*, Pergamon, Oxford.

Naik, J.P., 1982 "Education Planning after the Commission", quoted in Sundrum, R.M., *Growth and Income Distribution in India,* Sage Publications, New Delhi, 1987, p. 276.

Planning Commission, 1985, *Seventh Five-year Plan 1985-90,* Vol. II, Government of India, New Delhi.

Seers, Dudley, 1969. *The Meaning of Development,* Eleventh World Conference of the World Society for International Development, New Delhi.

Sharma, S.L., 1989. "Social Development: Reflections on the Concept and the Indian Experience", *Guru Nanak Journal of Sociology,* Nos. 1 & 2, pp. 37-53.

Shiva Kumar, A.K., 1991. "UNDP's Human Development Index: A Computation for Indian States", *Economic and Political Weekly,* Vol.26, No. 41.

Sundrum, R.M., 1987. *Growth and Income Distribution in India: Policy and Performance since Independence,* Sage Publications, New Delhi.

The World Bank, 1993, *World Development Report 1993,* Oxford University Press, pp. 276-77.

United Nations, 1990. *Study on the Development of Quality of Life Indicators in Asia and the Pacific,* ESCAP, New York, p. 39.

9

FEMINIST RESURGENCE IN INDIA
Towards A Gandhian Framework*

Like any other "ism", feminism also has got a large number of followers in India. But unlike many other "isms", feminism does not derive its theoretical or conceptual base from any single theoretical formulation. Hence there has been no specific abstract definition of feminism applicable to all feminist movements at all times. Women's organisations have tried to define feminism as an awareness of women's oppression and exploitation in society, at work and within the family, and conscious action by women and men to change this situation (Bhasin and Khan, 1986). Further, they have looked at it as a struggle to attain gender equality and dignity both at work and at home.

Though many of the earlier women's organisations in India had tried to wipe out the woes of women, they were seldom referred to as feminist. But the 1970s and 1980s have witnessed the emergence of feminist groups with specific aims and objectives. After two decades of intense ideological and practical struggle, feminists began to search traditional models for their ideological support. In this context, Gandhi's principles are of great help. As was the case with most issues in those days, Gandhi mingled women's issues with national liberation struggle. Yet in his Constructive Programme for attaining freedom for India, women's issues had a very prominent place. As Gandhi stood for an egalitarian, non-exploitative, friendly, and humane society, work for the dignity of women was of supreme importance. This chapter examines the background of feminist

---

* An earlier draft of this chapter was published in *Gandhi Marg*. This chapter is written jointly with Clymes Augustine.

movements in India and the place of women in Gandhian thought. It also suggests some solutions to women's problems in the Gandhian perspective.

BACKGROUND OF WOMEN'S MOVEMENTS

The advance of capitalism in the West has induced inequality, on the one hand, and inspired and broadened the search for equality on the other (Beck, 1993). Feminism in the West emerged in this context (Giddens, 1989). It argued that men and women should have equal civic rights and equal roles in society. It showed that women had been denied support within the home and access to the market-place because of discrimination and inadequate social institutions. Women's movements that emerged in the second half of the present century, also known as women's liberation movements, were the early social movements to press for demands to ensure women's equality (Radhakumar, 1969). Within the liberal tradition in women's movements in the West, the following two ideological positions were prominent: (i) moderate feminism; and (ii) radical feminism. Moderate feminists believed that there should be equal opportunity for all. Though they were not very critical of motherhood and family, they considered the institution of family as oppressive and motherhood as a curse. They were optimistic so far as their relationship with men is concerned. Radical feminists believe that exploitation of women by men has its origin in reproductive biology. They are of the opinion that liberation will be possible only when child-bearing and child-rearing become the responsibility of the society as a whole. Women and children should be given the freedom to choose the lifestyle that suits them best.

Feminists within the socialist tradition, influenced by Marx and Engels, strongly believe that the women's struggle is a part of the larger struggle based on class. Thus they should demand equal pay and equal opportunity in education and employment. They are of the opinion that the concepts of private property and class divisions are the root cause of women's oppression. In the modern capitalist society, women play a subordinate role in the family and at the workplace. Thus women's groups must work in collaboration with other socialist groups to transform society (Radhakumar, 1969). It is only in the future classless society that women would achieve a position of equality.

Organisationally, women's liberation movements had different origins in different Western countries. For example, in England, they sprang up as trade union movements, in Italy, as Marxist students groups, and in America, as the Black Power struggle, which as part of their programmes induced the women's consciousness. It may be noted that in the beginning, women's movements in the West emerged as loosely organised groupings outside the mainstream of orthodox politics and they were primarily concerned with liberal legislative reforms (Giddens, 1989). Voting rights for all including women was one of their main issues. From a sociological point of view, they projected issues which were constructed within and by the very systems of Western democracies (Oakley, 1989). Their main goal was to challenge male political and intellectual hegemony. They were often characterised as anti-male and anti-family. Women carried placards proclaiming "starve a rat—don't cook dinner" and "marriage is a form of slavery", and used unconventional methods of protests, strikes, and demonstrations. As the system started responding to women's movements by providing them equal civic rights, at least in theory, their issues became more feminist, coherent, and sharpened (Kelien, 1984). Today abortion, sexual choices, sexual harassment, and domestic violence are some of their major issues. Simultaneously, as women won political seats, their interests widened. They have started rethinking on hierarchy at workplace and restructuring of home and work in the light of women's qualities such as patience, nurture, and an emphasis on interpersonal relationships. Women have also participated in large numbers in ecological movements and anti-nuclear demonstrations. Mobilisation is important. It gives opportunity to meet with other women outside the family, kinship and community, and concentrate on issues other than the domestic. It infuses women with new aspirations, need for expression and enthusiasm for self organisation. Generally, there is some crisis in the system that leads to mobilisation but every time they participate in efforts to resolve a crisis, they are likely to take an irrevocable step of some kind and their collective consciousness is changed. They become conscious of their potential to grow into a viable political group (Kishwar, 1988).

Thus the women's movements in the West are also seeking new perspectives for social transformation. They are increasingly recognising the need for a change in development strategies through which a sustainable and equitable development paradigm may emerge. They are stressing the need to construct alternatives in production and said to be working for a feminist perspective on development, drawing from gender-based experience of economic and social change (Jain, 1991). Yet their approaches reflect their Western epistemological basis very clearly. Their outlook is materialistic and they are hardly concerned with problems of the poor countries or malaise of industrial civilization. They are working primarily to achieve greater legal and politico-economic equality. They are operating in a post-industrial society urging to redefine male-oriented ideology and social institutions and their models may not be of much help to women in agrarian and transitional societies.

WOMEN'S MOVEMENTS IN INDIA

During the Vedic period women were far more privileged. They enjoyed a fair amount of freedom and equality. Monogamy was practised and widow remarriage was allowed. Women had high status in family. During the period 1500 B.C. to 500 B.C., though they enjoyed high status in family, they were discouraged to be sent to teachers and centres of learning. Then during the period from 500 B.C. to 500 A.D., women were discouraged to participate in Vedic activities. Now to produce male progeny had become a religious duty as sons only could serve certain religious functions. After that, position of women continued to deteriorate. This is indexed by transition from the concept of *Kanyashulka* to *stridhana* and *kanyadan*, and from *kanyadan* to dowry. Social reform movements of the 19th century initiated both by heterogenetic and orthogenetic forces showed concern about women's issues but gradually they were subsumed under the national liberation struggle (Panda, 1987). Consequently, though women participated in freedom struggle, they did not raise women's issues as such.

In the post-independence period, there was complacency among women upto the late 1960s. Then as economic situation worsened and women who are associated with management of household in particular, experienced economic crisis, they started organising themselves against economic policies of the state. In 1975, International Women's Year was celebrated and that proved to be a turning point in women's movements in many countries. Eventually, several women's organisations sprang up. These organisations focused on issues such as dowry, rape, inequality, exploitation, laws and customs which discriminate against women, education, health, and family planning, thus creating organisational links between different action groups.

Women's liberaton movements in India are so diverse in their perceptions and programmes that it is difficult to classify them on the basis of certain common characteristics. Here we shall try only to highlight some of their activities in the last two decades. Women's movements of the post-independence period were initiated by Gandhians and socialists in the early 1970s but it was only much later that they began to be looked upon as feminist. During mid-1970s, a number of women's organisations had come up in major cities like Bombay, Delhi, Madras, Pune, Patna, Ahmedabad, and some other places. Though there was no particular uniformity among them, their members were drawn largely from the urban educated middle class. A serious onlooker certainly can categorise diverse strains of thought in the feminist ideology. During the early stages, women's organisations moved towards left and began to align themselves with socialist trade unions. They had a broad view of feminism, as an on going process, hand in hand with class struggle. The unfortunate spell of Emergency brought a halt to these activities. Later, many of the feminist idologies of Europe were brought in and discussed at great length. Women's equality, freedom, and social justice took the major toll of debate. They never took extreme steps such as "bride burning" or "lesbianism"; Indian feminists were more of a democratic socialist type from the very beginning.

In the 1980s, women's groups and their campaigns had started all over India and ranged from protesting dowry murders and police rape to unionising women workers, domestic servants, and slum-dwellers. The issues of dowry murders and rapes were exposed to public notice and caught attention of the press and the public. In the subsequent campaigns, they gained considerable confidence and support. By the mid-1980s, they could establish themselves in society based on a common ideology and programme.

Another significant development during this period was that all these small movements began to keep their identity separate and exhibited a sort of exclusiveness towards each other. This resulted in the fragmentation of the movement. Small women's organisations had come up depending upon their class position. Each of these organisations had tried to define feminism separately. Their class character was such that they often lost the larger vision neglecting the conditions of the marginalised and the poor. Bumiller observes that one can describe all the activities that are occurring on behalf of women in India as a movement, but one with three separate parts: first, the urban feminist groups; second, the larger, more rural oriented voluntary organisations; and third, mass peasant struggles. However, unlike American feminists whose first hand experience of economic and personal injustice influenced the movement to focus largely on such middle class issues as job discrimination and equal pay for equal work, Indian feminist leaders have come to realise that their efforts would be meaningless unless they attempt to change conditions of 80 per cent Indian women whose basic concerns—clean water, animal fodder and cooking fuel, are alien to their privileged world (Bumiller, 1990).

During the 1980s, feminists increasingly began to take part in other social movements like ecology and civil rights movements. In the Chipko movement, women's participation was tremendous. By the end of the

1980s, Indian society became more vulnerable to caste, communal, and divisive forces which itself is a reflection of the larger spectrum of inequalities, underdevelopment, growing awareness of exploitation, and miseries of the downtrodden. Feminists appreciably had taken a stand which is against these divisive forces on the one hand, and for a just and egalitarian social order on the other. To quote Tanika Sarkar (1991): "Feminists see light at the end of the tunnel of feminists exploration — a light leading us towards a social order which is just and humane, and for which feminism is trying to develop a perspective on all issues, economic, social, political, and cultural". At the same time, an attempt was made by some political groups to involve women in national and communal issues. Thus some of them became a communal subject also. In general, the history of women's movements in India shows three distinct phases:first phase in which women started participating in politics, the second phase in which they raised women's issues, and the third phase in which they have joined the other subaltern groups in fight for justice.

The debate on the ideology of feminism had stuck somewhere in the meantime. Though many of the radical and liberal feminist ideologies of Europe had been discussed at length, feminists were reluctant to accept them as ideologies for action. The issues raised by European feminists were either irrelevant to Indian conditions or too radical to be accepted. The Indian feminists', rift was more socialistic in nature. Though Gandhian organisations had taken up women's issues earlier, they refused to accept them as "feminist tasks". At the same time, feminists were looking at traditional philosophies in order to construct indigenous models for their action. Many of the traditional philosophies of India had been studied and evaluated. Nineteenth century reformation in India provided the best canvas to work with. And so did the freedom movement with leaders like Gandhi, Nehru, and Syed Ahmed Khan, which provided a vast literature related to women's issues.

A recent publication by KALI has aptly summarised the position of feminists in South Asia. It says three things: First, women must concern themselves about creating equality not only with respect to gender but also with respect to caste, class, etc. and help in solving ecological and communal tensions. Secondly, mothering should be as noble as other outside home jobs and a matter of choice, which anybody can do, mother or father. Thirdly, feminists are those who not only realise these things but also act (Bhasin and Khan, 1986).

It is widely recognised now that the position of women in India is precarious and needs attention. In a society which is steeped in inequality and underdevelopment, a society where the majority are fighting for their necessities of life and for their very survival, women constitute the most oppressed and exploited section. In this scenario, the functions of women's organisations are manifold. Women's groups have realised that like casteism and communalism, sexism is also an instrument of dividing masses by the ruling elite. They have also realised that the battle will have to be fought against casteism, communalism, and sexism simultaneously. Their major challenge is how should they cooperate with other movements (Patel, 1988). However, many Indian feminists could not shed their middle-class character even after three decades of practical work. They would not join the masses where the primary question is not of equality but of survival. Many of their ideologies are a hindrance to their own cause since they do not embrace the masses and are not holistic.

In general, women's movement in India is increasingly adopting the position that every issue is a women's issue. According to one movement, "women have become increasingly aware, in the campaigns against the dowry and other social ills, that they are only attacking the symptoms, not the disease itself." Women's position in India is a creation of interplay of patriarchy, class, caste, religion, and new technological colonialism. To change the *status quo,* women must show a global concern (Omvedt, 1991).

"The debate on the development crisis, crisis in key social institutions, the critiques of growth models and their national and international dimensions, analysis of new inequalities generated by the pattern of development, and new forms of exploitation emanating from world economic systems, have together given a new direction to the women's movement. The 'women in the development' literature which began exploring and explaining the realities of women's lives and interconnections between macro-processes of development and women's disadvantaged situation, found many areas of common concern: impact of technological changes on women's work and migration, female headed households, women in the informal sector and in home-based production, impact of industrialisation strategies (particularly in export-oriented industries) on women, women and environmental degradation, etc." (Sharma, 1992).

Thanks to efforts made by Gandhians including Dev Suman, Mira Behn, and Sarala Behn, Gandhian organisations, active in post-independence period, have taken interest in ecology and politics of survival. They have been quite successful in organising and conscientising women in the areas of their operation. Experience of activist women has shown that environment is an equilibrium of social space, religious merit, and community well-being (Parajuli, 1991). Even from a tactical angle, if women want to become visible and audible, they should recognise that by just involving in women's projects as, for example, media portrayal of women, household violence, gender issues, and contesting the patriarchal ideology of male supremacy, they have simply marginalised themeselves. It may be noted that due to differences in culture, Indian feminism will have to acquire a different form than feminism in the West. In the West, exploitation of women was rooted in a theodicy which favoured males. But India has been a plural society since ages which dealt with theoretical questions in a spiritual non-dualist framework. Therefore, India has always had a theoretical apparatus to fight with its own socially created hierarchies. That is why Gandhi gave the idea of revolutionising tradition to remove ills of contemporary society and modernisation. He related social justice with Kingdom of God and the Kingdom of God with rule of true self. Women's feminist-ecological movements in India seem to be moving towards this perspective. Others may also benefit from it in the future (Parajuli, 1991).

GANDHI ON WOMEN

As mentioned above, feminists in India are now in search of an "Indian" model. A review of the nineteenth-and early twentieth-century Indian history will clearly illustrate that many of the earliest agitators for women's emancipation were men. Social reformers like Tagore, Gandhi, Nehru, and Syed Ahmad Khan had raised issues related to women.

Patel believes that Gandhi's ideas fit very well into the new stream of consciousness in women's movement. He had created image of a new woman, a woman who could have strength, courage, patience and a capacity for suffering and thus could become a symbol of non-violence and peace. The Gandhian ideology assumes the following about women:

(a) men and women have separate qualities and spheres in society which are complementary;
(b) women are not plaything but creative individuals who play important roles as mothers and wives;
(c) in domestic space women show unsurpassable and superior qualities than men;
(d) to be good mothers they require knowledge of both domestic needs and outside world;
(e) women should fight against wrong practices existing in religious social systems;
(f) they should maintain purity;

(g) men and women must have equal political rights;
(h) to protect her purity a woman should be ready to kill herself;
(i) a woman should marry only for reproduction;
(j) the highest goal for women is to reject the reproductive role and work for the welfare of the poor.

However, it should be noted that Gandhi's ideology related to women developed over time and was contingent to his involvement in the political events occurring in the country and his response to them (Patel, 1988).

India's struggle for freedom had precipitated diverse strains of thought and a wide spectrum of ideas. It aimed at a thorough transformation of Indian society in every sphere of life. Among many other issues, women's issues were also brought to the centre-stage of activities. There were social practices and customs particularly related to women which were oppressive and exploitative. The leaders of the national liberation movement voiced their concern against these practices. Also, there emerged an array of women leaders who were trained in the humanitarian and socialist ideas of industrial England. They fought relentlessly in the freedom struggle and raised women's issues from a national platform. Through non-cooperation and civil disobedience, Gandhi enhanced the participation of women in the national movement.

Gandhi assessed rightly that in a long-drawn political struggle against the *Raj,* he would achieve its desired goal only when all sections of people work shoulder to shoulder and put in their efforts in a consistent and organised manner. He found that a larger section of our women needed a great deal of attention. To gear up such a mass of humanity for the national cause and prepare them for a long-drawn struggle required a unique strategy, persuasive methods, security and protection for them in the women's centres or *ashrams,* and training in vocations which could be economically viable (Bakshi, 1987).

Gandhi had sought the support of women for almost all of his political movements—non-cooperation, civil disobedience, and Quit India Movement. The role of educated women to implement Gandhian programmes was unique. They became inmates in the *ashrams* and promoted spinning, *khadi,* and other items of constructive programme. They resorted to picketing of foreign cloth shops and wine and liquor shops and succeeded in their mission. They gave up foreign cloth and celebrated their bonfires in public.

The Salt Satyagraha of 1930 witnessed the greatest participation of women who organised and participated in procession, hawked *khadi* from door to door, and courted arrests in different movements. The response of women towards national upsurge was tremendous. Many of them had sacrificed their personal and family lives for the national cause. At times, when they were standing as a picket or marching in processions, they were *lathicharged,* insulted and humiliated, and when arrested, they were put into unbearable jail conditions. But they accepted all these hardships without a murmur.

It may be seen that the national movement had provided the best platform for the awakening of women's consciousness in India. It is important to note that the ideology and programmes which were used for this purpose were profoundly indigenous. However, after Independence, this trend declined immensely. The tradition of national movement has given way to modernisation and urbanisation which sucked away the Gandhian tradition. Women's issues were increasingly sidelined as the national elite were reconstructing society in a modern scientific and industrial setting.

Though industrialisation and modernisation had not solved many of our problems, they provided a wider canvas for rational and scientific endeavours in ideology and praxis. The 1970s in India had witnessed a reawakening of women's consciousness. The contact with European feminist ideology helped them to locate themselves. During the national movement the rejuvenation of women was not essentially feminist in character. These movements were liberal-national and confined to the existing social framework. But the second phase represents a typical feminist upsurge. As the movement took roots in Indian soil, efforts have been made to seek traditional answers to women's problems. In this context, Gandhian idology reverberates its abundant richness and holistic character. Gandhi was the champion of women's emancipation during his times and produced a considerable amount of literature about them. For those who are seeking new perspectives for action, Gandhian ideology would be of great help.

On landing in India in 1915, Gandhi realised the fact that crores of people—men and women—living in more than half a million villages were quite ignorant of the ideology of *swaraj.* He emphatically declared that our first attempt should be directed towards creating, in the minds of as many women as possible, a consciousness of their present condition.

For Gandhi there was no basic difference between men and women with regard to the ultimate goal of life, namely, self-realisation. He maintained the view that women are equally capable of attaining it (Iyer, 1973). He wrote:

"My ideal is this: A man should remain man and yet should become woman. Similarly a woman should remain woman and yet become man. This means that man should cultivate the gentleness and the discrimination of woman and woman should cast off her timidity and become brave and courageous".

He further said that both men and women can become fearless. Man and woman are characterised by fear as long as both are subject to passions. So Gandhi suggested that by controlling passion women can overcome many of their shortcomings.

From the very beginning of his campaign, Gandhi emphasised the inner strength of women (Iyer, 1973). He wrote:

> "Only the self can raise the self; the self is the help of the self. Only women can raise women. This requires *tapascharya* and hard work. It is true that women are more capable of it than men; but the *tapascharya* must be intelligent. Today women merely toil on in a helpless condition like drudges".

Gandhi considered women as the incarnation of *ahimsa* which means infinite love which again means infinite capacity for suffering (Iyer, 1973). He wrote:

> "Who but woman, the mother of man, shows this capacity in the largest measure? She shows it as she carries the infant and feeds it during nine months and derives joy in the sufferings involved. She forgets them in the joy of creation. Let her transfer that love to the whole of humanity, let her forget that she ever was or can be the object of man's lust".

It is true that at times Gandhi adopted a traditional approach to solve many of the women's problems. He wanted to take women to a larger struggle—a struggle for the liberation and reconstruction of the nation. In an article entitled "To Women" in *Navajivan,* Gandhi preferred to send a massage of *swadeshi* on the eve of his birthday. He recommended that all women should devote at least one hour daily to spinning (Gandhi, 1921).

Gandhi stressed the need for education among women. Also, he spread the message of *charkha* and *khadi* through them. He believed that by doing productive work she can be self-sufficient. Gandhi also advised them to go to the houses of drink addicts and start picketing liquor booths. He maintained the view that a woman is the companion of man gifted with equal mental capacities. She had every right to participate in the very minutest detail in the activities of men and she had an equal right of freedom and liberty.

It can be said that Gandhi tried to make the women of India into a person, self-respecting, self confident. He was highly conscious of women's rights (Gandhi, 1971). He said: "I am uncompromising in the matter of woman's rights. In my opinion she should labour under no legal disability not suffered by man. I should treat the daughters and sons on a footing of perfect equality." In the field of social reforms, he strongly advocated the removal of social evils including *purdah* and child marriage which have brought about the downfall of women in this country (Mehta, 1981). Gandhi wrote in *Young India* (1930):

> "The sooner we recognise that many of our social evils impede our march towards *swaraj,* the greater will be our progress towards the cherished goal. To postpone social reforms till after the attainment of swaraj is not to know the meaning of *swaraj"*.

Writing against the *purdah,* Gandhi said that chastity is not a hot-house growth. It cannot be superimposed. It cannot be protected by the surrounding wall of the *purdah.* It must grow from within, and to be worth anything, it must be capable of withstanding every onslaught of temptation. He took a very strong stand against child marriage.

Throughout his writings and speeches one feels the throbbing note of Gandhi's sympathy for women. He tried to rouse her to the realisation of their true position in society. To quote him: "If non-violence is the law of our being, the future is with women" (Gandhi, 1930).

It needs to be emphasised here that in the Gandhi-Vinoba perspective, the causes of women's problems are as much socio-economic and political as religious. Materialism, violence in society, and their spiritual insignificance created by modern religious conception have all contributed to marginalisation of women (Bhave, 1989). All major religions of the world have maintained that men are different from women. In some religions, woman is treated as object of sexual gratification and instruments of reproduction and in other religions she is projected as a source of corrupting influence on man from which man must be saved. Even in India, where religion of salvation has had greater influence, social beliefs of people and various practices have treated woman as a source of man's downfall. Buddha too hesitated initially to accept women in *sanghas.* But finally, when he admitted them he preferred separate *sanghas* for men and women. Only Mahavir Swami was an exception who gave the same position to women as to men. Thus it may be noted that to raise the status of woman what society needs is a total revolution of which change in the world-view is an important component. The new world-view must assign them same spiritual status as to men. In this context, Gandhi's theory of *brahmacharya* is of great relevance. Gandhi wanted the whole society to practise *brahmacharya.* At the societal level, it implies two things: (a) complete socio-economic and political independence of women; and (b) cocivilness and coexistence including right to celibacy. Women must be recognised as independent persons and should not be defined in the framework of kinship or sexual relationship (Dharmadhikari, 1983).

Some people have criticised Gandhi for the fact that he was not interested in inviting women to participate in civil disobedience. Much of this criticism is based on a misunderstanding of Gandhi's approach. He thought that in the civil disobedience they would be lost amongst men. Also, there was a sense of chivalry that prevented Gandhi from accepting women in the movement. As Hindus do not attack cow, the British would not attack women and, therefore, as it is cowardice to take cow to Battlefield, it would also be cowardice to take women to salt *satyagraha.* It is also a fact that women could not have come for this purpose in as large a number as men. Moreover, it would not be difficult to get salt tax abolished, he thought. Still when many women wrote on this matter to Gandhi or met him and expressed their desire to participate in the *satyagraha,* he in a written massage invited women to participate in it. As a matter of fact, two great women, Sarojini Naidu and Mithubehn Petite were with him when he broke salt laws on 6 April 1930. Sarojini Naidu even led *satyagraha* at Dharsana against Congressmen's wishes (Agnew, 1979), Kamaladevi Chattopadhyaya, who met and disagreed with Gandhi on this issue, discovered later that he was right. She said: "Events proved that Gandhi was right" (Chattopadhyaya, 1983). To him, special fields for women were *khadi* and prohibition. Still he allowed all those women to participate in civil disobedience who could do so. In this way he showed sensitivity to both symbolic nature of the participation and the identity (Gandhi, 1971).

THE WOES OF INDIAN WOMENHOOD

A Gandhian Solution

The diversity of situation and problems arising out of the interplay of political economy and value systems is of great importance in Indian society. In the post-independence period, various strategies have been adopted to bring about change in society, which would provide the basis for an egalitarian social structure, a structure that would ensure equality and dignity of women, There have been some significant developments in the national scenario since the attainment of independence. Yet the belief that the advances in science and technology and other fields of prominence would trickle down to the masses and develop the entire society has not been proved right. The overall gains have benefited only a few: mainly the professionals, the rich and the big (Pethe, 1985). The conditions of the masses, especially in the rural areas, seem to have become more and more precarious defying solution within the framework of the prevailing social structure. It has been pointed out that science and technology have been used to discriminate against women (Adiseshiah, 1985). The quality of their life continues to be miserable and the environmental conditions in which they live continue to be unworthy of decent human existence. Despite apparent dynamism ushered in by modernisation and industrial development, the social structure in India still remains exploitative and reactionary in the countryside as well as in the urban areas. In this context, it can be argued that in a country where majority of the people are marginalised, liberation of women alone would be a myth. However, the ideology of women's liberation would add a new dimension to the total struggle for social justice and equality.

In recent years, there has been an alarming increase in dowry deaths, sexual violence, and harassment of women, which reveals a large-scale societal breakdown. Women's position is worsening practically in every sphere, with the exception of some gains in education and employment for middle-class women (Desai and Krishnaraj, 1987). Women are still found in least-paid jobs, long working hours, and bearing full responsibility for the home also by fetching fuel and water, by doing work in family production units, without being paid for the labour, by bringing up children and looking after the sick and the aged. There are growing cases of violence against women, rape, wife battering, family violence, dowry deaths, and prostitution. This is the stark reality for millions of women in India which reflects the wide range of disparity and estrangement of the whole population. How can a Gandhian framework be applied in this situation?

The central philosophy of Gandhi has been named *sarvodaya, i.e.,* the survival and development of all. It was the vision of a moral society based on the cardinal principles of truth and non-violence—a society which aims at a thorough transformation of individuals through vows which he practised in his *ashrams. Sarvodaya* was a moral order in which the fullest expression of human freedom, creativity, cooperation, and justice would blossom and flourish. The economic institution of *sarvodaya* stressed simplicity of life, *khadi* and village industries, decentralisation of economic units, self-reliance, *swadeshi,* and cooperation in economic affairs. Gandhi also introduced constructive programme to ameliorate social and economic injustices which were rampant in his days. In his order of *sarvodaya,* political institutions would be decentralised where leaders become servicemen rather than party bosses. The state would remain as a symbol of non-violence with the least interference in individuals' matters.

Gandhi stood for the emancipation and welfare of all, irrespective of caste, class, creed, and gender. For him, collective self-reliance is the way towards a harmonious society. A society which accepts truth and non-violence as its central philosophy would recognise and promote emancipation of women in every walk of life. Gandhi emphasised the inner regeneration of the country. In his constructive progremme, he promoted widow remarriage and, abolition of *purdah, sati,* and other evil social customs related to women. Like his philosophy, Gandhi's strategies were also multipronged. It is clear that by reconstructing the social order towards *sarvodaya,* he was visualising an egalitarian society based on social and gender justice, equality, freedom, and fraternity.

On the level of praxis, Gandhi was a relentless fighter against injustice and untruth but in order to fight them Gandhi adopted a non-violent moral weapon of *satyagraha.* For him, *satyagraha* is the vindication of truth. It is a moral weapon which is superior to all other weapons of warfare. Gandhi's major contribution in this respect is his attempt to put into practice a non-violent programme for fighting evil. He had declared that the method of persuasion, whether in internal or external affairs, is the only human and civilised way open to man. He wanted to rule out physical force and substitute in its place the use of moral pressure, namely, *satyagraha.* For the building up of *satyagrahis,* Gandhi suggested eleven vows, the practice of which would lead towards an inner revolution. In his *ashrams,* he put these vows into practice and men and women freedom fighters were expected to follow them.

Therefore, several feminists feel that Gandhian ideology and practice can be of immense importance for women's movements. First, in a Gandhian framework women have to realise their own potential and inner strength. Simultaneously, they must accept truth and non-violence as their guiding principles. It needs to be stressed that most of the problems of modern society stem from material progress and devaluation of spiritual life. In this situation only an inner revolution can intensify women's moral fight against injustice. Also, there is much to be desired on the organisational and agitational front. It is encouraging to note that women's movements in contemporary India despise hierarchical organisational structures.

Most of them have informal structures where all members participate in decision-making. They spring as grassroots organisations and keep themselves away from party politics. Social malaise like dowry, family violence, and *sati* would not go unless there is a social action against these evil social practices. In this respect, development of *satyagraha* techniques would be of great help to remove them. Gandhi wrote (Iyer, 1969):

> "If she learns *satyagraha*, she can be perfectly independent and self-supporting. She will not have to feel dependent upon one. This does not mean that she shall not take any help from others. She will certainly. But if such help be not forthcoming, she will not feel destitute".

Before we conclude, it may also be important to note that women in India have to go a long way to attain the complete enjoyment of policical, economic, social, and cultural freedom. The first attempt should be primarily to improve her religious and social conditions. A change in this respect has been rather slow. Perhaps the contribution of Gandhian ideas in this respect can be more in the direction of creating an awareness of the injustice done to women, of the need to raise their religious and social status, and in the field of actually effecting changes (Unnithan, 1979).

Concluding Remarks

The significant contribution of the feminist movement in India is that it helped to spread some kind of women's consciousness throughout the country. The three decades of feminism in India have witnessed intense ideological as well as practical debate over the issues related to women. Recent trends reveal that feminists are increasingly coming out to support civil rights, ecological, health and other related social movements in order to seek alternatives in every walk of human life. As many of these movements are taking nourishment from Gandhian ideology, feminist ideology is also turning towards Gandhian principles. For a theoretical framework of feminist ideology, the *sarvodaya* philosophy of Gandhi would be the best frame of reference. Gandhi's insistence on truth and non-violence, equality and justice, the moral weapon of *satyagraha* in order to attain social, economic as well as political freedom with the emphasis on decentralisation and people's participation would be of a great help in building up a theoretical as well as a practical alternative. There are trends that in the organisational set-up, the cult of dedication, collective decision-making, service and sacrifice of Gandhian movements is getting imbibed. On the agitational front, the spirit of *satyagraha* needs to be revitalised. Thus the feminist movement in this country has enough indigenous resources with which it can certainly look towards the twenty-first century. It will then present new alternatives. While the Western feminism is moving towards promoting a more feminist consciousness of the human existence, the Indian feminism has potential to go beyond gender and help in building a society in which gender differences become redundant for meaningful existence of humans.

REFERENCES

Adiseshiah, Malcolm, S., 1985, *Science and Technology for Women,* Tamil Nadu State Council for Science and Technology, pp. 1-3.

Agnew, Vijay, 1979, *Elite Women in Indian Politics,* Vikas Publishing House, New Delhi, pp. 34-61.

Bakshi, S.R., 1987, *Gandhi and Status of Women,* Criterion Publications, p. 103.

Beck, Ulrich, 1993, *Risk Society,* Sage Publications, pp. 103-54

Bhasin, Kamla, and Khan, Nighat Said, 1986, *Feminism,* KALI for Women, New Delhi, pp. 1-2.

Bhave, Vinoba, 1989, *Stri Shakti,* Sarva Sewa Sangh Prakashan, Varanasi.

Bumiller, Elisabeth, 1990, *May You be the Mother of a Hundred Sons,* Penguin Books, Calcutta, pp. 125-281.

Chattopadhyaya, Kamladevi, 1983, *Indian Women's Battle for Freedom,* Abhinav Publications, New Delhi, p. 107.

Desai, Neera, and Krishnaraj, Maithreyi, 1987, *Women and Society in India,* Prentice-Hall, p. 394.

Dharmadhikari, Dada, 1983, *Sarvodaya Darshan,* Sarva Sewa Sangh Prakashan, Varanasi.

Gandhi, M.K., 1930, *Young India,* 10 April and 17 April.

Gandhi, M.K., 1971, *The Collected Works of Mahatma Gandhi,* Vol. 43, Ministry of Information and Broadcasting, New Delhi, pp. 189-98, 350-60.

Giddens, Anthony, 1989, *Sociology,* Polity Press, 1989, pp. 156-80.

Iyer, Raghavan, 1969, *The Moral and Political Thought of Mahatma Gandhi,* Oxford University Press, Clarendon.

Iyer, Raghavan, 1973, *The Moral and Political Writings of Mahatma Gandhi,* Clarendon Press, Oxford, Vol. 3, pp. 1-2, 394.

Jain, Devaki, 1991, *Development,* Vol. 1, p. 75.

Kelien, Ethel, 1984, *Gender Politics: From Consciousness to Mass Politics,* Harvard University Press, p. 126.

Kishwar, Madhu, 1988, "Nature of Women's Mobilisation in Rural India: An Exploratory Essay", *Economic and Political Weekly,* December 24-31, pp. 2754-63.

Mehta, Hansa, 1981, *Indian Women,* Butala & Co., Delhi, pp. 110-11.

Oakley, Ann, 1989, "Women's Studies in British Sociology: To End at Our Begining", *The British Journal of Sociology,* Vol. 40, No. 3, p. 443.

Omvedt, G., 1991, "Rural Women Fight for Independence", *Economic and Political Weekly.*

Vol. 29, pp. 910-33.

Panda, A.C., 1987, *Contemporary Social Movements in India*, Unpublished Ph.D. thesis, I.I.T. Kanpur.

Parajuli, Pramod, 1991, "Power and Knowledge in Development discourse: New Social Movements and the State in India", *International Social Science Journal*, Vol. 127, pp. 173-90.

Patel, Bibhuti, 1988, "Emergence and Proliferation of Autonomous Women's Groups in India: 1974-1984", in Ghadially, Rehana (ed.), *Women in India*, Sage Publications, New Delhi, pp. 249-56.

Patel, Sujata, 1988, "Construction and Reconstruction of Woman in Gandhi", *Economic and Political Weekly*, February 20, pp. 377-86.

Pethe, V.P., 1985, *State of Knowldege and the Demographic and Social Reality*, Poona, pp. 3-4.

Radhakumar, 1969, "The Women's Movement", *Seminar*, March.

Sarkar, Tanika, 1991, "The Women as Communal Subject: Rashtra-Sevika Samiti and Ram Janmabhoomi Andolan", *Economic and Political Weekly*, Vol. 26, No. 35, pp. 2057-62.

Sharma, Kumud, 1992, "Contemporary women's Movement in India: Its Dialectics and Dilemmas", *The Indian Journal of Social Science*, Vol. 5, No.2, pp. 1-31.

Unnithan, T.K.N., 1979, *Gandhi and Social Change*, Rawat Publishers, Jaipur, p. 149.

10

ENVIRONMENTAL DEGRADATION AND CONTROL

A Gandhian Perspective

India is quite rich in natural resources. If these natural resources are properly managed they can continue to yield high returns for several centuries. Yet the capitalist development initiated during the British period and speeded up after independence is causing serious human and ecological problems. Social scientists feel that to have sustainable development natural resources will have to be made available continuously over time and, therefore, a serious thought has to be given to planning and use of natural resources. In this context, attempts are needed to look into nature and causes of environmental degradation and ways to control them. This chapter discusses these and related issues. It may be noted that environmental management, a term encompassing environmental planning, protection monitoring, assessment research, education, conservation and sustainable use of resources, is now accepted as a major guiding factor for national developent in India (Planning Commission, 1985).

Starting with the Fifth Five-Year Plan and stepped up during the Sixth and Seventh Plans, the Government of India has taken up some major activities in the area of environment. They include water and air pollution monitoring and control, environmental impact assessment, natural living, resource conservation, special project on wildlife, ecological studies, eco-development programmes, environmental research promotion, and environmental information, education, training and awareness. As a result of these efforts, about one-third of large and medium industries have installed pollution control equipments. A network of about 120 monitoring stations has been created to check water pollution. Also zoning and classification of all the 14 major inter-state rivers have been completed to provide a basis for water quality management.

Air and Water Pollution and their Control

The two greatest environmental problmes of our times are air and water pollution. The former is caused mainly by the combustion of fossil and, to a lesser extent, biomass fuels. The latter is caused by a wide range of activities on land, often due to lack or the excess of economic and industrial growth. The growing human population and their land use, agricultural modernisation, deforestation, modern fisheries, urban development, tourism and industry, all have polluted marine environment. In a large number of cities both in the developed and the developing countries air quality has deteriorated greatly and caused increased incidence of respiratory diseases and other health problems.

Degradation of air and marine environment are no more local problems; they are transboundary. In the developing countries in particular, indoor air pollution produced by the traditional burning of low quality biomass fuels (such as dung or waste wood) and fossil fuels (such as low quality coal) has harmed the health of women and children.

Greenhouse gases including carbon dioxide, methane, nitrous oxide, halocarbons and atmospheric water vapor, are emitting today at unprecedented rate through energy conversion, as well as through agricultural and industrial activities. "At the same time, the forests and soils that provide natural sinks for carbon dioxide, the most important greenhouse gas, are being threatened by air pollution, land clearing and degradation and other harmful man-made processes (UNCED, 1972).

One immediate consequence of mismanaged water resources in the country is shortage of clean drinking water. Pollution of ponds, river water and sea has adversely affected fisheries. Contaminants include sewage, agricultural run-off, pesticides and fertilisers, synthetic organic compounds, sediments, litter and plastics, metals, radionuclides, oil/hydrocarbons, and polycyclic aromatic hydrocarbons. It has not been understood that fresh water which is indispensable for the sustenance of life on earth, is a finite resource. Development is not possible without water sources. Moreover, water is also a carrier of diseases. Estimates show that about 80 per cent of all diseases and above 33 per cent of deaths in developing countries are caused through pathogen-loaded or desease-vector-loaded water. Diseases caused by microbiological pollution of water supplies, transmitted by water-associated vectors, or related to inadequate sanitation and absence of clean water are widespread. According to UNCED (1972), this problem has been aggravated by the rise in water consumption due to economic growth and population increase, resulting in greater volumes of sewage requiring treatment and disposal. The 1988 report on status of India's environment prepared by Gandhi Peace Foundation and Science and Environment Centre, New Delhi, has discussed causes and consequences of environmental degradation in India. It has clearly brought out that environmental degradation is a direct consequence of economic development and is a socio-political problem.

Economics of Ecodevelopment

Consciousness of ecological consequences of ozone depletion, climate change, soil degradation, loss of biodiversity and the increasing pollution of air, water and land has led to questioning of the old notions of development in most countries. The new paradigm gives as much importance to revitalisation of growth as to sustainability, *i.e.,* to developmental processes that last and ensure a constant stock of assets" (Pearce, 1988). It is consistent with:

— Justice in respect of the socially disadvantaged
— Justice to future generations
— Justice to nature, and
— Aversion to risk arising from our ignorance about the nature of the interaction between environment, economy, and society, and the social and economic damage arising from low margins of resilience to external "stock".

Rifkin and Howard (1980) asserted that *Homo sapiens* are not made for a highly industrialised petrochemical environment. Due to modern practices in various walks of life and constantly increasing energy flow, "entropy" is continuously rising. To them entropy is a measure of the amount of energy no longer capable of conversion into work. Increase in entropy means decrease in "availabe energy". In this respect air and water pollutiion is simply the unavailable energy or entropy. Rifkin and Howard argued that modern medicine and modern economic growth take their cue from the Newtonian worldview. They have caused such long range debilities that it is impossible to know them fully today. Supporting a transition from a mechanical worldview to entropic worldview, they said that the Eastern religions had understood the value of minimising energy flow. The traditional Christian approach to nature has been a major contributing factor to ecological destruction becuase it overemphasised the "other world" the world of God, not our own world. Their position in favour of minimising energy flow is the position of ecodevelopment. As said above, it does not reject economic growth but it says that human welfare depends on economic processes which in turn depends on man-made and natural capitals. Also both the man made capital and natural capital cannot be raised simultaneously. Man-made capital can be raised only at the cost of natural capital. Here we may actually visualise a kind of trade-off between the two.

One result of the mechnical worldview of economic development is that the economic development proceeded at the cost of the rural poor, and natural and survival economies. Ecological movements, occurring in various countries, aim at reversing this trend and provide justice to the disadvantaged. Berry (1988) observed that we are now entering the third mediation, earth-human mediation. For thousands of years, our ancestors stayed in divine-human mediation, then sometime during industrialisation human society entered the interhuman mediation which marginalised the vast mass of humanity. The dream of the earth during earth-human mediation is to strengthen human and natural processes based on a holistic rather than scientific analytical perspective on development. To quote:

> "Within the new Cosmology, we recognize man as a part of and an extension of the evolving cosmos. The evolution enables us to attribute sanctity to man. His evolution-rooted sanctity makes man free of the tyranny of absolutes, in which earlier forms of sanctity are bound and, at the same time, allows him to transcend moral nihilism and relativism, with its arbitrariness and lawlessness" (Skolimowski, 1981).

Ecological man envisages the human condition as defined by at least four components; compassion, wisdom, suffering, and love. Serious suffering, of course, must be reduced but it is through suffering that we learn the sense of the human condition and meaning of life. Gandhian philosophy provides the basic framework in which this idea can further be developed and practised.

Cost of Development, Ecology and Knowledge

In 1928, Gandhi wrote in *Young India:* "God forbid that India should ever take to industrialism after the manner of the West. The economic imperialism of a single tiny island kingdom (England) is today keeping the world in chains. If an entire nation of 300 million took to similar economic exploitation, it would strip the world bare like locusts". At that time the population of India was around 300 million. Today, when it is close to reaching 900 million the above observations of Gandhi bacome particularly more relevant.

Ecology movements in independent India have shown that the development processes in independent India have benefited mostly the elite. Yet the cost of development has been borne by the economically poor and powerless people whose natural resources base has narrowed down either because resources have been transferred away from the basic needs or because the forces of economic growth have destroyed those ecological processes that ensure renewability of the life-supporting natural resources. For long, ecosystem was maintained in India efficiently. People used natural resources cautiously and according to well defined norms. They showed great concern about vegetation, soil and water use and the caste/community management of resources did not permit too much exploitation of resources by selfish interests. During the British rule the ever increasing resource demands for the English industries were largely met from colonies like India. For this they not only reorganised resource use on a more private or state basis they also raised development aspirations among those who owned them. The indigenous systems of production and consumption were systematically destroyed and replaced by resource hungry urban industrial systems. To quote:

> "Modern science and technology is not always used as a brutish tool by the rich and powerful to dispossess the poor. It has also been used subtly to undermine the confidence of the poor in their own resources and resource use patterns. Particularly if a natural resource used traditionally by people is so widely available that it just cannot be monopolised. every effort is made in the name of scientific progress to discredit that natural resource as archaic and useless. The drive to discredit a resource is undertaken to the extent that even the poor who often have no alternative except to use that resource, look forward to the day when they can do without it"(Agarwal, 1986).

What the Western institutions have done in the field of knowledge (Dharampal, 1983) is equally true about ecology. Speaking in London in 1931 Gandhi said: "The British administrators, when they came to India, instead of taking hold of things as they were, began to root them out. They scratched the soil and began to look at the root, and left the root like that and the beautiful tree perished".

Modernisation has been destructive of the environment. It has steadily transformed the very character of nature. It produced a tendency to reduce diversity in nature and transform it into a nature that is full of high yielding monocultures. Thus farmers were made to adopt high yield variety (HYV) irrespective of farm size and tenure, soil quality, access to irrigation water, and other biophysical-agroclimatic conditions. Thus they have become prone to increasing incidence of pest, disease and weed problems, sometimes aggravated by pesticide use itself. There is now enough evidence of diminishing returns to investment in HYVs and high payoff inputs. Thus, the ability to maintain productivity, whether of a field or farm or nation, in the face of stress or shock has declined enormously.

From ecological point of view the shortcomings of modern scientific knowledge economics are three (Shiva, 1991):

"1. It identifies development merely with sectoral growth, ignoring the underdevelopment intorduced in related sectors through negative externalities and the related undermining of the productivity of the ecosystem.
2. It identifies economic value merely with exchange value of marketable resources, ignoring use of more vital resources and ecological processes.
3. It identifies utilisation merely with extraction, ignoring the productive and economic functions of conserved resources".

Shiva, a Gandhian feminist ecologist, argued that due to the above false identifications development planning has failed to recognise ecosystem linkages and natural ecological processes and has created severe ecological problems. The modern scientific knowledge is reductionist and fragmented. The modern technology based on this science is more resource-intensive. Rational choice framework which evaluates them merely in terms of efficiency of need satisfaction capability is incapable of providing a real alternative choice. The knowledge framework of ecology requires

"1. A knowledge system with an ecological understanding of nature.
2. A technological system for processing resources to satisfy human needs with minimum resource waste.
3. Rationality criteria for demarcating vital and non-vital needs and between resource destructive and resource enhancing technologies."

In addition to environmental destruction caused by modern science and technology, in the developing countries there is an another cause of ecological problems also. That is under-development. In the West, the degradation of environment is due to stresses of over-development. In India, as in many other less developed countries, the problems of environment is due to poverty and consequent inadequate care of environment (Nagchaudhuri and Bhatt, 1987). In developing countries, millions continue to live far below the minimum levels required for a decent human existence. They are deprived of the minimum necessities of life, food, clothing, shelter, education, health and sanitation. Moreover, almost all the developing countries are undergoing rapid population growth. Their rates of population growth are generally well above 2 per cent per year. Therefore, they will have to direct their efforts to development. Ironically, quite often it is in the name of abatement of poverty itself that the state in less developed countries pursues its modernisation aims.

In this situation the aim of ecodevelopent cannot be separated from economic development altogether. However, the economic development must meet the following objectives:

— Satisfaction of basic needs of all
— Economic development with sustainability
— Equal distribution of both the benefits and cost of development.

Lastly, there is a need to distinguish between knowledge framework of the elite and that of the people. The elitist framework of ecological development can broaden its objectives to incorporate interests of the people only to a limited extent. What we need urgently is to establish a dialogue with the ecological movements and mobilisations of the subaltern groups. Their knowledge framework can make a tremendous contribution to our understanding of ecological management for a better future. In this respect fresh attempts would be required to define development. Development can no longer be perceived as process of generation of income but it must be defined critically as a process through which micro-cultures can achieve their own values and develop capacity to survive. If there is a conflict between income and survival, survival should get precedence and peace should be placed above both income and survival. There has to occur a shift from a simple mechanical and deterministic view of the physical world towards a more holistic view (Harrison, 1993).

Role of Scientists and Technologists

In order to solve environmental issues, all major groups, *e.g.* women, children and youth, indigenous people, farmers, local authorities, non-government organisations, trade unions, business and industrial establishments, scientists and technologists have to play an important role. The united Nations Conference on Environment and Development, held in June 1992 at Rio de Janeiro, has assigned a special role to scientific and technological community. To quote:

> "The scientific and technological (S&T) community, with its enormous capacity for generating possible solutions to the many problems the Earth faces today, can greatly contribute towards environmentally sound and sustainable development. Yet its potential has been far from fully realized, due in large part to insufficient communication. It is imperative that links between this valuable human resource and both decision makers and the public be expanded and strenghtened". (UNCED, 1992).

According to the Agenda 21 *improved communication and cooperation among the S&T community, decision-makers and the public* can help implement more effective strategies for environmentally sound and sustainable development. The best available knowledge should provide the basis for it. Moreover, such cooperation would assist the S&T community in evolving new priorities for research and suggesting constructive solutions. Needless to say, this requires a paradigm shift—a shift from the present undimensional thinking on development to holistic thinking underlying the Gandhian thoughts. It has to be stressed that economics must be subservient to the basic goals of human life (Misra and Lakshmanan, 1988).

To quote UNCED (1991):

> "National scientific and technological activities should be more responsive to sustainable development needs as part of an overall effort to strengthen national research and development systems. In this respect, the membership of national scientific and technological advisory councils, organizations and committees should be strengthened and widened, with the particular aim of making them more representative of the various strands of public opinion. Mechanisms should be developed for increasing scientific input into international collaborative and negotiating processes towards international agreements. Scientific and technological advice should be heard at the highest levels of governments and intergovernmental organizations."

Scientific and technological professionals at universities and research instittutions bear a special responsibility to disseminate their results, not only to peers in other fields but also to decision makers and the general public as well, says the report. Thus those active in generating knowledge about forces of sustainability should be recognised and supported. National scientific research publications should be made simple and relevant to local needs. In this way S&T community could better serve society. Communication between the scientific and technological institutions and industry need to be improved. New ways should be found to disseminate information on sustainable development. This time the spur is not resource shortage but impact of wastes. Intervention is needed right across the board, in population, consumption and technology and everything that affects them. The goal of this is to reach sustainable balance with our natural environment (Harrison, 1993). The role of women and the backward classes in the scientific and technological disciplines must be promoted and strengthened. Voluntary action groups, grassroots organisations, ecological movements and *Sarvodaya* workers should be involved. Altruism is needed to community, future generations and other species.

> "An important need is the *promotion of codes of practice and guidelines* in order for the S&T community to best advise the development process. A broader and more extensive national and international effort should develop a full range of codes of practice and guidelines regarding environmentally sound sustainable development, taking into account the Rio Declaration. This would involve reviewing and amending relevant national and international environment and development of legal instruments to ensure that this new ethos is reflected in regulatory machinery, as well as the establishment and strengthening of national advisory groups focusing on environmental and development ethics. Their integration into national reaseach priorities and education and training curricula is therefore, necessary. Fundamentally, these codes of practice and guidelines should mirror the changing global society".

The essential means to protect the environment could be envisaged as:

— A new holistic conception of development
— Information for decision-making
— National and international cooperation for building survival capacity
— Science for sustainable development

— Environmentally sound technology
— International and national legal instruments and arrangements
— Voluntary action

The above obviously involve all, scientists and technologists, politicians, planners, administrators, journalists and activists. Scientists and technologists have, however, most significant role to play. They can influence decision makers as consultants and advisors. Scientists should also act as citizens to mobilise general opinion in favour of having ecologically sound policies and defending the dispossessed. In the Indian context, Haribabu (1990) maintains that for protection of environment, pollution control and safeguarding the interest of the poor, scientists and technologists should participate in politics and promote values of equity and environmental development. They should make sustained efforts to influence state policies and pressurise the industrial interests to minimise pollution in the short-run and to replace pollution causing technologies by pollution eliminating technologies in the long-run.

REFERENCES

Agarwal, Anil, 1986, "Politics of Environment", *Gandhi Marg*, Vol. 87. pp. 137-62.

Berry, Thomas, 1988, *The Dream of the Earth*, Sierra Club Books, San Francisco.

Conway, G.R. and Edward B. Barbier, 1988, "The Green Revolution: Sustainable and Equitable Agricultural Development", *Futures*, Vol. 20, No. 6, pp. 651-70.

Dharampal, 1983, *The Beautiful Tree*, Biblia Impex Private Limited, New Delhi.

Gandhi Peace Foundation and Centre for Science and Environment, 1988, *Our Environment*, GPF and CSW, New Delhi.

Haribabu, E., 1990, "Economic and Political Dimensions of Pollution: Need for Political Action for Environment Protection" in Sharma, Anuradha, and Sharan, Raka (eds), *Social Responsibilities of Technologists, Scientists and Managers*, Gian Publishing House, New Delhi.

Harrison, Paul, 1993, *The Third Revolution: Population, Environment and a Sustainable Development*, Penguin Books, London.

Misra, R.P. and Lakshamanan, T.R., 1988, "Introduction" in Misra, R.P. (ed.), *Gandhian Model of Development and World Peace*, Concept Publishing Company, New Delhi.

Nagchaudhuri, B.D. and Bhatt, S., 1987, *The Global Environment Movement*, Sterling Publishers Private Limited, New Delhi, p. 50.

Pearce, David, 1988, "Economics, Equity and Sustainable Development", *Futures*, Vol. 20, No.6.

Planning Commission, 1985, *Seventh Five Year Plan*, Government of India.

Rifkin, Jeremy, and Howard, Ted, 1980, *Entropy*, The Viking Press, New York.

Shiva, Vandana, 1991, *Ecology; and the Politics of Survival*, Sage Publication, New Delhi.

Skolimowsky, Henryk, n.d., *The Ecological Man*, Eco-Philosophy Publication, Madras.

Skolimowsky, Henryk, 1981, *Eco-Philosophy: Designing New Tactics for Living*, Marion Boyans, Boston.

UNCED, 1992, *The Global Partnership for Environment and Development: A Guide to Agenda 21*, UNCED, Geneva.

11

POPULATION AND URBAN FUTURE

There seems to be a revival of interest in urban future of India and the relationship between urban and rural area. Of late sociologists, demographers, planners, administrators and politicians, all have shown growing concern about urban trends. Uninterrupted series of decadal censuses of population, urban surveys, administrative statistics and projections of future population have provided a good data base to examine urban questions in the new light. There are several such questions: Can India be as urban as some of the developed countries are? Does urbanisation lead to modernisation of the whole country or does it lead to marginalisation of the rural areas? What are going to be the major problems of cities in the future? What paradigm of urban future do we have? Will it solve some of our existing problems? In this context, this chapter attempts to draw scholars' attention to the role of urban areas in India. It is divided into two parts. Part I characterises the state of urbanisation today in the light of theory of urbanisation held by experts and planners. Part II discusses the implications of present day trends and suggests an alternative theory which may help India achieve the utopia of no-poverty, non-violent integral society.

PART I

The Concept of Urbanisation

Urbanisation has been defined in different ways in different countries and by different scholars. For our purpose, urbanisation may be defined as a process of population concentration. In operational terms, it may be shown by a rise in percentage of population living in urban areas. Indian censuses have classified all localities into urban and rural. Seats of local administration, localities of size 5,000 + and density above 400 per square km., localities having at least 75 per cent of male working population engaged in non-agricultural activities, and certain other localities showing "urban" traits are classified as urban. Large urban areas (or groups of neighbouring urban areas) and their outgrowth are called urban agglomerations (UAs). All the remaining localities are called rural. Thus urbanisation is essentially a domographic process. It may be associated with processes of modernisation, industrialisation, demographic transition, or cultural change but it is not necessarily an index of any of them. As such it is caused by natural increase, rural-urban migration, definitional changes, and growth and absorption of rural localities (NIUA, 1988). It does not necessarily reflect improvement in the quality of population in urban or rural areas.

The State of Urbanisation in India

There are two important measures of urbanisation. They are called level and speed of urbanisation. The level of urbanisation refers to percentage population living in urban areas and the speed refers to rate of change in the level of urbanisation during a reference period.

According to 1991 Census data, the level of urbanisation in India was 25.72 per cent (Census of India, 1991). As compared to developed and many developing countries also India has a rather low level of urbanisation. The speed of urbanisation in the post-independence period has shown an erratic pattern. In 1951, the level was 17.29 per cent. Thus during 1951-91 the average annual increase in the level of urbanisation was only 0.21 (Table 11.1). In this period highest speed was observed during 1971-81 and lowest during 1951-61. During 1981-91 per cent urban grew at an average annual exponential rate of 3.09 per cent. Contrary to economists' expectations the early decades of rapid industrialisation and infrastructural development did not exhibit any significant change in the level of urbanisation (Bose, 1978). Yet India has a very large urban population. In 1991 in all in 3,768 urban areas of varying sizes 217,177,625 people were enumerated. Their size is more than the size of countries like Indonesia, Nigeria, Australia, Japan, Bangladesh, Pakistan, Brazil, etc.

Census data on urban population is classified according to size of urban area. In Indian census, total urban population is divided into six such classes. The 1991 census shows that 65.20 per cent of urban population was living in 296 Class-I cities of size 100,000+. Another 10.95 per cent lived in Class-II towns of size 50,000 - 99,999 (Table 11.2).

TABLE 11.1: Trend of Urbanisation in India

Year	Number of UAs/Towns	Urban popul-ation	Per cent urban	Decennial growth rate of urban population %	Annual exponential growth of % urban
1901	1,827	25,851,873	10.84	—	—
1911	1,815	25,941,633	10.29	0.35	0.03
1921	1,949	28,086,167	11.18	8.27	0.79
1931	2,072	33,455,989	11.99	19.12	1.75
1941	2,250	44,153,297	13.86	31.97	2.77
1951	2,843	62,443,709	17.29	41.42	3.47
1961	2,365	78,936,603	17.97	26.41	2.34
1971	2,590	109,113,977	19.91	38.23	3.21
1981	3,378	159,462,547	23.34	46.14	3.83
1991	3,768	217,177,625	25.72	36.19	3.09

Source: Census of India, 1991, *Provisional Population Totals: Rural-Urban Distribution,* Paper-2 of 1991, Registrar General & Census Commissioner, India, New Delhi, p. 13.

Percentages of urban population living in Class III (having population between 20,000 - 49,999), Class IV (having population between 10,000 - 19,999), Class V (having population between 5,000 - 9,999) and Class VI (having population below 5000) are 13.19, 7.77, 2.60, and 0.29, respectively. Thus in all towns and urban agglomerations of size 50,000+ lived 76.15 per cent of the urban population.

Caused by both natural increase and migration—almost equally—urban population of India is growing at little less than double the rate of growth of the total population. Certain large cities are growing much faster, probably beyond the sustainable or optimal size. Data show that proportion of urban population living in Class I cities has been continuously rising since 1901. This is partly due to high population growth of large cities and partly due to the fact that with expansion of population many Class II cities have become Class I cities on various dates. Also proportion of urban population in Class II cities has remained more or less unchanged and that of other towns has declined.

This rapid expansion of urban population confined mostly to large cities has caused enormous ecological problems for urban areas themselves and also for the country as a whole. Majority of people in large cities live in slums or inadequate houses (Bhargava, 1981). For example, in Bombay, flats constitue only 20 per cent of all dwelling units; chawls are 61 per cent and huts are another 7 per cent (Muttagi, 1989). Similar is the

TABLE 11.2: Percentage Distribution of Urban Population by Size

Census Year	All Classes	I (100,000 and above)	II (50,000-99,999)	III (20,000-49,999)	IV (10,000-19,999)	V (5,000-9,999)	VI (below 5,000)
1901	100.00	26.00	11.29	15.64	20.83	20.14	6.10
1911	100.00	27.48	10.51	16.40	19.73	19.31	6.57
1921	100.00	29.70	10.39	15.92	18.29	18.67	7.03
1931	100.00	31.20	11.65	16.80	18.00	17.14	5.21
1941	100.00	38.23	11.42	16.35	15.78	15.08	3.14
1951	100.00	44.63	9.96	15.72	13.63	12.97	3.09
1961	100.00	51.42	11.23	16.94	12.77	6.87	0.77
1971	100.00	57.24	10.92	16.01	10.94	4.45	0.44
1981	100.00	60.42	11.63	14.33	9.54	3.58	0.50
1991	100.00	65.20	10.95	13.19	7.77	2.60	0.29

Source: See Table 11.1, p. 32.

situation of other large cities such as Calcutta, Delhi and Kanpur. Urban renewal programmes seem to be inadequate to solve urban problems in poor countries. Efforts of planners to improve living conditions in cities may often lead to greater immigration and thus yield little. The planners have still not found an appropriate answer to the problems of filth, poverty, pollution, slums, squatting, crime and rapidly rising informal sector in urban areas.

Table 11.3 presents data on growth of population by size class during 1981-91. It exhibits that 78.48 per cent of the urban population growth was contributed by Class I cities. On the other hand population of Class V and Class VI towns declined. An interesting aspect of the urban growth pattern revealed by the latest data is that urban areas of all sizes have shown a declining rate of growth. The smaller urban areas are, however, worst affected by fall in their growth rates. Growth rate of Class III towns is least altered.

On the administrative front there is a constant erosion of municipal council authority in all the States. The local administration is marked by corruption, inefficiency, excessive politicisation, lack of finances and withdrawal of certain financial resources like octroi, motor vehicle tax and professional tax. Quite often the democratically constituted bodies are known to be enjoying less power than the bodies nominated by State departments. There is also a political constraint to reserve 50 per cent seats in both councils and administration for members of the Scheduled Castes and Tribes, Other Backward Castes and women, which though important

TABLE 11.3: Increase/Decrease of Population in each Size Class, 1981-91

Size	Class	Population increase/ decrease during 1981-91		Contribution to India's total urban population		Decadal growth rate of population	
		Absolute	Per cent	1981	1991	1971-81	1981-91
All	All	56,447,569	100.00	100.00	100.00	46.23	36.09
100,000+	I	44,298,200	78.48	60.42	65.20	54.35	46.87
50,000-99,999	II	5,119,439	9.07	11.63	10.95	55.75	28.14
20,000-49,999	III	5,670,186	10.04	14.33	13.19	30.85	25.30
10,000-19,999	IV	1,600,767	2.84	9.54	7.77	27.54	10.72
5,000-9,999	V	-70,982	-0.13	3.58	2.60	17.82	-1.27
-5,000	VI	-170,071	-0.30	0.50	0.29	65.73	-21.70

Source: See Table 11.1, p. 29.

from social justice point of view may cause some problems in initial days.

Urban ecology in India has had a tradition of ethnic segregation. Of late, cities have increasingly become victims of terrorism, large scale political mobilisation, communal riots and communal and casteist politics, violence and state repression. This situation breeds insecurity, ethnic identity orientation, divisionism and alienation, and thus generates a positive feedback cycle of unrest. High rate of unemployment, both among the educated and the uneducated, easy availability of means of violence, new radical ideologies and rising suspicion between state and civilisation have also contributed to this sorry state of affairs.

At the same time much of the national wealth is concentrated in urban areas. In 1951, the share of agriculture in the gross domestic product GDP was about 60 per cent. By 1990, it had declined to 31 per cent indicating that more wealth is now created in non-agricultural sector. In 1990, the percentages of share of industry, manufacturing and services, etc. in the GDP were 29, 19 and 40, respectively (The World Bank, 1992). All institutes of excellence (in education) and research centres are all located in urban areas. Cities have well developed civic amenities, health facilities, hotels, recreational activities, and organisations for games and sports. They are the powerful political centres. Even for the urban poor who are found engaged in low-productivity activities and living on pavements or in slums, migration towards urban areas seemed to have been a better choice than continuing to stay in their native village. Now since everywhere cities are surrounded by backward countryside they are fast becoming centres of political attack by peasant leaders. The Indian mind is fast developing a feeling that city size is a crucial basis of stratification in the country, that developing the underdeveloped requires that resources are shifted from urban to rural areas, services to agriculture (Bang, 1984; Bang, 1987; Narayan, 1986).

The 1991 census has revealed certain reversals. First of all, the decennial growth rate of urban population, which was 46.14 during 1971-81, has declined to 36.19 per cent during 1981-91. Accordingly, the annual exponential growth of per cent urban has declined from 3.83 per cent during 1971-81 to 3.09 during 1981-91. This has resulted largely from fall in the rate of rural-urban migration. Secondly, the fall in decadal growth rate of urban population during 1981-91 is observed for all classes of towns/urban agglomerations (Table 11.3). The fall in growth rate in urban areas belonging to classes II,IV, V and VI is particularly noticeable. As a matter of fact population of towns of classes V and VI has declined even in the absolute sense. Thirdly, average population per urban agglomeration/city of size million plus has declined from 3.51 million to 3.07 million. Fourthly, a large number of million plus cities such as Calcutta, Delhi, Madras, Bangalore, Ahmedabad, Pune, Nagpur and Surat have returned a decreased decadal growth rate in the census. Fifthly, in many States, *viz.* Bihar, Karnataka, Meghalaya, Orissa, Punjab, Sikkim and Tamil Nadu, the increase in urban population during 1981-91 was less than in the previous decade. Have the pull-factors become less pulling or have the push factors in rural areas become less pushing? Are Indian cities reaching their carrying capacity?

In 1990, the Population Crisis Committee conducted a study of life conditions in 100 largest metropolitan cities of the world. The study ranked these cities on a 100 point scale developed by considering 10 indicators: public safety, food costs, living space, housing standards, communication, education, public health, peace and quiet, traffic flow and clean air. Nine cities of India were included. Their growth rates in 1980s and life conditions scores are given below.

They show that the life condition score had a miximum value of 86 for Melbourne and a minimum value of 19 for Lagos. The study showed that living conditions in cities of the developing countries are deteriorating fast. In some cases, the bulk of the city's population lives in slums and lacks basic urban amenities. In India, the 2 million plus cities were found to be having poor living conditions. However, there were significant differences between Indian cities. Ahmedabad and Madras are found to

City	Growth rate	Life condition score
Ahmedabad	1.98	43
Madras	2.86	42
Hyderabad	3.08	39
Bangalore	4.20	37
Delhi-New Delhi	3.93	36
Bombay	3.31	35
Calcutta	1.82	34
Pune	3.58	34
Kanpur	2.93	33

be on the upper side of life conditions and Pune and Kanpur are on the lower side.

Regional Differences in Degree and Speed of Urbanisation

India is a large country having great regional variations in patterns of urbanisation due to historical, socio-economic and ecological differences. Table 11.4 gives data on the degree and speed of urbanisation in States and Union Territories of India. While degree has been measured by per cent urban, speed has been mesured by per cent change in the degree of urbanisation during 1981-91. Among the major States having 10 million plus population Assam, Bihar, Haryana, Madhya Pradesh, Orrisa, Rajasthan and Uttar Pradesh have lower degree of urbanisation than the national level. Andhra Pradesh, Gujarat, Karnataka, Kerala, Maharashtra, Punjab, Tamil Nadu and West Bengal have higher degree of urbanization than the national level. Among the major States of India, the degree of urbanisation varies from 11.08 per cent in Assam to 38.73 per cent in Maharashtra. Among all States of India, Himachal Pradesh is the least urbanised (8.70 per cent) State and Mizoram is the most urbanised State (46.20 per cent). Except Dadra & Nagar Haveli, the Union Territories are all highly urbanised.

On the whole during 1981-91 the degree of urbanisation in India has risen by 10.20 per cent. In the preceding decade, *i.e.*, during 1971-81 it had risen by 15.43 per cent. These figures show a declining speed of urbanisation for the country. The States and Union Territories which have grown at a lesser speed than the country as a whole are Bihar, Karnataka, Manipur, Punjab, Rajasthan, Sikkim, Tamil Nadu, West Bangal, A & N. Islands, Chandigarh and Delhi. Sikkim, Chandigrah and Delhi, have shown a declining trend in urbanisation also. Arunachal Pradesh and

TABLE 11.4: Degree and Speed of Urbanisation in States and Union Territories, 1981-91

India/State/U.T	Degree of urbanisation			Speed of urbanisation (% change in the degree)	
	1971	1981	1991	1971-81	1981-91
India	20.22*	23.34	25.72	15.43	10.20
States					
1. Andhra Pradesh	19.31	23.32	26.84	20.77	15.09
2. Arunachal Pradesh	3.70	6.56	12.21	77.30	86.13
3. Assam	—	9.88	11.08	—	12.15
4. Bihar	10.00	12.47	13.17	24.70	5.61
5. Goa	—	32.03	41.02	—	28.07
6. Gujarat	28.08	31.10	34.40	10.75	10.61
7. Haryana	17.66	21.88	24.79	23.90	13.30
8. Himachal Pradesh	6.99	7.61	8.70	8.86	14.32
9. Jammu & Kashmir	—	21.05	23.83	—	13.21
10. Karnataka	24.31	28.89	30.91	18.84	6.99
11. Kerala	16.24	18.74	26.44	15.39	41.09
12. Madhya Pradesh	16.29	20.29	23.21	24.55	14.39
13. Maharashtra	31.17	35.03	38.73	12.38	10.56
14. Manipur	13.19	26.42	27.69	100.30	4.81
15. Meghalaya	14.55	18.07	18.69	24.19	3.43
16. Mizoram	11.36	24.67	46.20	117.16	87.27
17. Nagaland	9.95	15.52	17.28	55.98	11.34
18. Orissa	8.41	11.79	13.43	40.19	13.91
19. Punjab	23.73	27.68	29.72	16.65	7.37
20. Rajasthan	17.63	21.05	22.88	19.40	8.69
21. Sikkim	9.37	16.15	9.12	72.36	-43.53
22. Tamil Nadu	30.26	32.95	34.20	8.89	3.79
23. Tripura	10.43	10.99	15.26	10.10	38.85
24. Uttar Pradesh	14.02	17.95	19.89	28.83	10.81
25. West Bengal	24.75	26.47	27.39	6.95	3.48
Union Territories					
1. A & N Island	22.77	26.30	26.80	15.50	1.90
2. Chandigarh	90.55	93.63	89.69	3.40	-4.21
3. Dadra & Nagar Haveli	—	6.67	8.47	—	26.99
4. Daman & Diu	—	36.75	46.86	—	27.51
5. Delhi	89.70	92.73	89.93	3.38	-3.02
6. Lakshadweep	—	46.28	56.29	—	21.63
7. Pondicherry	42.04	52.28	64.05	24.35	22.51

Source: Census of India 1981, *Provisional Population Totals: Rural-Urban Distribution*, p. 26; and Census of India, 1991, *Provisional Population Totals: Rural-Urban Distribution*, p. 15.

*Figure does not match with that shown in table 11.1 due to adjustment.

Mizoram are two fastest urbanising States. During the last census decade majority of States and Union Territories have shown a declining speed of urbanisation. State which have shown the rising speed are only three: Himachal Pradesh, Kerala and Tripura. The rise in Kerala and Tripura is particularly significant. It appears that pulling capacity of urban areas or the centripetal forces are universally weakening in India. Wherever centripetal force has increased it has more to do perhaps with national and international political situation rather than economic growth and industrialisation.

An important aspect of urbanisation in India is that urban population is concentrated mostly in large cities. For majority of Indian States and Union Territories this is true. Table 11.5 shows the distribution of urban population in urban agglomerations and towns by size class. It is evident from the table that in majority of States and all the UTs more than half of urban population is living in Class I cities. In West Bengal, as much as 81.71 per cent of urban population lives in cities. Similarly, in Maharashtra 77.85 per cent urban population lives in Class I cities. Only in Himachal Pradesh, urban population is more or less equally distributed between Class I cities and Class III-VI towns. Arunachal Pradesh and Sikkim are tow outliers. In Arunchal Pradesh whole of the urban population is distributed between Class IV and Class V towns and in Sikkim the whole urban population lives in Class III localities. While the heavy concentration of population in large cities offers an advantage of economy of scale, it also shows that development in the country has been lop-sided and there is little integration of urban and rural economies.

Theories of Urbanisation

Based on the Western experience, sociologists had envisaged a positive relationship between development and urbanisation in 1950s when urban studies started in India. Many Western sociologists believed that there is a positive and symmetrical relationship between development and urbanisation. In other words, urbanisation was seen as both measure and cause of economic development. Even now many social scientists use levels and trends of urbanisation as independent variables determining the course of development. This thinking also provides the framework of development among the planners (Sharma, 1987; Government of India 1985). In addition, sociologists viewed city as a source of Westernisation and spread of urbanity. Urban man was characterised as rational, marginal, secular, alienated, modern and having a scientific outlook.

TABLE 11.5: Urban Population by Size Class in States and Union Territories of India

State/UT	All classes	Class I	II	III	IV	V	VI
1. Andhra Pradesh	100.00	66.88	12.60	16.53	3.30	0.64	0.05
2. Arunachal Pradesh	100.00	—	—	—	66.14	33.86	—
3. Assam	100.00	37.56	11.65	25.61	18.89	4.53	1.76
4. Bihar	100.00	52.62	17.58	20.80	7.03	1.79	0.18
5. Goa	100.00	—	51.84	6.59	22.22	15.42	3.93
6. Gujarat	100.00	66.43	12.73	10.52	7.69	2.42	0.21
7. Haryana	100.00	58.54	15.11	11.95	10.43	3.74	0.23
8. Himachal Pradesh	100.00	24.70	—	19.60	21.87	14.17	19.66
9. Karnataka	100.00	64.60	7.35	17.68	7.73	2.09	0.55
10. Kerala	100.00	66.34	7.22	19.08	6.78	0.58	—
11. Madhya Pradesh	100.00	50.38	13.94	12.82	16.15	6.58	0.13
12. Maharashtra	100.00	77.85	6.49	10.39	4.13	1.03	0.11
13. Manipur	100.00	39.66	—	17.96	15.44	24.19	2.75
14. Meghalaya	100.00	67.54	—	20.18	8.01	4.27	—
15. Mizoram	100.00	48.68	—	17.79	12.87	10.08	10.58
16. Nagaland	100.00		52.38	21.71	17.74	8.17	—
17. Orissa	100.00	44.43	14.65	19.73	16.97	3.94	0.28
18. Punjab	100.00	54.36	19.79	12.89	10.46	2.03	0.47
19. Rajasthan	100.00	50.09	13.67	21.31	13.08	1.82	0.03
20. Sikkim	100.00	—	—	67.52	—	—	32.48
21. Tamil Nadu	100.00	65.96	15.21	11.19	6.11	1.38	0.15
22. Tripura	100.00	37.62	—	27.59	24.66	7.97	2.16
23. Uttar Pradesh	100.00	55.99	11.46	13.94	12.25	5.86	0.50
24. West Bengal	100.00	81.71	6.58	7.66	2.59	1.35	0.11
Union Territory							
1. A.N. Islands	100.00		100.00	—	—	—	—
2. Chandigarh	100.00	100.00	—	—	—	—	—
3. Dadra & Nagar Haveli	100.00	100.00	—	—	—	—	—
4. Daman & Diu	100.00	100.00	—	—	—	—	—
5. Delhi	100.00	99.38	....	....	0.22	0.28	0.12
6. Lakshadweep	100.00	100.00	—	—	—	—	—
7. Pondicherry	100.00	77.64	11.97	3.93	4.04	2.42	—

Source: See Table 11.1, pp. 397-403.

Besides the urban-industrial theory the demographic transition theory was also projected by some Western scholars as another theory of urbanisation. According to this theory, a primitive society is marked by dispersal of population, high and fluctuating mortality, natural fertility and stability of population size. Advances in medical science, economic development and education lead to reduction in mortality. Thus a transitional type of population exhibits rising rate of population growth. However, population growth in itself does not cause urbanisation. Technological development during this period raises productivity of labour force in manufacturing as well as in agriculture. Since the demand for agricultural produce is less elastic than in the manufacturing, and mechanised agriculture does not require much manpower, the population growth results into large scale rural-urban migration. Eventually, concentration of highly mobile and heterogeneous population in centers of modern activities produces radical changes in social institutions, values and processes. People begin to see that family size is expanding which is not conducive to mobility. With this awareness they limit their family size and fertility starts falling. Society again stabilises, though at low levels of mortality and fertility (Mc Gee. 1979).

Data from India and many other developing countries show that urbanisation in these countries does not conform to the Western model. For example, in present day India the share of non-agricultural (*i.e.*, manufacturing and services) manpower is much higher than that was in the West at correspsonding levels of urbanisation about 100 years ago. Unlike Western countries Indian States exhibit a high degree of city primacy. In a number of Indian States, the ratio of population of the largest city to that of the second largest is quite high and the distribution of city size does not support the famous rank size rule —a rule that size of a city is reciprocally related to its rank according to size

Historically, urbanisation is not new to India. In ancient times, there were many cities in India. They existed as centres of trade, administration, education, and religious and political activities. Cities are part of larger society and, therefore, as time passed and political economy of India changed, cities of India also underwent great historical movements. During the British period the imperial forces made various attempts to destroy Indian industry. As a result of this people engaged in industry returned to land. This led to continuous ruralisation of the country and India became a newly formed agricultural colony of the industrial England. The colonial cities were connected to the hinterland through railways essentially for the colonial purposes . After independence many efforts were made to raised rural productivity and standard of living in villages. But there has been no change in the basic structure of the economy. More or less same relatioinship between city and countryside that evolved during colonial rule continued in the post-independence period. In 1951, the percentages of workers engaged in primary, secondary and tertiary sectors were 72.1 10.6 and 17.3, respectively. In 1981, the percentages were 69.3 12.9 and 17.8, respectively (Korpardekar, 1986). Table 11.6 exhibits the percentages of main workers engaged in agricultural sector in urban and rural areas of Indian States in 1991. They include cultivators and agricultural labourers but exclude workers engaged in livestock, forestry, fishing, hunting and plantations, orchards, and also allied activities. Thus actual percentages in primary sector are higher than given in the table by at least 2 per cent. In 1981, the percentage of main workers engaged in livestock, forestry, fishing, hunting, plantations, orchards and also allied activities was 2.2 per cent and we may safely assume that at present it is at least 2 per cent. In the absence of structural transformation, the real income of majority of households in rural areas changed little. Growth of income has been confined largely to service sector and urban areas. Moreover, as the share of agriculture in GDP has constantly declined, the gap betwen rural and urban areas has widened.

The most important issue is that urban economy in India has not been integrally linked with the national economy. Whatever industrial advancement has occurred in urban areas, that has been functionally associated primarily with the demands of international economy and only secondarily with the interests of the vast majority of Indian people. Earlier, in the imperialist framework, and now in the name of development (or catching up with the Western countries), the urban processes have always exploited the need based rural economy. Modernisation of the country has consistently ruined rural crafts, village industries, pauperised the rural poor and strengthened the chain of international imperialism, as the theorists of underdevelopment have been asserting for quite some time.

Different factors have been found to be responsible for urbanisation in different States. Analysis of data shows that in some States urbanisation was caused by improvement in agricultural productivity and in some other States it was caused by agricultural stagnation. Some States urbanised due to rapid industrialisation too. Even the reclassification of localities has caused urbanisation in some States during this period. However, in general urbanisation has been associated with transfer of rural based secondary and tertiary sector activities to urban centres of all sizes. In particular in the poor States, manufacturing and agricultural stagnation caused significant acceleration in urbanisation (Mohan, 1985).

TABLE 11.6 : Percentage of Main Workers Engaged in Agricultural Sector in Urban and Rural Areas, 1991

India /States	Percentage workers in agriculture		
	Total	Urban	Rural
India/State	64.90	11.65	80.24
1. Andhra Pradesh	68.52	15.92	80.80
2. Arunchal Pradesh	65.96	6.79	72.77
3. Assam	64.13	6.17	71.04
4. Bihar	80.62	20.80	88.05
5. Goa	23.97	7.10	35.60
6. Gujarat	56.44	8.09	76.78
7. Haryana	58.91	10.56	74.79
8. Himachal Pradesh	98.71	6.87	74.48
9. Karnataka	63.11	14.02	79.70
10. Kerala	38.04	14.95	46.06
11. Madhya Pradesh	75.37	15.51	88.20
12. Maharashtra	59.72	7.96	83.13
13. Manipur	66.38	40.65	73.97
14. Meghalaya	69.58	6.43	79.63
15. Mizoram	64.62	38.61	83.22
16. Nagaland	72.96	19.79	82.40
17. Orissa	73.06	14.63	80.94
18. Punjab	56.14	10.79	75.63
19. Rajasthan	69.31	12.76	83.14
20. Sikkim	66.23	1.01	72.12
21. Tamil Nadu	59.10	11.74	77.58
22. Tripura	61.57	9.50	70.74
23. Uttar Pradesh	72.07	15.25	84.48
24. West Bengal	52.95	5.32	70.12

Source: Census of India1991, *Provisional Population Table: Workers and their Distribution* Registrar General & Census Commisioner, India, New Delhi, pp. 433-37.

In the above context following things have happened: (a) demographic transition has not led to significant rise in proportion urban, but it has expanded urban population manifold, (b) urbanisation has not produced urbanism and urban areas have exhibited a process of ruralisation, for they have been acquiring many cultural traits of rural population; (c) urban areas have high incidence of poverty and a large informal sector; (d) in place of diffusing secularism and scientific outlook to villages, cities have strengthened identity crisis, ethnic divisionism and social conflicts; (e) sharpening of urban-rural contradictions, rising aspirations, relative deprivation and politicisation have produced a situation in which rural masses have started asserting themselves and asking for greater resources to be spent on rural development. Thus, in addition to ethnicity, the urban-rural division has become a serious political question. This has created a need for building a new theoretical model to look at urban processes in the context of developing countries. So far sociologists have made Western theories their focus of study and tested them with data and arguments from various angles. Now there seems to be a general agreement regarding the inadequacy of Western theories and approaches. But a comprehensive positive alternative is yet to come. It is time that we focus upon the urban changes afresh.

PART II

Implications of Present Day Patterns

Before we take up the issue of planning for the urban future it is imperative to ask: what will be the consequences of urbanisation if the present trends continue? True it is risky to indulge in predictions. Yet we must not overlook the strikingly rapid social changes occurring at the national and international levels. We need projections to plan for the future more rationally. Mohan (1985) has projected future urban population of India by the famous U.R.G.D. method. According to these projections:

1. The level of urbanisation was expected to be around 27-28 per cent in 1991, and around 31.32 per cent in 2001.
2. There will occur a large absolute increase in the urban population raising it to a level of about 235 million by 1991 and about 320 million by 2001.

Projections showed that in 2001 about 230 million urban population would be living in class I cities. In metropolitan cities alone the total population would be 97 million. These figures revealed that even though the level of urbanisation may not exceed 32 per cent, urban areas in general and cities in particular would undergo rapid expansion due to both high natural increase and population transfer. It may be noted that depending on the degree of success with which the Government of India and various State governments can industrialise the backward regions, some rural and small-town migrants may move towards new towns, but it will neither check expansion of large cities nor help in alleviating poopulation pressure on rural resources. The 1991 Census has of course returned lower degree of urbanisation than predicted, but the substantive nature of Mohan's argument still holds valid.

Eastimates show that economic contradictions between urban and rural areas may sharpen further; urban per capita income is expected to continue to rise faster than rural income (Mohan, 1985). It is unlikely that gains in urban income will be distributed equally among various sections of urban population. Filth, housing shortage, lack of satisfactory transport facilities, health problems, pollution, environmental problems, crime and problems of "development refugees" and expanding informal sector with low productivity may rise to new heights. Cities are already facing severe problem of unemployment among the educated youths. Constant rise in the army of the unemployed may become a breeding ground for violence and terrorism. Some thinkers may call it a process of rise in entropy. Rifkin and Howard (1980) say that rise in entropy means not only greater uncertainty in the system but also increase in quantum of energy that is no more available for use. It is an unfortnate trend that society is increasingly getting polarised along class, caste, communal, linguistic and regional lines. Political leaders exploit public sentiments to further their ends. This may lead to more violence. Real issues such as population control, structural transformation of the economy, poverty and ecological deterioration may then occupy a back seat.

Of course this does not mean that no good thing will happen. New initiatives will be taken in selected industries. Industrially advanced countries have also developed a vested interest in shifting manufacturing activities from developed countries to less developed countries so as to keep the latter dependent through technological innovation (U.N., n.d.). There will be more Westernisation, particularly in the newly created islands of affluence in cities. They will be enjoying the highest benefits of progress occurring anywhere in the world.

On the welfare side, it may be stressed that in the West urban renewal programmes have solved some problems of urban environment. In India, amidst the ocean of poverty, there will be little political will and administrative commitment for replanning and comprehensive redevelopment of land structures, physical and social infrastructure, and conservation and rehabilitation of areas in need of conservation. Urban renewal programmes were developed in the Western context (Prasad, 1989). The Western system emphasises the role of city authorities and concentrates on population control, infrastructural development, employment creation and special measures to remove poverty (Oberai, 1989). In India, the problmes are so great and have so many dimensions that special assistance programmes and infrastructure development approaches yield little results. Therefore, to maintain *status-quo* the economic and political elite are resorting to give ethnic colour to problems created basically by inappropriate development planning. Using an ethnic approach to strains of social structure they refuse to see that they are leaving a fractured and burning India for the next generation. How unfortunate it is that the country has been made to face a great turmoil that ensues from politics of reservations while there are not even 1 per cent jobs to be reserved. Financial crisis in government-run institutions, employment-freeze and privatisation have made the issue virtually meaningless. How unfortunate it is that in place of showing light to illiterate villagers cities are spreading communal hatred. They are the places where places of worship are destroyed causing violence and turmoil in the whole country. Why are we not focusing upon the basic causes of agricultural backwardness and methods of improving village life? Is there a way out?

New Imperatives

Planning for the future fundamentally requires that objective function of planning be clearly defined. What do we want to do in the future in India? Should we continue to strive to catch-up with the powerful market economies? Should we work for a socialist reconstruction of society? Should we have some alternative conceptions of development and social justice? Let us first look at what our constraints are and what is feasible. Large scale modernisation of the whole India having little less than 70 per cent labour force dependent on agriculture and large tribal regions is impossible. We neither have sufficient capital nor training to achieve full modernisation of the urban economy that has a large informal sector. With meagre growth of per capita income at a level of 2 per cent or less we cannot catch-up even with an average less developed country not to talk of competing with the West. In the West, rise of capitalism has been attributed to asceticism. Is it possible to inculcate asceticism in our modernising country today, when the West has rejected it long ago and our youths have been socialised to develop rising aspirations? Simulation exercises can easily show that ecologically also it will not be possible to raise standards in poor countries to the level of developed market economies.

Scientific socialism of Marx could not be sold in India at large. Socialist revolution assumes three conditions: belief in unending industrial progress; class contradictions as the main form of social conflicts, *i.e.*, a fair degree of ethnic homogeneity; and radical revolutionary orientation among the people. India did not ever fulfil any of these conditions. Intellectuals have virtually rejected the theory of infinite development in favour of sustainable development (Norgaard, 1988). India is a plural society and there are many cross-cutting conflicts, not necessarily converging around class. China, Slavic Russia, and many other socialist countries were ethnically highly homogeneous during their times of struggle. It has also been argued that the radical revolutionary conception never took roots in Indian consciousness, the key concept of inter-subjective processes in India remained ethnical, transcendental or individualistc.

Should we then not learn from the intellectual systems of those native thinkers who were aware of world historical movments occurring in their times and also needs of our own society. It is our contention that Gandhi, Lohia, J.P. tradition provides us an alternative to work for integral growth, humanism and a no-poverty society, but not an exploitative affluent society (Skolimowsky and Henryk n.d.; 1983; Norgaard, 1988; Pearce, 1988; Dasgupta, 1985).

In response to a letter by an English friend Gandhi (1930) wrote in *Young India:*

> "It should be remembered that India is a predominantly rural civilization. Before the devastating British occupation the seven hundred thousand villages of India were so many self-contained republics. It was left for the marvellous organizing British ability, used not for the welfare of the land as the writer imagines, but misused for its systematic exploitation, to disturb the placid and comparatively happy life of the villager. Rulers have before now come and gone leaving these villages untouched and without leaving chaos behind. Why should the disappearance of British rule result in chaos?...... Ruthless exploitation of India is too great a price to pay for securing the so-called orderly government."

Gandhian theory of society is discussed in Chapter 6. It may, however, be mentioned here that Gandhi developed his concept of *Ramrajya* (kingdom of God) around autonomous villages. As a visionary he could foresee that sustainable progress rests with the system of concentric circles in which a man lives for his family, the family for the village, the village for the region, the region for the state, the state for the country, and the country for the World. India of his dreams must emerge as a world-nation and not as one among the few most powerful nations of the world. His concept of *sarvodaya*—*i.e.*, rise of all—entails correcting two errors which we have made in the past: (a) shift of values from the arena of morality to the arena of materiality; (b) shift from village to city.

In the present system villages have developed a great dependence on cities and the cities on the international technologcal imperialism. In the self-rule or the kingdom of God these relationships will be reversed. Then, in the future, cities would be the centres of certain vital national activities and act as clearing houses for the village produce. There would be an integral link between the urban and the rural areas and the rural-to-urban migration would be minimal as nobody would need to leave his native place in search of livelihood or security. This requires a small modification in the Gandhian theory: the idea of antonomous villages has to be supported by the idea of autonomous urban areas. In Gandhi's days urban population was small. Now it is very large both proportionately and absolutely. It also has to have self-rule and self-reliance. With active involvement of students in productive systems free education would be available to all, irrespective of his ethclass. Then there would be no slums; environmental problems would be minimum. There would be no conflict between urban and rural areas, and no concentration of population in metropolitan cities. It implies:

(a) sustainable development in agriculture by a methodology combining traditional wisdom and modern science;
(b) promotion of *Khadi* and village industries;
(c) removal of income inequality between urban and rural areas, and between various sectors of economy;
(d) promotion of certain key industries related to defence, science, ecological planning, transport and communication, etc. in public sector at the national level;
(e) developing urban areas as centres of diffusion and integration of regional and village cultures rather than using them as gatekeepers of Westernisation.
(f) decentralisation of political power;
(g) ban on sale of liquor or drugs;
(h) promotion of education as part of agricultural and industrial processes; and
(i) popularising *khadi* and other rural based produce in urban areas.

Can the above goals be achieved in today's world? The task is certainly difficult. It cannot be achieved through law or by force. It can be achieved only trough non-violent methods, changing public opinion, and making constructive use of everything existing and not by destruction or disowning them. Political leaders and specially created social institutions would be required for educating the masses. Scientist including social scientists can help by spreading scientific education about urbanisation, environment, and economic principles. Philosophers and religious workers would be required to demonstrate power of non-violence and spread the age-old wisdom of religion. They must stress that there is a dialectical relationship between moral and physical bases of power and that the true interest of man lies in raising moral power. Some intellectuals are needed to show how some latest scientific theories have come close to eastern mysticism and what the implications of latest developments in philosophy of science are.

In sum, it may be said that planning for the future of urban India is an absurd project if it is not made part of the bigger project of planning for the future of villages. In the present conditions, isolated efforts to raise scale of living in cities or to plan the urban ecology would only sharpen the conflict between urban and rural areas which may lead to new forms of political mobilisation or to common harm of interests of both urban and rural areas. There is an urgent need for truncating both ends of income distribution in the spirit of cooperation and intersubjective development. Gandhian tradition provides an alternative frmework in which issues of future planning may be looked at. Unrestrained freedom for all irrespective of power and moral concerns cannot solve our problems. There is un urgent need to operationalise ideas of *gram swaraj* and *nagar swaraj* in the context of open and global systems.

REFERENCES

Bang, Thakurdas, 1984, *Kissan Mazdoor Ki Loot,* Sarva Seva Sangh Prakashan, Varanasi (in Hindi).

Bang, Thakurdas, 1987, *Swatantrata ke Char Daskak,* Sarva Seva Sangh Prakashan, Varanasi (in Hindi).

Bhargava, Gopal, 1981, "Slums of Urban India: Planning and Policy Framework", in Bhargava, Gopal (ed.), *Urban Problems and Polcy Prespectives,* Abhinav Publication, New Delhi.

Bose, Ashish, 1978, *India's Urbanization: 1901-2001,* Tata McGraw Hill Publishing Company Ltd., New Delhi.

Census of India 1991, Provisional Population Totals, Paper-1, Registrar General & Census Commissioner, India, New Delhi.

Census of India 1991, *Provisional Population Totals: Rural Urban Distribution*, Paper-2, Registrar General & Census Commissioner, India, New Delhi.

Census of India 1991, Provisional Population Totals: Workers and Their Distribution, Paper-

3, Registrar General & Census Commissioner, India, New Delhi.

Government of India, 1985, *Seventh Five Year Plan: 1985-90* Vol. II, Planning Commission, New Delhi.

Capra, Fritjof, 1983, *The Tao of Phsics: Exploration of the Parallels between Modern Physics and Modern Mysticism.* Boulder Publications, Shambhala.

Dasgupta, Sugata, 1985, *Towards a Post-Development Era: Essays in Poverty, Welfare and* Development, Mittal Publications, New Delhi.

Korpardekar, H.D., 1986, *Social Aspects of Urban Development,* Popular Prakashan, Bombay.

Mc Gee, T.G., 1979, *The Urbanisation Process in the Third World,* Bell & Hyman, London, pp. 13-30.

Mohan, Rakesh, 1985, "Urbanization in India's Future", *Population and Development Review* Vol. II, No. 4, pp. 619-46.

Muttagi, P.K., 1989, "Urban Environment - The Bombay Scene", *Nagarlok,* Vol. 21, No. 2.

Narayan, J.P., 1986, *Aamne Samne,* Sarva Seva Sangh Prakashan, Varanasi, (in Hindi).

National Institute of Urban Affairs, 1988, *State of India's Urbanization,* National Institute of Urban Affairs, New Delhi.

Norgaard, Richard B., 1988, "Sustainable Development: A Co-evolutionary View", *Futures,* Vol. 20, No. 6, pp. 606-20.

Oberai, A.S., 1989, "Rapid Population Growth, Employment and Housing in Megacities in Developing Countries" in IUSSP, *International Population Conference,* Vol. 2. IUSSP, Belgium, pp. 187-200.

Population Crisis Committee 1990, *Life in the World's 100 Largest Metropolitan Areas,* Population Crisis Committee, Washington.

Prasad, D.R., 1989, "Introduction", in Prasad, D.R. (ed.), *Urban Renewal: The Indian Experience,* Sterling Publishers Private limited, pp. 1-25.

Pearce, David, 1988, "Economics, Equity and Sustainable Development", *Furutes,* Vol. 20, No. 6, pp. 598-605.

Rifkin, Jeremy, and Howard, Ted 1980. *Entropy,* The Viking Press, New York.

Sharma, A.K., "Social Implications of Urbanization in India", *The Journal of Sociological Studies,* Vol. 6.

Skolimowsky Henryk, n. d., *The Ecological Man,* Eco-Philosophy Publication, Madras.

The World Bank, 1992, *World Development Report 1992: Development and the Environment,* Oxford University Press, New York.

United Nations, n.d., *Report and Selected Papers of the Regional Seminar on Ecological Implications of Rural and Urban Population Growth,* Economic Commission for Asia and the Far-East, Bangkok.

12

KNOWLEDGE
Theory and Social Issues

Analysis of knowledge has always been a matter of great concern to philosophers and sociologists. Philosophers have focused largely on concepts of knowledge, truth, true opinion, validity of evidence, etc. (Chischolm, 1966) and sociologists on the interrelationship between structure of society and social processes on the one hand, and structure of knowledge, on the other (Merton, 1973). It may easily be shown that what constitutes knowledge and chracteristics of knowables vary remarkably across cultures and ages. For example, in different cultures and times "knowledege" has varyingly referred to knowledge of true self, knolwdge of God, complete knowledge of religion including jurisprudence, knowledge of ethic, knowledge of some specific area of science, knowledge of witchcraft, and knowledge of working of expert systems, etc. The concepts of knowlege are product of society. Moreover, knowledge at least in our age is no more private. Production, distribution and implications of knowledge are for all, even for those who do not contribute to knowledge directly. Therefore, it is important that like any other cultural product knowledge is subjected to social considerations. Unfortunately, due to reasons of practical expediency in India, knowledge has been taken more seriously than sociology of knowledge. Consequently, sociology of knowledge has not taken roots in Indian soil. It is only now that scientists and social movement theoreticians have started questioning so far unquestioned belief in scientific knowledge. In this context, this chapter attempts to raise the following issues regarding relationship between society and knowledge:

1. Sociology of knowledge perspectives;

2. Society and modes of reflection;
3. Instrumentality of and values in science: power and knowledge in development.
4. Ethics in science; and
5. New imperatives.

This chapter shows that cognitive processes are inseparable from social processes. Various sociology of knowledge perspectives have, however, viewed cognitive processes in different frameworks depending on their basic and prescientific modes of reflection and examine the rationality assumptions and interests. They also attempt to distinguish between scientific and pre-scientific modes of reflection and examine and examine the rationality criterion. Each society defines knowledge in its own manner. Also knowledge plays a crucial role both in maintaining and transforming society. It raises the question of ethics in science. It may be said that further development of society in our age needs a redefinition of knowledge which places same or perhaps more emphasis on science of man and institutions than on science of matter and which subjects science to universal ethical values of life. The author maintains that this has always been the framework of knowledge in ancient India. It was only rediscovered by Gandhi. After independence it was abandoned by the national elite. But recently a critical examination of science, particularly by ecologists has drawn attention of the people to alternatives including pre-modern Indian modes of reflection.

Sociology of Knowledge Perspectives

In the sociology of knowledge perspective, the term knowledge is rarely defined with any high degree of precision. According to Merton, sociology of knowledge "must be interpreted very broadly indeed, since studies in this area have dealt with virtually the entire gamut of cultural products (ideas, ideologies, juristic and ethical beliefs, philosophy, science, technology). But whatever be the conception of knowledge, the orientaion of this discipline remains largely the same: it is primarily concerned with the relations between knowledge and other existential factors in the society or culture". For Habermas (1970) there are three categories of possible knowledge: "information, which increases the extent of our technical command, interpretation which enables an orientation of action in the light of common traditions, and analysis, which sets the consciousness free from its dependence on hypostatised forces". It may be said that in most societies in our age a sharp distinction is made between the social and the natural. "People invariably distinguish two spheres of belief, one relating to a world of objects, facts or concrete events, one to a system of values, obligations, conventions and institutional categories. Both spheres are taken for granted as permanent and valid; both, in this sense, are real. But, today, it is our construction of the natural or physical world which is the most secure and unquestioned" (Barnes, 1974). Thus the main concern of the sociology of knowledge has been to examine the beliefs in the natural sciences. "The sociology of knowledge came into being with the signal hypothesis that even truths were to be held socially accountable, were to be related to the historical society in which they emerged" (Merton, 1973). Thus sociology of knowledge differs from philosophy of knowledge in the sense that in philosophy of knowledge may be defined in terms of observation and observation being a concept of physiology and psychology, it may be defined in terms of these sciences and without reference to knowledge (Chisholm, 1966) but in the sociology of knowledge the sciences themselves are held to be socially accountable, to be reflective of the historical society in which they emerge.

Remmling (1973) says that there are two approaches to sociology of knowledge: diffuse and focused. The first approach fuses sociology of knowledge with related subfields such as historical sociology, socio-linguistics, sociology of art, literature, occupations and professions, popular culture, religion, etc. and the sociology of sociology. The second approach focuses on the origin of sociology of knowledge, present state and further development. "The basic postulates of the sociology of knowldege include conceptions of reality which emphasize the dynamic, historically flowing, relative nature of the world and its division into strata of unequal ontological significance. The concept of historicism expresses the relativistic desire to interpret the world as a dynamic unity undergoing contant socio-historical changes: ideology conceptualizes the assumption that the ideal and ideational spheres are ontologically less real than the social stratum of existence".

Remmling suggested that sociology of knowledge originated during 1924-25 when first Max Scheler and then Karl Mannheim used the term to define and delimit the nature, purpose, and scope of the subdiscipline though Mannheim argued that it emerged with Marx. More recently Holzner and Marx (1979) have shown that the origin of sociology of knowledge is to be found in the expansion of critical thought and skepticism. To quote:

> "It was the rigorous search for truth that also led to the relativization of truth. The context was the debate with eighteenth century thought

> with the legacy of the enlightenment. Enlightenment thought upheld reason as the critical measure of social institutions and their suitability for man's nature. It presumed that essential rationality could lead him to freedom. It looked toward the perfectability of humanity and society. Being infinitely perfectible, people could secure for themselves greater degrees of freedom through social critiques and institutional modification. This in turn would enable them to actualize their potentially creative powers. But these powers were inhibited and repressed by existing institutions; being tradition bound and nonrational, they were not in accord with man's basic nature."

Needless to say there are as many sociologies of knowledge as sociologies proper. Functionalists, Marxists, evolutionary sociologists, structuralists, cyclical sociologists, all have looked at knowledge in their own framework. Thus one can talk of both conservative and radical traditions, macro and micro traditions, and empirical and theoretical traditions in sociology of knowledge. Auguste Comte is called the founder father of sociology. In his study of social physics, he was obviously referring to what was later known as sociology of knowledge. To quote.

> "There is a connection, profound, though indirect, between the conceptions of Aristotle about terrestrial and celestial physics, the scholastic doctrines of the Middle ages, and the social contract of Rousseau. The spirit is the same, extending itself to a new order of ideas."

Comte argued that in his time society was entering the positive or physical phase, and scientific men and industrial chiefs represented the spiritual and temporal organisation (Fletcher, 1974). He said that "scientific men ought in our day to elevate politics to the rank of a science of observation". Comte believed that a primitive society may be characterised by a theological stage from which it moves towards metaphysical stage and then towards positive stage. In the theological stage paramount is always contingent upon the supremacy of military regimes. The gods and the generals go together. In the mataphysical stage occur religious and political upheavals. Finally, positive stage is marked by the supremacy of industry and technology. "Man in spite of himself belongs to his epoch. Those who oppose, as they believe, the greatest resistance to the progress of civilizations unconsciously obey its irresistible influence, nay themselves second it" (Fletcher, 1974).

Durkheim's sociological theory of knowldege further developed the Comtean idea that social structure and social consciousness are interdependent. In his major work he focused on the interaction between primitive social structure, religious behaviour and the origin of basic logical categories.

The nature of relationship between individual psychological factors—personality, attitudes, drives, cognitive properties—on the one hand, and socio-economic and political factors on the other has been a matter of great concern to social theoreticians. Theorists have distinguished between manifestations and deeper reality. Various terms have been coined for the two. They all show a reductionist bias in orthodox social positions. As stated above, Durkheim reduced individual psychological properties and anthropological variables to social structure or social facts. Contrary to this Max Scheler argued that "substructure" consists of psychological factors rather than socio-economic ones and there is a sharp line drawn between the two spheres (Mannheim, 1978).

Scheler (1982) identified seven main types of knowledge and subjected them to the problem of their social origin and forms of movement. He replaced the traditional concept of natural world view by the concept of relatively natural worldview. To him, in the order of "artificiality" the chief knowledge types are": (1) myth and legend, (2) knowledge in the folk language, (3) religious knowledge, (4) the basic forms of mystic knowledge, (5) philosophic-metaphysical knowledge, (6) the positivistic knowledge of mathematics, the natural sciences and (7) technological knowledge. Each of these knowledge types has its own language and style for the expression of knowledge. They originate from the collective urge to save their existence and for that purpose to relate to the "overpowering and holy" intellectual feeling of wonder leading to metaphysics, and the search for experiences leading to striving for power and rule. Kant had believed that the human mind is structured in a universal pattern of organisation somewhat akin to the universal structure of the human body. Knowledge was, therefore, necessarily universal in nature, even though all knowledge was distinctly and specifically human (Holzner and Marx, 1979). In sociology, Scheler had the same universalistic conception of science.

Marx has perhaps made the greatest contribution to critical tradition in sociology of knowledge. Marx was a realist who viewed science as "a progressive, potentially and actually a liberating force, increasing man's power over nature and his own destiny" (Roy, 1983). Marx showed that consciousness and social structure is grounded in organisation of economic activities or in relations which human beings historically develop in the sphere of production. Marx believed in constant development in mode of production. He attempted to show that corresponding to a certain mode of production has been a certain shape of relations of production and during their historical development when mode of production comes in conflict with social structure, revolutionary changes in society follow. Marx divided a changing society into two antagonistic groups of the exploiters and the exploited. He believed that the conflict of interests between these two basic classes is reflected in the battle of ideas in society. Thus one can think of two systems of knowledge including sciences existing at the same time—one legitimising and promoting interests of the dominant class and the other those of the subordinate class. Like Comte, Marx believed that "to assume one basis for life and a different basis for science is *a priori* a falsehood." Natural science and science of man will in time incorporate each other.

In the area of theory sociology of knowledge has added a new perspective in sociology. This new theoretical position has been called the constructivist position. Woolgar (1983) says that regarding the connections between documents (which may be in the form of words, utterances, conversational extracts, signs, gestures, events, etc.) and reality *(i.e.,* motives, intentions, desires, interests of actors, etc.) we may have three positions: reflective, mediative and constitutive. According to reflective position the real world entities have their own existence (independent of documents). They reside outside the description and descriptions are attempts to capture them. The mediative position is that the accounts of realities are not straightforward rather they are products of the social, cultural and historical circumstances which intervene between reality and the accounts. This position has led to constructivist study of science in general and constructivism in particular. The constitutive position is that the accounts are themselves constitutive of reality. In this perspective, sociology of science tells more about the circumstances of its production rather than reality of science that it purports to describe. Today, majority of researchers have adopted mediative position. This has shifted attention of sociologists from aspects of social structure to micro-sociology or to studies of what actually happens in the laboratory. Due to increasing influence of ethnographic and ethnomethodological studies today the question of HOW receives more importance than WHAT or WHY. The inference of these studies is that instead of relying on scientists' accounts as indicators of scientific practice, we first have to improve our understanding of these accounting practices (Knora-Cetina and Mulkay, 1983).

Further, Remmling (1983) has shown that not only works of

sociologists in different milieus exhibit different perspectives but changes in environmental conditions lead to changes in the theories of same men over time. For this he takes up the case of Karl Mannheim, one of the founder fathers of sociology of knowledge. His life was divided into four distinct phases. In the first phase, 1922-32, during which he produced *IDEOLOGY* and *UTOPIA*, he was concerned with sociology of knowledge. During this time he accepted absolute, historicism had suspicion of ideology and treated knowledge as socio existentially determined. During the second phase, 1933-38, he concentrated on sociology of planning. In *Man and Society in an Age of Reconstruction,* which he wrote after arriving in England, he developed theory of democratic social planning. He argued that time had come to overcome "functional rationality" of industrialists (which related social actions of associated individuals to objective ends) by the "substantial rationality" (which would enable the majority of people to grasp the interrelationship between social facts and processes. In the third phase, 1939-44, after, experiencing the Second World War, his attention shifted to sociology of religion, values and education. In the book *Diagnosis of Our Time* he questioned his earlier belief that the rationality framework was adequate to understand man. He realised that emotional and volitional variables are of great importance and emphasised religious behaviour, rejuvenation of public education and Christianity in the interest of social reconstruction. Finally, in the last phase, 1945-47, during which he wrote *Freedom, Power and Democratic Planning*, Mannheim developed serious interest in cold war. He stressed the study of power, and, thus, problems of political and military power.

Society and Modes of Reflection

Sociologists in our age have often been sceptical about the notion of truth in general and scientific truth in particular. They have asked: how does science differ from pre-scientific world of knowldege? What are differences between magic, religion, mysticism, and science? If science is viewed as a rational enterprise, what is the criterion of rationality? What are differences between sciences of action such as economics, sociology and politics, historical interpretative sciences and empirical analytical sciences?

In order to distinguish sicence from non-science, Willer (1971) divides all thought connections into three categories: empirical, rational and abstractive. He says that empirical thinking connects observable to observable, rational thought consists of concepts and their mental connections, and abstractive thinking connects the theoretic and observational levels. To him magical knowledge is practical; as a type of knowledge system it may be classified as empirical. Mystical knowledge also depends on empirical thought but, unlike magical knowledge, mystical knowledge attempts to escape from the empirical world. Religion achieves just the reverse of it. Religious knowledge combines rational connection of concept to concept with the abstractive connection of concept to observable. Scientific knowledge is based on connections at both theoretic and observational levels.

Obviously, if scientific knowledge has to deal with connections at both theoretical and empirical levels, it has to have certain notions of truth and objective validity. For long sociologists have debated the criteria of rationality. Among those who believe in what has been termed the reflective approach above some have used models of inductive inference, and others have used the anti-inductive epistemology suggested by Popper. According to the former, knowledge may be represented by a set of statements with initial probabilities. Based on empirical observations these probabilities are revised. Each revision of probabilities is viewed as a step towards growth of knowledge. And according to the latter, scientific activity takes theories and attempts to falsify them. In the process statements are derived from theories and tested empirically with the help of agreed methodology. Here theories are not directly related to facts. Rather statements derived from theory (original statements) are falsified. In neither approach is there any reflection on how do the original statements or theories arise. There is also no proof that after a number of repetitions all sets of initial probabilities lead to the same reality or that all belief systems can be objectively established to be falsifiable.

Merton suggested that ethos of science are universalism, communism,disinterestedness and organised scepticism, all of which have been coming under heavy criticism by contemporary philosophers of sicence, since the publication of Kuhn's *The Struture of Scientific Revolution.* Kuhn (1970) showed that at a given point of time scientists work within a definite paradigm. Scientists agree on problems, methodologies, beliefs, etc. and their scientific activities may be equated to puzzle solving. Then suddenly some new problem arises that cannot be handled within the paradigm, leading to alternatives. Competition between paradigms eventually produces a new paradigm. Needless to say the process of paradigm shift may be complex and irrational. However, in philosophy of science this paradigm shift has not yet occurred. There are many sociologists of sicence who believe that selection of objects of knowledge and the forms of mental processes are determined sociologically but the content and objective validity of knowledge are to a large extent independent of social interests.

Barnes (1974) has argued that there are no appropriate rationality criteria of truth or logic to be found. Regarding truth he says that all societies use the dichotomy of true/false and good/bad to institutionalise natural beliefs and a system of roles but to know meaning of language, categories, etc. we have to share natives' point of view. Thus there is no universality of observations and language. Regarding logic he says that "contradiction is endemic and routinely accepted in everyday utterances, despite their high general level of consistent usage." People including scientists hold contradictory beliefs and make contradictory utterances. At the same time, scientist is able to "elaborate upon his everday utterances progressively removing contradictions and diffculties, turning 'loose' statements into precise ones, articulating unstated assumptions, qualifying the scope of statments to eliminate contradiction and so on". Yet in doing this he would dig into his cultural resources as a scientist.

Barnes assigns rationality of beliefs not to logical relationship between the elements of abstractly conceived belief systems but to their functions in practical activity. Thus he suggests that in place of constructing abstract criteria of rationality sociologists' understanding must start with actors' normal practice and its inadequacies as they themselves define them. To quote:

> "He must make action intelligible through detailed and extensive insight into the nature of actors' perspectives, their categorie and typifications, the assumptions which mediate their responses, the models which organize their cognition, the rules they normally follow. Then he must construct theories which treat this material symmetrically. This is, as yet, the approach of a minority in sociology, including 'idealists, phenomenologists, ethnomethodologists' and some 'symbolic-interactionists'. Nonetheless it is, essentially, a correct approach, and one which is universally applicable."

Instrumentality of and Values in Science: Power and Knowledge in Development

Social power and social knowledge have always maintained a close mutually reinforcing relationship. In the West, both in market economies and socialist political economies political and knowledge powers had a tendency to get concentrated in the same hands. Recognising the implications of mutuality of the two, Indian philosophers in the ancient times made an attempt to dissociate the two sources of power. However, due to various orthogenetic and heterogenetic influences facing contemporary society and the long run relationship between social and cultural developments this separation could not last very long even here. It was, therefore, soon replaced by a transcendental perspective of *vedanta.*

In our times, the mass production techniques and the ideologies of development have normally served the political interests of the dominant elite. The political institutions have exerted great influence on production of ideas, science and transfer of Western technology. State has made conscious attempts to improve pace of industrialisation, plan economic development and create the "scientific temper". State has legitimised science. It has questioned the validity of pre-scientific cognitive theories and in theocratic contexts it has given a "scientific" colour to religion. History shows that state, reformatories, experts and social engineers have often used scientific arguments to pursue their political programmes such as restriction of immigration, prevention of breeding of criminals, curtailment of civic liberties and vasectomy of youths to curb excessive masturbation (Waites, 1989). Marxists have argued that the doctrine of "mental testing" in Britain had legitimised and provided the technology for a crude educational functionalism which matched education system to social order and social needs.

Willer (1974) says that societies are of two types: (a) politically empirical, and (b) political theology such as communist Russia and Nazi Germany. While a politically empirical society supports and is supported by sicence, political theology eliminates sicence in favour of empiricism which poses no threat to the autoritarian system of knowledge and could be immediately of use. He also said that the present power circles are centres of magical empirical power. They want to control sciences, including political and eocnomic sciences. To quote:

> "If social science were to develop scientifically, it is probable that its scientific power would replace the present magical power in these societies and the whole basis of the present power structures. It is doubtful, however, that this development would be popular in the present power circles; the economic and political structures, as long as they are based on magical power, will continue to reserve support for physical sciences and for empirical work only in the social science. Social science, if it develops, will have to develop on its own".

Willer used the above argument to explain why social science is less developed than physical science. He believed that in the magical empirical context to destroy the empiricist power system and its technological base, the imbalance between various sciences would extremely necessary. For this social sciences have lagged dangerously behind. He wants social sciences to be developed rather than integrated with physical sciences. This, he envisaged, will be the approach to transform the nexus between political and knowledge institutions for self-correction.

Recently, Parajuli has stressed that in the developing countries the real transformation of state within the framework of civil society requires struggle against the knowledge system as part of political programmes of neo-social movements. He argues that the social movements will have to evolve distinctive knowledge system which could represent the experiences of subaltern groups by using alternative ways of producing and validating knowledge. To quote:

> "I am not proposing that women's, dalit's and indigenous people's knowledge be integrated into a ready-made body of dominant development discourse. For developmentalist knowledge is in many ways antithetical to the best interest of these groups. What I am proposing is a two fold task for the new social movements. First, the folkloric commonsensical knowledge of those people must be regenerated and made relevant to the contemporary struggles. Second the language of the dominant development discourse must be reconstructed in appreciation of these knowledge claims from the bottom."

Looking at knowledge from this angle, the author finds that one of the most recent attempts in this direction has been made by environmentalists such as Anil Agarwal, James Lovelock and Vandana Shiva. Agarwal articulated that science and technology have not only dispossessed the poor, they have also subtly undermined confidence of the poor in their own experiences and resources use. In the name of scientific progress, widely available resources have been discredited and the poor who have no other alternatives have started looking to the day when they can manage without them. Shiva has divided sciences into two groups: partisan science and public interest sicence. In her view the modern scientific knowledge is partisan. It identifies development merely with sectoral growth. It defines economic value merely as exchange value of marketable resources and ignores use value of more vital resources and ecological processes. Also it indentifies utilisation with extraction and ignores functions of conserved resources. This partisan science has a reductionist character. It assumes that natural resources are isolated and non-interacting and they acquire economic value only when they are exploited. "Reductionist science leads to the human transformation of nature which is successful in creating artefacts and generating exchange value, but which fails to maintain the essential life-support systems on which human survival depends. Reductionism is not an epistemological accident. It is a particular response to an economic need of a particular form of economic organisation. The reductionist worldview, the industrial revolution and capitalist organisation are the philosophical, technological and economic component of the same process.

As an alternative to the above, partisan science is the knowledge created by the people whose interest lies in sustainable livelihood of people and satisfaction of their basic needs. The public interest science has questioned the "neutral and independent" role of the dominant science in conflicts over natural resources. In other words it acts as a critique of the dominant development discourse. The economic objectives of this new ecological knowledge are: (a) satisfaction of all basic needs, (b) sustainable development and (c) equality of costs of development. It is notable that this knowledge aims not merely at equality with respect to fruits of development but also equality with respect to costs. It has been amply demonstrated by ecologists that the elite have not only benefited most from economic development, they had to bear lesser cost of development than the masses. Ecological knowledge or public interest science, should, therefore, exhibit the two-dimensional attack of economic growth and conventional economic knowledge on interests of the people. It should prepare them to acquire new ways of constructing knowledge and to act accordingly.

However, there is a problem here. The ecological knowledge has failed to change people's perceptions. Unless they are attacked directly by negativities of development they have not shown any sustained concern about ecology. One may argue that the dominant science has successfully marginalised not only the pre-development modes of reflection but also the ecological alternatives. The reason is that in majority of cases it carries the same materialistic epistemology to the people which the dominant science has. Consequently, while it may raise the environmental understanding of society, it may not change consciousness of the people whom it claims to help. The real alternative, if ever achieved, will lie in the people's knowledge framework which destroys the basic psychological and epistemological foundations of the development discourse. *Sarvodaya* concept of Gandhi may offer this alternative.

Max Scheler who attacked the positivist school of sociology and attempted to explain knowledge in terms of permanent attitudes and essential features of mind distinguished between Europistic orientation and Indian and East Asian science. He was of the view that positivistic sociologists have committed a fallacy of mistaking West European movement of knowledge in the capitalist phase of religious and metaphysical decadence for the law of development of the whole mankind. Scheler stressed that cultures of the world vary greatly with respect to ability of three kinds of knowledge systems, *viz.* religion, metaphysics and positive science. In his opinion the Indian and East Asian culture is characterised by the predominance of the metaphysical attitude over the religious and positive-scientific one. The aim of science in India and China has been the forming of man, not knowledge of rules by which nature can be directed. Thus while European science ascends from the inanimate over the animate world to the soul and God, Indian science starts at the soul. From soul it descends to the order of the inanimate world. While the European classes aim at achievement and control, the Indian classes aim at forming of man. "To each kind of science belongs a kind of technics: to the Asian ideal of knowledge, the bio-and psychotecnics of self-salvation (objectification of all wishing and willing, of all passions and affects before a purely contemplative mind); to the European ideal, the inorganic technics of the control of nature" (Scheler, 1982). Ecological knowledge to be effective requires promotion of this Indian Science.

The above review shows that in the past in different forms theoreticians have distinguished between three classes of knowledge: knowledge of values, knowledge of material support for values, and knowledge of action. It has been observed that man knows that he wants freedom for which he has to solve certain problems of man's behaviour. His goals and means are clear to him. It has also been observed that he can accept suffering and is equipped with great mental faculties for progress. Yet he has been notoriously slow to learn and timid in using what in his own knowledge will change his circumstances. Bryson (1947) attributed this to his submission to ancient patterns of fairy tales, dreams and violence (which have failed him before) and sociologists have attributed this to relativistic or situated knowledge systems.

Let us take the case of demographic knowledge in India. Demography is one of the most developed social sciences in the country as far as data, analytical procedures, measurements and size of research operation are concerned. State has encouraged researches in this area with liberal grants. Many international donor organisations have continuously been supporting generation of new knowledge. Many Indian demographers have made significant contributions to the descipline at the international level. But where is the theory? Why have Indian demographers failed to theorise about Indian demographic patterns? Why has Indian society, one of the most active societies in creating knowledge base in population matters has failed to benefit from what it knows? Bryson would explain this anomaly in terms of inertia, traditional beliefs about reproduction, religious hinderances, etc. Myrdal (1970) explains this in terms of softness of state in India. Marxists at one time maintained that India did not face population problem. It is the semi-feudal semi-capitalist state that created the myth of population problem to divert attention from real issues of economy. Sharma (1991) argued that the new imperatives have destroyed the traditional knowledge base but have remained ineffective due to mismatch between new concepts and traditional structure. Common man may complain about lack of political will. Now the social movement theorists are asking: has the decision been made? Is the developmentalist knowledge the only valid system and is the commonsensical knowledge inferior knowledge? Would the subaltern groups benefit politically from accepting the dominant development discourse and declaring indigenous people's knowledge absurdist?

Habermas stressed that sciences in our times have served their interest largely by setting them free from political interests. "The sciences earn the respect that is their by applying their methods imperturbably and without thought for their guiding interest. By being methodologically ignorant of what they are doing, the sciences are the more sure of their discipline, that is, of methodological advances within a non-problematic frame. This inadequate awareness of theirs has a safeguarding function, for at the self-reflective level the sciences lack the means of protection against the risks of a too clear view of the connection between knowledge and interest. Thus science may be projected as the pure wisdom which, may be misused by the political system. It is in the same perspective that Steinkraus mentioned that the present day technology is not scientific technology but industrial technology. For him it would, therefore, be necessary to take continuous and circumspect cognisance of the effects and impacts of science and technology on human life. He believes that health and harmony, satisfaction and happiness in human life, individual and social, are the ultimate values. He desires that continuous attempts be made to harness science for these values. Adiseshiah (1985) claims that in the past science in India was used not to remove disparities but to strengthen disparities. What is needed in this contest is to use more science and technology, including more social and human science, to enable man to eradicate gender and class differences many of which are creation of his own science.

Ethics in Sciences

As mentioned above, the term knowledge as used in the literature has two connotations: knowledge as a value and knowledge as an area of cultural activites. This distinction is more pronounced in the case of science. Science as a value refers to "scientific temper" and as an activity it refers to achievements of scientific developments. In the second sense science is used as means for attaining universal values of development other culture specific values of societies. Both ways scientists must conform to certain ethical standards or norms. Originally, in the functional perspective it was maintained that people engaged in production of knowledge must be objective, free from any ideological bias and should be dedicated to promotion of true knowledge. They should be ready to make sacrifices and not use knowledge for sectarian political purposes. Thus Merton suggested that there are certain scientific norms which may be expressed as communalism, universalism, disinterestedness, originality and scepticism. Accordingly, science is public knowledge, freely available to all. There are no privileged sources of scientific knowledge. Science is done for its own sake. Science is the discovery of the unknown, and scientists take nothing for trust (Ziman, 1984). Steinkraus stated that science is based on three normal presupposition: (a) principle of integrity; (b) avoidance of personal or other bias; and (c) principle of cooperation. To him a scientist who states facts and does not hide facts contradicting his theory is an honest scientist. Thus science (even technology) was viewed as neutral; its practical results were viewed as reflections of human will (Bishop, 1976). Technology has different values from values of knowledge or science.

The above realisation has led to the thinking that knowledge in general and scientific knowledge in particular must be treated as any other cultural product. It should not be treated as epistemologically superior to any other system of belief. Ziman (1984) states that this is the "strong programme" in the sociology of knowledge. Researches have shown that research process in the natural sciences has seldom conformed to formal norms of scientific rationality. This implies that science must be viewed as a social enterprise and must be subject to social evaluation. In what framework is knowledge to be evaluated?

Oberai says that there are three dimensions of civilisation: cosmology or the reality or the world, epistemology or truth and ontology or man. They deal with three important questions: What is world? What is truth? What is man? The modern Western science has developed largely in the positivistic framework of Saint-Simon. Not just that it is unsuitable or irrelevant for India, China or some other country in one extrinsic respect or another, *e.g.* in relation to applications of technology, at some time it took wrong direction in the intrinsic sense (Oberai, 1978). It may be said that its findings, theories and techiques are all largely untrue, misleading and senseless for mankind as a whole. No one should, therefore, believe in the magic of modern science or bow before its superior intellectual authority. Oberai feels that the possible future alternative of the Western science lies in using the integral framework of Goethe. We must realise that cosmology, epistemology and ontology are "inseparable aspects of one and the same regime of thought and life that we call civilization or culture, so that one cannot formulate the answer to any one question to the other two fundamental questions".

Comte, one of the earliest sociologists of knowledge, recognised that the industrial society would need spiritual power for its maintenance and development. Yet his notion of spirituality in this context was ethical and not cosmological or ontological. To quote:

> "However great the progress of civilization may be, it must ever remain true that if the social state is, in certain respects, a continuous state of individual satisfaction, it is also, under other not less necessary aspects, a continuous state of sacrifice. To speak more precisely, each person in every personal act, must experience a certain degree of satisfaction without which society could not exist and a certain degree of sacrifice without which it could not maintain itself, having regard to the opposition of individual tendencies which is, in some degree, absolutely inevitable".

The above notion of spirituality implies that scientists as individuals make sacrifices for society. Scientists must not use science for promotion of their own professional or scientific interest alone. A sense of sacrifice is necessary not only for growth of knowledge but also for social development of modern society. Has it happened? Unfortunately, deviation from scientific ethos has not been uncommon in research. Scientists are known to have manipulated their findings to suit their academic, economic or political interests. It has been so particularly in social sciences or knowledge systems which have direct bearing upon political and social policies. Tehri dam and Mandal Commission controversies are good examples of this. Recently, IIT Delhi organised a workshop on the responsibilities of technologists, scientists and managers (Sharma and Sharan, 1990). Majority of participants in the workshop felt that there was a need to stress the promotion of humanistic and scientific values in science. The discussion on ethos in science and technology that took place there had a systems perspective.

In the Marxist perspective, there are no universal ethos independent of social formations. For Marxists social standards are part of the superstructure which is determined by the infrastructure of relations of productions. Thus ethical/moral standards are viewed simply as reflections of political interest of the basic classes that constitute a class society. Only in socialist or classless society social standards are universal, and benefit all. Since, according to Marxist belief, a proletarian revolution is essential and inevitable, only those scientists, philosophers, educationists, artists, journalists and other connected with knowledge, who contribute to social transformation from capitalism to socialism show true ethical standards. In commenting on bourgeois knowledge Marx had himself classified the different schools into four main categories: fatalist school, ramantic school, humanitarian school, and philanthropic school. The falalists are indifferent to faults of bourgeois production. Romantics are modern blase fatalists and cognates. The humanitarian school is based on the distinction between theory and practice. The philanthropic school is the humanitarian school carried to its perfection. It denies the necessity of antagonism; it wants to turn all men into bourgeois; it wants to realise theory in so far as it is distinguished from practice and contains no antagonism.

New Imperatives

The above discussion has shown that construction of knowledge is a socio-cultural process, the aims and determinants of which are social. It has also shown that sociologists have used all the sociological perspectives to examine contents of knowledge. That knowledge is a social enterprise is a relatively new realisation that has led to attempts to scrutinise both nature of knowledge at the structural level and nature of knowledge processes in labs. However, one can look at sociology of knowledge itself in a sociological perspective . Recently, some Gandhian thinkers have taken interest in knowledge and they have indirectly explored sociology and psychology of sociology of knowledge. Their works and works of many other sociologists have shown that sociology of knowledge is rooted in the Western philosophy which has gradually replaced God by society. Now when the crisis within sociologistic tradition is clearly evident in both theory and practice there is perhaps a need to examine alternatives.

Bang (1986) in his essay on direction of science stressed that we need a holistic perspective on science. Science must be related to knowledge of true self. Gandhi had a belief that the methods of science must be applied in the spiritual area and science must be done in a spiritual framework.

The evils of modern science are obvious. Modern sicence has led to urbanisation, industrialisation, centralisation of power, destruction of nature, environmental problems, violence and anomy and alienation. It has happened largely because science (knowledge of external world) was pursued at the cost of wisdom (knowledge of self). In the process an image of rational-utilitarian individual, a self-seeking individual, was built motivating him to maximise his own gains in society. Consequently, science became a tool in the hands of powerful exploitative elite and was used to cause only ignorance, unemployment, hatred, diseases and helplessness among the masses. Gandhian theorists have argued that the remedy for this pathological state of society lies in spiritualising knowledge which is true sociology of knowledge and which involves a back journey from society to self. It may be noted that on 24th June 1981 about 51 Nobel prize winning scientists had to make an appeal from seven cities of the Western world that the powerful people of the world must read the writings on the wall. They said that everywhere centralised political power and economy had committed a fraud against common man. This centralised system is crushing crores of people. Hesitation to change this system may lead to destruction of the whole world. If the powerful people fail to understand this, the powerless people of the world will have to prevent this suicide through peaceful Gandhian movement (Bang, 1986). Schumacher (1979) declared that industrial society is an evil and technology is essential and even the crucial base of industrial society.

Gandhian theory of knowledge may be constructed on the following assumptions: (a) there is no difference between true individual value and true social value and qualities such as *brahmacharya* and non-possession which are needed by individuals for freedom from bondage or truth realisation are also needed for good society; (b) urban life promotes consumerism and inequality and it leads to abuse knowledge by the power elite; (c) redemption of knowledge is possible by rejecting consumerist society and envisaging a spiritual society. To him as a rule, knowledge in urban industrial society creates unemployment, violence, wastages in economy, poverty, wars and destruction of nature. Contrary to this, knowledge in *gram swaraj* (self-ruled villages) contributes to sustainability, quality, peace, natural balance and independence. Most countries of Asia and Africa have less (per capita) land and capital and more population. They should have adopted a more labour intensive model of development rather than capital intensive model. Westernisation and industrialisation of these countries have created artificial ornamental development. They have marginalised and alienated large sections of society. The knowledge perspectives generated in these artificial islands of development (affluence) will further destroy the basic fabric of society. Knowledge is power. If knowledge is not produced in the framework of humanity, its consequences may be horrifying. Gandhi had warned that if India accepts Industrialisation, it will one day have to produce another Chingiz Khan also.

Gandhi envisaged a total and integral development of all human faculties and all parts of society. As mentioned above, in our age science has become an instrument of promoting industrial—political interests of the elite. Thus industrial elite use science for raising their competitive edge over others and for accumulation. For Gandhi, accumulation is inconceivable without exploitation and violence. Gandhi was not against science and technology as such but he wanted that science and technology should be developed to serve all (parts of society and human needs). It may be said that on the one hand, he admired the progress made in medical health and surgery in the Western countries, he even allowed some disciples to go for surgical operation, but on the other he opposed even nature cure if this knowledge is not produced in India and makes us dependent on the West. In revising his position, earlier expressed in *Hind Swaraj,* he had accepted industrialisation of India if it lessens India's dependence on the colonial power as a beginning towards the self-rule. It may be noted that Gandhian theory projects two reversals: at societal level reversal of increasing dependence of the marginalised on the Western power; at the individual level reversal of increasing dependence of the self on materiality. The project of knowledge should relate to these reversals.

Concluding Remarks

Sociology of science has clearly established that conception, level and nature of application of science are social choices. And at the same time these choices are shaped by the worldview—non-scientific or scientific leading to a reciprocal relationship between science and society. If the Third World countries including India have dependent or destructive (of ecology) science, it reflects the choices made by their elite on behalf of their social structure. It is also partly due to their uncritical acceptance of the Western worldview and uncritical technology transfer. As a remedy for this sickness it may be suggested that they must first evolve holistic concepts of man and social development. They must place scientific worldview in a proper perspective. The Gandhian model of revolutionising tradition to counter evils of Westernisation is one such conceptual framework. Students of knowledge may, therefore, find a ready framework in Gandhian theory for evaluation and modification in sociology (and philosophy) of science. They must not only ask what is knowledge doing to society and its various constituents but also ponder on how do the scientific notions relate to society and self.

REFERENCES

Adiseshiah, Malcolm S. (nd.), 1985, *Science and Technology for Women,* Tamil Nadu State Council for Science & Technology, Madras.

Agarwal, Anil, 1986, "Politics of Environment", *Gandhi Marg,* Vol. 87, pp. 137-62.

Ananthu, T.S., 1990, "Going Beyond the Intellect: A Gandhian Approach to Scientific Education", in Sharma, Anuradha, and Sharan, Raka (eds.), *Social Responsibilites of Technologists, Scientists and Managers,* Gian Publishing House, New Delhi.

Bang, Thakurdas, 1986, *Vigyan Ki Sahi Disha,* Sarva Sewa Sangha Prakashan, Varanasi (in Hindi).

Barnes, Barry, 1974, *Scientific Knowledge and Sociological Theory,* Routledge & Kagan Paul, London.

Bishop, D.H., 1976, "Science, Technology and Value", in Pandeya, R.C., and Bhatt, S.R. (eds.), *Knowledge Culture and Value,* Motilal Banarasidass, Delhi, pp. 51-52.

Bryson, Lyman, 1947, *Science and Freedom,* Columbia University Press, New Delhi.

Chischolm, Roderick, 1966, *Theory of knowledge,* Prentice-Hall, Inc.

Elisa, Norbert, 1982, "Scientific Establishments", in Elias, Norbert, Martins, Herminio and Whitley, Richard (eds.) *Scientific Establishments and Hierarchies,* D. Reidel Publishing Company, London.

Fletcher, Ronald, 1974, *The Crisis of Industrial Civilization: The Early Essays of Auguste Comte,* Heinemann Educational Book Limited, London.

Habermas, Jurgen, 1970, "Knowledge and Interest", in Emmet, Dorothy, and Macintyre Alasdais (ed.), *Sociological Theory and Philosophical Analysis,* Macmillan, pp. 36-54.

Holzner, Burkart, and Marx, J.H., 1979, *Knowledge Application: The Knowledge System in Society,* Allyn and Bacon, Boston.

Judith, Willer, 1971, *The Social Determination of Knowledge,* Prentice-Hall, Inc., Englewood Cliffs, New Jersey, pp. 20-141.

Knorr-Cetina, Karin D. and Mulkay, Michael, 1983, "Introduction: Emerging Principles in Social Studies of Science", in Knorr-Cetina, Karin D., and Mulkay, Michael, (eds)., *Science Observed,* Sage Publications, New Delhi, pp. 1-18.

Kuhn, Thomas, 1970. *The Structure of Scientific Revolution,* University of Chicago Press, Chicago.

Lovelock, James, 1989, "The Greening of Science", *Resurgence,* No. 138, pp. 12-19.

Mannheim, Karl, 1973, "Sociology of Knowledge from the Standpoint of Modern Phenomenology: Max Scheler", in Remmling, G.W. (ed.), *Towards the Sociology of Knowledge,* Routledge & Kegan Paul, London, pp. 187-201.

Marx, Karl, 1978, *The Poverty of Philosophy,* Progress Publishers, Moscow, pp. 112-17.

Merton, R.K., 1973, *The Sociology of Science: Theoretical and Empirical Investigations,* University of Chicago Press, Chicago.

Myrdal, Gunnar, 1970, *The Challenge of World Poverty,* Penguin Book.

Parajuli, Pramod, 1991. "Power and Knowledge in Development Discourse: New Social Movements and the State in India" *International Social Science Journal,* Vol. 127, pp. 173-90.

Oberai, J.P.S., 1978, *Science and Culture,* Oxford University Press, New Delhi.

Remmling, G.W., 1973, "Existence and Thought", in Remmling, G.W. (ed.), *Towards the Sociology of Knowledge,* Routledge & Kegan Paul, London, pp. 3-43.

Remmling G.W., 1973, "The Significance and Development of Karl Mannehim's Sociology", in Remmling G.W. (ed.), *Ibid*, pp. 217-28.

Roy, Bhaskar, 1983, "Science", in Bottomore, Tom (ed.), *A Dictionary of Marxist Thought*, Oxford University Press, Delhi pp. 434-36.

Scheler, Max, 1982, "On the Positivistic Philosophy of the History of Knowledge and its Law of Three Stages", in Curtis, J.E., and Petras, J.W. (eds.), *The Sociology of Knowledge: A Reader*, Praeger Publishers, London, pp. 170-86.

Scheler, Max, 1982, "The Sociology of Knowledge: Formal Problem" in Curtis, J.E., and Petras, J.W. (eds.), *Op cit*, pp. 161-69.

Schumacher, E.F. 1979, *Good Work*, Harper and Row, New York.

Sharma, A.K., 1991, "Gandhian Theory of Population: Relevance and Implication", *Indian Journal of Family Welfare*, Vol. 37, No. 4, pp. 32-45.

Sharma, Anuradha, and Sharan, Raka, 1990, *Social Responsibilities of Technologists, Scientists and Managers*, Gian Publishing House, New Delhi.

Shiva, Vandana, 1991, *Ecology and the Politics of Survival*, Sage Publications, pp. 13-60.

Steinkraus, W., 1976, "Transcultural Value Pre-suppositions of Science", in Pandeya, R.C., and Bhatt, S.R.(eds.) *Knowledge, Culture and Value*, Motilal Banarsidass, Delhi, pp. 63-66.

Vadekar, D.D., 1978, "Science, Technology and Value", in Pandeya, R.C., and Bhatt S.R. (eds.), *Knowledge, Culture and Value*, Today and Tomorow Publishers & Printers, New Delhi, pp. 25-36.

Waites, Bernard, 1989, "Social and Human Engineering", in Chant, Colin (ed.) *Science, Technology and Everyday Life, 1870-1950*, Routledge.

Woolgar, Steve, 1983. "Irony in the Social Study of Science", in Knorr-Cetina, Karin D., and Mulkay, Michael (eds.), *Science Observed*, Sage Publications, New Delhi, pp. 239-66.

Woolgar, Steve, and Malcolm, Ashmore, 1988, "The next Step: An Introduction to the Reflexivity Project", in Woolgar, Steve (ed.) *Knowledge and Reflexivity*, Sage Publications, New Delhi, pp. 1-11.

Ziman, John, 1984, *An Introduction to Science Studies: The Philosophical and Social Aspects of Science and Technology*, Cambridge University Press, Cambridge.

—

13

MUSLIM FERTILITY IN URBAN U.P.
A Qualitative Study

India is a land of many religions. The various religious communities in the country are known to have been responding differently to master processes of change (*e.g.* urbanisation, industrialisation, demographic revolution) in terms of their theodicy and socio-economic characteristics. Thus today when the country is known to be passing through the second stage of demographic transition (low mortality and declining birth rates), significant fertility differentials are known to have emerged between ethnic groups including religious communities. As a matter of fact, as early as 1951, the noted demographer and sociologist, Davis had observed such religious differentials in India. His study was a comparative study. It was based on child-women ratios. Subsequently many others have shown presence of such differentials in censuses, administrative statistics, and sample survey data (Sharma and Misra, 1978; Gupta, 1986; Saseendran and Kumar, 1989, ORG; n.d., Bhatia, 1990). One aspect of religious differentials in fertility is that they are rooted in differentials in ideal family size (NFHS, 1995). Muslims not only show higher fertility than Hindus, they have higher ideal family size than Hindus too. Also, the relationship between fertility and fertility goals on the one hand, and socio-economic status on the other, is far from being downward sloping linear (Khan, 1976; Gupta 1986; Srivastava and Saksena, 1989). For example, among the Muslims in Kanpur city, initially fertility increases with rise in literacy/education levels to be followed by declining fertility at higher levels of literacy/education.

A large section of urban Muslims may possibly have higher fertility than rural Muslims. In this context, a study was conducted in Kanpur to explore various dimensions of Muslim fertility in the urban setting.

Kanpur is the largest city of U.P. with a considerably large Muslim population. This chapter discusses findings of the study.

Theoretical Framework

Sharma (1989) developed a theoretical framework to explain patterns of Muslim fertility in India. Criticising the prevailing strands of thought on this issue—socio-economic theory, cultural theory, and minority-status hypothesis—he said that it requires explanation why is Muslim fertility in India higher than Hindu fertility but lower than fertility in most of the Muslim countries, and even lower than fertility in neighbouring Muslim countries such as Pakistan and Bangladesh. This explanation would require a sound understanding of the Indian situation and the historicity.

According to Sharma, Muslims in contemporary India seem to show three tendencies: marginalisation, modernisation, and Islamisation. Undoubtedly, these tendencies are conditioned by economic factors. The poor are marginalising, the rich are modernising and the middle strata are Islamising. These three tendencies are, however, not completely independent of each other and quite often Islamisation results from the failure of much desired modernisation to deliver goods. Sharma also stressed that for Indian Muslims in contemporary India Hindus are as much a reference group as Muslims in Pakistan or Saudi Arabia. There is emerging a much more self-confident Westernised elite group among the Muslims which can relate to both *ulema* and the Westernised Hindu elite. The elite have a more rational attitude towards religion, are sensitive to Indian socio-economic and cultural milieu, are individualising, and want to work in cooperation with Hindus and others. Many of them, for historical reasons, are influenced by the Hindu thought categories. Their reaction against such aims and processes of modernisation which are not explicitly and symbolically associated with Hindu tradition is weakening. Among the elite there is rather a sense of competition. Consequently many behavioural differences between Hindus and Muslims including reproduction have been dissolved at the higher levels of education and modernity.

Because of the fact that different categories of Muslims exhibit different reproductive tendencies, explanation of urban Muslim fertility would require a *theory of rotating coordinates system.*[1] Broadly speaking, their fertility would depend on:

(a) Religiosity and perceptions of Islamic position on fertility and family planning;

(b) The degree of residential segregation between Muslims and others; and

(c) Socio-economic conditions.

Thus it could safely be assumed that fertility would be higher among families which are (a) highly religious and traditional in their outlook, (b) live in segregated areas, and (c) belong to lower socio-economic strata.

Methodology

Since the purpose of the present study was not to estimate levels of fertility, and fertility differentials but to explore the dimensions of urban Muslim fertility, a qualitative method was adopted. Of late, great advances have been made in application of qualitative methods (Misra, 1993; Theis and Grady, 1991). To some extent the differences between qualitative and quantitative methods have become unimportant. Development theorists have increasingly taken a stand that all methods can be used freely depending on the purpose of the enquiry. Initially, the author felt severely constrained by a number of factors. He did not have an interdisciplinary team of researchers that could facilitate use of triangulation which would suit the study most. The topic of the study is highly personal. The city of Kanpur has become communally sensitive. In urban areas people are normally busy during the day time and to make them collect at one place for focused group discussion is difficult. Therefore, the author had to satisfy himself only with interview method. He visited various parts of Kanpur, both mixed areas and purely Muslim areas and interviewed people of different socio-economic and demographic backgrounds. In majority of cases he established contacts with respondents through local professionals such as doctors, social workers, and common friends. In some cases direct contacts were also made. Some members of voluntary organisations (such as Shramic Bharati) working in Muslim areas and professionals of Kanpur branch of Family Planning Association of India (FPAI) were also interviewed. These interviews were conducted during July-September 1993.

Findings

In urban areas population may broadly be divided into three groups: the elite, the commoners, and the poor. The elite are those who own industry, run big business enterprises, belong to the class of professionals or are simply property owners. The poor have submarginal existence, irregular jobs, low income, live in slums or slum-like conditions. Many of them are new migrants. A great majority of them are engaged in the informal sector. The percentages of the elite and the poor may roughly be around 5 and 40, respectively. The rest are commoners.

The first significant learning that the author had in the field was that not the religion but perceptions of religion should be related to behaviour. In the past researchers have analysed behaviour in terms of religious constructs obtained from holy books (Anonymous, 1987; Khan 1991; Sawhney *et al.*, 1990; Swee-Hock, 1989), *i.e.* from the great tradition of Islam. That may not help much. No doubt people's understanding at the grassroots level is a reflection of great tradition but the two never match fully. Wherever religion is important it is fundamentally the perceptions of religion which influence behaviour. The author observed the following four responses among Muslims:

(a) *Religious Non-actualists.* They have high regard for religion and religious life and keep religion always at high pedestal. Yet their behaviour including fertility behaviour is governed almost fully by material conditions of life. They may not even be aware of religious position on issues of practical interest. In other words, among these people the traditional unity of cosmology, metaphysics and ethics, a unique characteristic of Islam, has been broken and ethical concerns are increasingly shaped by material conditions. Cosmology and metaphysics may remain unchanged for long but their power to affect behaviour is very limited. The elite and some socially mobile commoners belong to this category.

(b) *Religiously Rationalising Secularists.* They are the people who either due to compelling circumstances or due to influence of change, desire to act according to secular considerations. However, their conditions are such that they generally fail. Then they rationalise their failure in religious terms. Quite often they look religious but they are failed secularists. They are mostly commoners. For example, lack of quality of family planning services among the less educated artisans may result into unwanted delays in family planning acceptance or accidental pregnancy. Then they say that children are in the hands of *Kudarat* (God). One of our respondents said that he wanted to adopt family planning after two children. So after having two he and his wife got ready. One day they were about to go to the hospital for tubectomy. All of a sudden his father-in-law came and told that his wife's *mausa* (mother's sister's husband) had died. Then his wife went with her father and tubectomy could not be done. After her return, he used *nirodh* but his wife conceived. Thus they had the third baby. After that also something happened and his wife could not be sterilised. Finally, after four she was sterilised by laproscopy method. Luck was not with them. After laproscopy too his wife conceived. Since his wife had been sterilised he thought that there was some health problem causing swelling on her stomach. Their local doctor confirmed that it was a case of simple swelling. A few days later she went to her father's place from where she wrote that swelling was rising. The village doctor still believed that it was a simple swelling . On return she was taken to a proper lady doctor who confirmed pregnancy. Thus she delivered her fifth baby. Our respondent believes that today everybody wants small family. But whether one will have 10 children or none is decided by God—no matter what man does, he is helpless. As another respondent says: "There are some couples who have done everything for it but they have had no child but there are many who get child even if husband just smells his wife".

If good quality family planning services are available and they succeed in preventing births, religious rationalisers change. They may even liberally accept sterilisation for health and family planning.

(c) *Rationalised Religious Idealists.* They are those commoners whose decisions are purely secular but who would like to believe that they are truly Islamic. They have their own interpretations which show religion in highly positive and scientific image. One such respondent who had only two children and was working in I.I.T. said that those who practise Islam can have only 1-2 children. To him none of their *wali ullahs* such as Hazrat Ali, Abdul Kadir Jilani, Khwaja Garib Nawaz had more children although many of them had married. The reason is that a person who is really religious and spiritual, who is all the time remembering God, he will not think of worldly pleasures (including sex). He did not accept family planning methods and believed that people truly practising Islam would not need them. For those who have not yet achieved high religious level, people having rationalised religiousity may permit use of conventional contraceptives but not abortion or sterilisation. To them, of course, religion does not allow to think about negative consequences of having children but it certainly ordains one to use brain for his benefit and benefit of his children. "If one has 12 children, he is all the time worried about maintenance of family, how can he pray?"

(d) *Religious Orthodoxy.* Those who have read religious literature only (in Urdu or Arabic), who have theological degrees such as *Hafiz, Kari* or *Alim* are orthodox. They think that as soon as boys and girls begin showing signs of adulthood ("boys between 12-15 years and girls between 9-12 Years") they should be married. They believe that Islam is opposed to all family planning methods and abortion. They believe that *Allah* has made arrangements for all souls sent in the world. To think that large family may lead to misery is to commit a sin, a great sin. This orthodoxy is maintained by *maulvis* and *maulanas* (religious priests) and given the monolithic nature of Islam the poor are mostly guided by such ideas. The influence of priests is highest among those who are poor and who live in segregated areas. They have read only Urdu literature. They read books like *Khamind Musalmaan* by Idris which deals with how should Muslim householder behave. The book is against family planning and propagates the view that children are sent by God. Man's will is unimportant. Their children go to *madarasa* rather than secular schools. After fifth standard, there is a high chance that they will drop out. They engage in menial jobs. The vicious circle of ignorance-orthodoxy continues.

Influenced by these ideas many Muslims, even some educated and in modern jobs, feel that family planning is against Islam. A sterilised man cannot perform *namaz* (prayer), he cannot become *pesh imam* (*i.e.*, he cannot lead congregation at the time of *namaz*). To be sure he is not allowed to go for *haj* (pilgrimage to Mecca and Madina). One *maulvi* said that Islam orders to bring girl of that family in marriage which has 30 children so that she bears large number of children and spreads Islam.

The above are urban Muslim perceptions of religion and their implications for fertility are obvious. Things are certainly changing under economic pressures. Interestingly, one *sunni*-Hanafi *maulana* of age 26 years holding the degree of *Alim* and believing that a boy should marry between 12-15 years had not married yet. He earned Rs. 500-1000 a month from performing *milad sharif* (religious preachings lasting about an hour) and around the same money from fees that children paid in Urdu school run by him between 1.00-3.00 p.m. He was still waiting for his economic condition to improve before marriage. He was learning scooter repair work from a local mechanic. When the author asked why had he not married till then, as per Islamic injuction, he told that Islam is more liberal towards boys; girls should definitely be married in time lest they commit sin or bring disrepute to family. Is it not the same argument as offered by the poor Hindu in rural areas?

At this stage one may ask: what are the sources of religious perceptions? Though religion and religious institutions have been highly explored areas in sociological researches, it is still quite intriguing to examine causes and forms of religiosity. On the face of it, religious perceptions are product of socialisation. They are shaped by complex interplay of socio-economic and political forces. For example, the elite class children, socialised in the nuclear mobile urban family, raised in heterogenous neighbourhood, exposed to modern ideas, going to best schools in the city, and aspiring to become professionals are likely to grow as irreligious or religious non-actualists. They are individualists and they have competitive relationship with other members of society. The members of the upper middle class, educated in schools and universities, working in modern secular organisations and yet confronting the fundamentalist Islamic ideology or religious revivalism are likely to reflect rationalised religiosity. They are essentially religious apologists. This tendency not only satisfies certain sociological needs but also responds to their anxieties, uncertainties need for meaning and alienation. Political forces in the present day India, leading to emergence of ethnic religious identities have partly produced this tendency.

Religious orthodoxy is usually a poor segregated class phenomenon. It is as much socio-psychological in nature as political. It is often a response of a peripheral community on defensive expressing occasionally in a kind of tribal militancy. The author has known that in certain Muslim dominated areas in Kanpur not only the family planning workers but the municipal or electricity workers also fear to enter. And if they visit them at all, the purpose is simply to show visits on papers to save their jobs and not to act. The peripheral community develops a strange sense of power by putting an iron curtain around it and maintaining its full distinction.

Majority of the people reflect the religious rationalising tendency. They are members of the vast middle class. They may be religious but their behaviour is governed by secular factors. They are in no way different from Hindu middle classes. Since the middle class has more of failures and frustrations, they seem to rationalise them in the religious framework. Absence of access to good quality condoms or other clinical services and contraceptive failure or discontinuation are common reasons why ordinary people say that children are sent by God.

By and large socio-economic factors and degree of segregation are more important than religion as explanas of reproductive behaviour. Many people, marginal to urban economy, *e.g.* migrant labourers, domestic servants, those engaged in menial jobs are hardly religious. They are Muslims only in the sense that they perform *namaz* (prayer) on Id. Otherwise they live among non-Muslims, work among non-Muslim, have no interest and opportunity to learn religious texts. Religion is important no doubt but life is above religion. Even in segregated poor localities many people tend to develop a feeling that like "Constitution of India" Islamic ethics had developed in special circumstances, that change should occur with time and place. But they cannot come up openly due to fear of strong *ulema*. They seem to be trapped in the process of Islamisation. The middle class is clever enough to take full advantage of modernisation. Yet their Islamisation and fundamentalism caused by political forces and identity formation have served as great barriers in the modernisation of the poor.

Thus socio-economic situation cannot be ignored. Literature show that normative factors, health facilities, income, rational thinking, and costs and benefits of children are important determinants of fertility. As discussed above, socio-economic factors interact with religion and determine how significant influence of religion would be on fertility and family planning behaviour. Table 13.1 shows the status of correlates of fertility among urban Muslims. Certain observations need to be stressed—(a) the notion that the poor produce more children as a source of income does not seem to be true rather the poor produce children without thinking and their poverty forces them to do menial jobs early in life; (b) all sections of urban society have moderate-to-high levels of aspirations; (c) both the commoners and the poor lack access to quality family planning services; (d) due to seeming by increasing number of cases of uterine and intestinal problems attitudes towards sterilisation are softening; (e) in poor localities it would be vulgar and cruel to approach people straight for family planning acceptance for whatever may be the nature of relationship between population and poverty at the macro level, high fertility does not appear to them as the most deciding factor in their marginalisation; and (f) benefits like old age security are losing ground.

The table 13.1 shows that there is hardly a need for family planning work among the elite. Among them there is hardly any utiity of children other than "consumption utility"[2] but the costs of children are quite high. Among the poor concentrated in certain Muslim dominated areas direct appeal to limit family size will be hardly effective. Perhaps it will be better to approach them through *ulema*. Possibly community work can make

TABLE 13.1: Status of Correlates of Fertility among Urban Muslims

	Correlate	Socio-economic status		
		The elite	The commoners	The poor
1.	Impact of religion	No	Some	Yes
2.	Nature of religiosity	Weakend due to Westernisation	Rationalisation of religion - formation of identity	Religious orthodoxy trap
3.	Is decision about children (costs and benefits) conscious	Yes	Yes	No
4.	Life	Individualised competitive	Competitive cooperative	Cooperative (isolation at the extreme level of poverty)
5.	Medical facilities	Easy access	Costly	Inadequate
6.	Family size norm	Small family	Changing towards small family	Natural fertility
7.	Cost of children	High	Middle	Small
8.	Cost of children relative to income	Low	High	Low
9.	Utility			
(a)	Old age Security	Not expected due to functional alternatives	Uncertain but expected	Strong expectation
(b)	Work-income utility	Nil	Some	High
(c)	Dependence on extended family	Absent	Some	Strong (absent in extreme poverty)
10.	Attitude towards sterilisation	Liberal	Conditional — largely depending on health grounds	Sinful to accept sterilisation
11.	Attitude towards conventional contraceptives	Methods accepted	Methods accepted	Accepted if approached properly
12.	Attitude towards abortion	Liberal	Conditional, as per Islamic beliefs	Rejection
13.	Quality of family planning services	Good	Poor	Very poor
14.	Proper approach	Nothing needed	Improve quality of services	a. Approach through *ulema* b. Imporve quality of services c. Community incentives

government or voluntary organisations to develop rapport with the poor. And then quality care should make some dent on fertility plateau. Among the poor there are also many who live among the Hindus and others. They are not very orthodox. Government or voluntary organisations can more easily communicate with such people. Finally, quality service is the only thing that commoners require. Providing access to effective methods and facilitating success experience in limiting births should be the best modes of communication among people. This will generate greater self-confidence, efficacy and greater rationalisation of the worldview. This should also weaken the religious opposition to family planning if it exists at all.

Nobody desires to have large family, not even the poor. Of course the poor may not realise that small family is a happy family and that they should adopt family planning methods. At Jajmau, in a predominantly Muslim locality, inhabited by tannery workers, the author asked: "Which is a happy family, a small family or a large family?" The answer was: "It depends on circumstances." Further, one's thinking on such matters depends on behaviour patterns prevalent in the neighbourhood. Surprisingly, the poor seldom meet their neighbours and discuss social issues. Due to fear of the powerful groups they do not think of organising themselves even for improving civic facilities.

Another change of great importance occurring among the urban Muslims is that dependence on brothers is being increasingly replaced by dependence on wife in almost all sections. In need people look for help from wife, parents and father-in-law in that order. Help from brothers is less expected. Even the poor who live in joint families cannot expect much from brothers who themselves are poor. More than brothers they depend on moneylenders who may even be Hindus.

Sex-preference among the Muslims seems to be less than among the Hindus. Muslims do not have so much dowry as prevalent among Hindus. But due to the fact that girls are married off, women are expected to remain in *purdah* and old age security expectations, commoners and the poor would desire to have a son also. However, once people start thinking about lmiting family size, they may not produce many children in anticipation of son if they have none.

Concluding Remarks

The present study of Kanpur Muslims shows that fertility among the urban Muslims is largly a socio-economic problem. We cannot deny that religion can sometime appear as a great barrier to family planning adoption. Yet the effect of religion depends heavily on the socio-economic structure. This is true that Islam forbids a Muslim to think that large family (*i.e.* more children) will lead to starvation. Islam forbids Malthusianism but Islam says that God has given wisdom to man and man should make use of it for advancing his secular and religious welfare. The real impact of Islamic teachings regarding birth prevention is confined olny to the segregated poor people; in mixed areas and in abject poverty Muslims hardly bother about religion. In urban areas, pressure of economic forces is so great that once they start thinking about the economics of reproduction the family size norm will reduce to 1-2 children in all socio-economic classes. Except for the segregated communities, the people do not pay much heed to *maulana* now. Even though at one time (during Emergency days) *maulanas* from mosques had issued *FATWAS* against sterilisation, hospital records as well as records of Kanpur branch of FPAI show that many Muslims had been accepting sterilisation as well as abortion.

The author feels that resources need not be wasted on changing the hard core *ulema*. Conspicuous efforts to involve *ulema* can often be counterproductive. Motivated *ulema* can easily be stigmatized by other due to internal politics of community of preachers and will be ineffective as change agents if is less risky to engage in indirect communication and not leave the impression as some community is a special target of the programme. If good quality family planning services can be made available (initially free or at negligible cost) and the isolation of the poor class is removed through development programmes, religious differentials in fertility and family planning will reduce substantially.

Notes

1. Prof. P.C. Sexena, IIPS Bombay, is a great admirer of the theory of rotating coordinate system in social sciences. The author also believes that facts and their interrlationships depend heavily on perspectives and contexts.
2. According to Leibenstein (1975) consumption utility of children is a kind of direct emotional utility, not as a means for other instrumental utilities such as old age protection, income utility, etc.

REFERNCES

Anonymous, 1987, "Islam and Family Planning", *Asia Pacific Population Journal,* Vol. 2, No. 3, pp. 78-79.

Bhatia, P.S., 1990, "Population Growth of Various Communities in India-Myth and Reality, *Demography India,* Vol. 19, No. 1. pp. 121-30.

Davis, Kingsley 1951, *The Population of India and Pakistan,* Princeton University Press, Princeton.

Gupta, Ravindra, 1986, *Fertility Tables: Uttar Pradesh Series 22, Part VI-A & B*, Registrar General and Census Commissioner, Government of India.

Khan, Irfan, 1991, *Fertility Behaviour and Birth Control among Muslims in India: A Study of a Village in Bihar State*, Unpublished Ph.D. thesis, HSS Department, IIT Kanpur.

Khan, M.E. 1976, *The Correlates of Muslim Fertility in Urban Setting: A Case Study of Kanpur City*, Unpublished Ph.D. thesis, HSS Department, Kanpur.

Khan, M.E. 1978, *Birth Control Among Muslims in India*, Manohar Publication.

Leibenstein, H., 1975, "Relation of Economic Development to Fertility" in Tabah, Leon (ed.), *Population Growth and Economic Development in Third World*, IUSSP, Vol. 2, pp. 437-508.

Misra, B.D., 1993, *Area-Specific Approach in Health and Family Welfare-Uttar Pradesh*, State Institute of Health and Family Welfare, Lucknow.

National Family Health Survey 1992-93, 1995, *India*, International Institute for Population Sciences, Bombay.

Operations Research Group, n.d., *Family Planning Practices in India-Second All India Survey*, ORG Baroda.

Saseendran, P.P., and Kumar, Mithilesh, 1989 *Determinants of Family Welfare Programme in U.P. :An Analytical Study of CPR and Socio-Economic Variables*, Population Centre, Lucknow.

Sawhney, Nirmal, Mithilesh, Kumar, and Saseendran, P.P., 1990, *Socio-Religious Dimensions of Family Welfare Programme: A Case Study of Muslim Elite*, Population Centre, Lucknow.

Sharma, A.K. 1989, "Muslim Population in India", *The Eastern Anthropologist*, Vol. 42, No.4, pp. 353-64.

Sharma, A.K., and Misra, B.D., 1978, "Fertility Defferentials in India-An analysis of Census Fertility Data", *The Journal of Family Welfare*, Vol. 25, No. 2.

Srivastava, J.N., and Saksena, D.N., 1989, "Hindu-Muslim Defferentials in Family Size Ideal by Socio-Economic Status", *The Journal of family Welfare*, Vol. 35, No. 4, pp. 38-48.

Swee-Hock, Saw, 1989, "Muslim Fertility Transition", *Asia-Pacific Population Journal*, Vol.4, No. 3, pp. 31-40.

Theis, Joachim, and Grady, H.M., 1991, *Training Manual: Preparing a Participatory Rapid Appraisal Training*, International Institute for Environment and Development, London.

14

POPULATION POLICY
Need for A Holistic Theory

There is a great unresolved controversy on whether in the less developed countries rapid population growth is a cause of or is caused by poverty, underdevelopment or unsustainable development, or in other words whether it is development that leads to wide acceptance of contraceptives or it is contraception use that leads to development. Many things can be said to support or reject arguments on both sides. This is also true that rapid population growth reduces investment and raises such demands which may deteriorate environment. This is also true that in all countries rate of environmental degradation (no matter how is environment quality measured) far exceeds the rate of population growth. Moreover, in the developed countries, consumption standards being very high, total population impact of addition of one person to the population of developed countries is thirty to forty times the similar impact in less developed countries. Could we not say that rapid population growth and underdevelopment are two great problems before the developing countries and both must be tackled appropriately and in time? This chapter summaries the developments in family planning programme in India and emphasise need for a holistic perspective.

Government of India has been very much concerned about population planning since the beginning. India has certainly the distinction of being the first country in the world to launch a Government sponsored family planning programme. Many experiments have been made and learning from these experiments Government has revised its policies and programmes several times. Undoubtedly much has been achieved and still much remains to be desired. This is the time to rethink about population policy.

As is well known around 1951 Government of India adopted the "Gandhian approach" in family planning. The reason was that during the early 1950s, then Health Minister of India, Rajkumari Amrit Kaur, was a close associate of Gandhi. She favoured self-control. In the First Five Year Plan, the Government focused on research into the dynamics of population growth, experiments and studies about the acceptability of the rhythm method, and research on different aspects of contraception. Then the Government adopted the clinical approach whereby the Ministry of Health opened a large number of clinics in urban and rural areas where the needy could come and obtain family planning services and advice. In the Second Five Year Plan, it was proposed to set up one clinic per 50,000 population in urban areas and 1,800 clinics in rural areas. The clinical approach did not work. The 1961 Census showed that the growth rate of population had increased to a level close to 2 per cent. Thereafter the Government decided to go for the extension approach. In between mass vasectomy camps were organised in several States and IUCD was introduced in the programme in 1965. Finally, the cafeteria approach came to stay in the family planning programme (Sharma, 1985) of India.

In 1976, during the Emergency period, the then Minister of Health and Family Planning, Dr. Karan Singh issued the first official statement on National Population Policy. The statement listed measures that the Government had envisaged to promote family planning acceptance to achieve the target of reducing birth rate from the prevailing level of 35 per thousand to 25 per thousand at the end of the Sixth Plan. They included: (a) programmes to raise marriage age; (b) freezing of representation in the Lok Sabha and the State Legislatures on the basis of 1971 Census until the year 2001; (c) decision to consider only 1971 Census figures in the allocation of Central assistance to State Plans, devolution of taxes and duties and grants-in-aid till the year 2001; (d) programmes to raise female literacy; (e) incentives for acceptance of sterilisation; (f) introduction of group incentive for family planning acceptance; (g) decision to involve voluntary organisations; (h) multi-media motivational strategy; and (i) experimentation with the idea of compulsory sterilisation in those States where facilities to perform large number of sterilisations were adequate. As far as planning for birth control is concerned (there is still no clear policy on migration, etc.) the policy was well thought out and a comprehensive one. However, the inclusion of the idea of compulsory sterilisation proved to be a boomerang which harmed the family planning programme greatly during late 1970s. The Congress party lost the parliamentary elections held subsequently in which compulsion in family planning was one of the major issues. Janata Party won the elections and in June 1977 another statement of Population Policy was issued. In his address to the Parliament on 28 March 1977 the President said:

> "Family planning will be pursued vigorously as a wholly voluntary programme and as an integral part of a comprehensive policy covering education, health, maternity and child care, family welfare, women's rights and nutrition"

The statement mentioned that the Prime Minsiter had on a number of occasions underlined the vital importance of family planning as a means of individual and national development and well being and the government was totally committed to the Family Welfare Programme and would spare no efforts to motivate the people to accept it voluntarily in their own interest and in the interest of their children as well as in the larger interest of the nation. As such the second policy statment contained almost all the points contained in the first statement except the idea of compulsory sterilisation but it had a few additional points. These points were: (a) change of name of the programme from family planning to family welfare programme; (b) a comprehensive scheme of training of indigenous dais; and (c) a decision that the performance of Family Welfare in the States should be reviewed intensively by the Union Cabinet at least once a year and the programme should be carefully monitored in coordination with other connected programmes of welfare.

During the Sixth Plan, the Working Group on Population Policy (appointed in 1978) recommended the adoption of long term demographic goal of reducing Net Reproduction Rate (NRR) to one by 1976 for the country as a whole and by 2001 in all the States, from the prevailing level of 1.67. The implications of this were as follows:

"(a) the average size of family would be reduced from 4.2 children to 2.3 children;

(b) the birth rate per 1,000 population would be reduced from the level of 33 in 1978 to 21;

(c) the death rate per 1,000 population would be reduced from the level of 14 in 1978 to 9 and IMR would be reduced from 129 to 60 or less;

(d) as against 22 per cent of eligible couples using family planning methods at present, 60 per cent would be protected; and

(e) the population of India will be around 900 million by the turn of the century and will stabilize at 1,200 million by the year 2050 A.D."

In the Seventh Five Year Plan an attempt was made to divide the States and the Union Territories into three groups: A,B and C on the basis of their family planning performance. The Plan said: "Taking into consideration the realities of the situation, different sets of targets have to be fixed for different States, both in terms of level of CPR to be attained and in terms of the method-mix of the acceptors". Group A included Andhra Pradesh, Gujarat, Haryana, Himachal Pradesh, Kerala, Maharashtra, Punjab, Tamil Nadu, Chandigarh, Delhi, and Pondicherry. Group B included Assam, Karnataka, Madhya Pradesh, Orissa, West Bengal, Andaman & Nicobar Islands, Dadra and Nagar Haveli, Goa, Daman and Diu, and Mizoram. Group C included Bihar, Jammu and Kashmir, Rajasthan, Uttar Pradesh, Manipur, Meghalaya, Nagaland, Sikkim, Tripura, Arunachal Pradesh, and Lakshadweep. The years by which NRR of 1 was to be attained by States in A, B and C categories were 1991-92, 1996-97, and 2000-02, respectively.

"The Revised Strategy for Family Welfare Programme 1986" presented a very comprehensive analysis and policy statement on family planning. For the first time the Government of India had accepted that we require differential area, region and group specific approaches; members of lagging groups and communities should be involved for motivational work and for providing services so that variations within groups would be reduced. It was also proposed that the family planning programme should have greater linkage with poverty alleviation programme—that is, while selecting beneficiaries under any of the poverty alleviation schemes, preference should be given to those who accept the small family norm. Couples with a two-child certificate and youths who voluntarily give a pledge to limit their family may be selected as beneficiaries (Sharma, 1989).

Recently, the Department of Family Welfare, Government of India, invited Pravin Visaria, S.N. Misra and J.K. Satia (1993) to attempt a rough draft of what might go into a national population policy for the 1990s and beyond. Visaria, Mishra and Satia have prepared the "zeroth draft of the possible policy" which is under circulation for facilitating discussion. The draft has noted that the provisional data for 1991 (birth rate: 29.3; and death rate: 9.8) suggest a decline in the rate of natural increase to a little below 2 per cent. Thus India is in the advanced 2nd stage of demographic transition. Sample Registration Scheme and other data have established the order of change in birth and death rates in India. Further, data on family planning acceptance show that the couple protection rate has a level of 43-44 per cent (Fig. 14.1). The draft also shows that at ages above 25 years there has been a considerable fall in age specific fertility rates

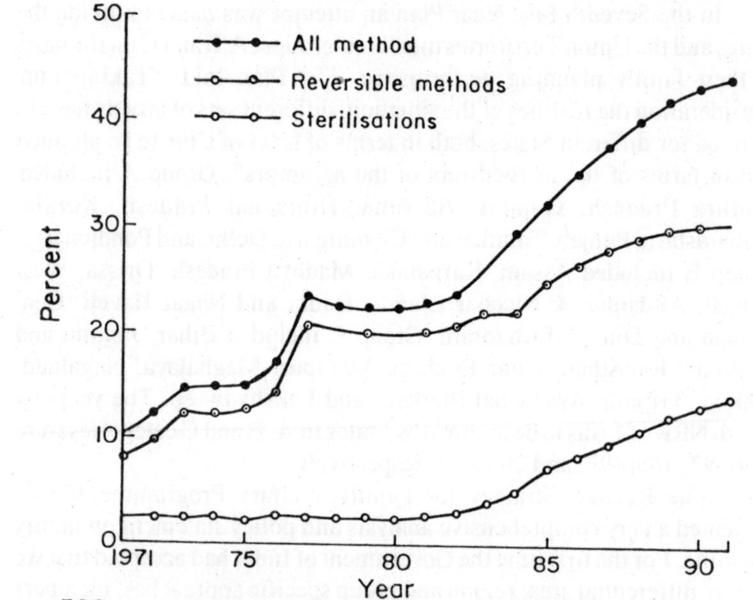

FIG. 14.1: Couple Protection Rate by Method, India: 1971-91

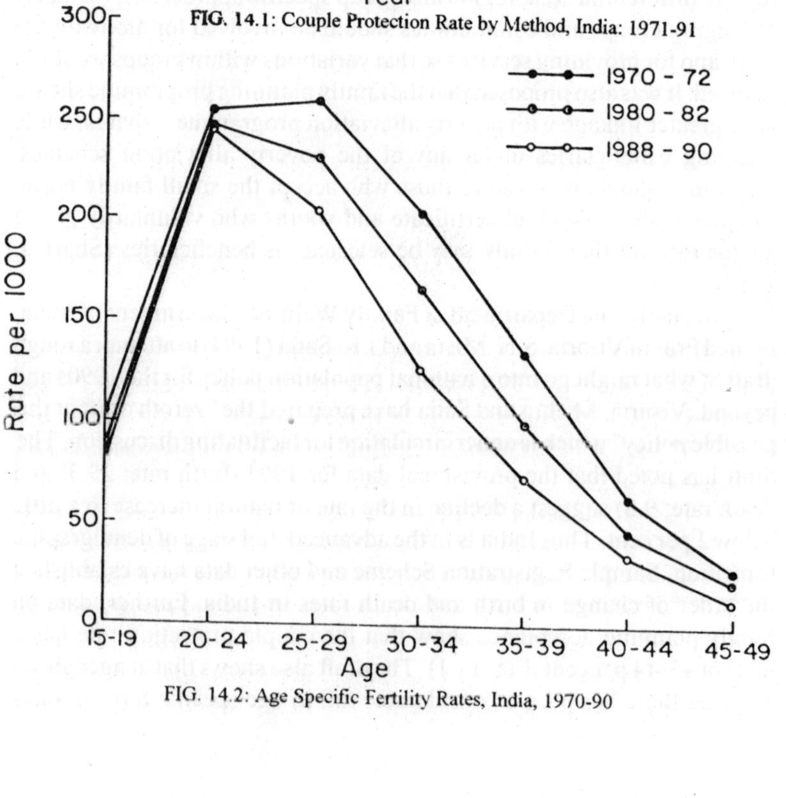

FIG. 14.2: Age Specific Fertility Rates, India, 1970-90

(Fig. 14.2). Kerala, Goa and Tamil Nadu have low fertility. In Maharashtra, Andhra Pradesh, Karnataka, Gujarat, Punjab and Himachal Pradesh birth rates have reached the moderate levels. The main problem of high fertility and high mortality exists in four large northern States of U.P., Bihar, M.P. and Rajasthan.

The above draft shows that to achieve NRR of 1 couple protection rate (CPR) of 75 will be required. However, if age of marriage in all the States can be raised to the level of Kerala, NRR of 1 can be achieved with a CPR of 68 per cent also. Among the specific measures to achieve NRR of 1 the draft includes: (a) promotion of reversible methods of contraception; (b) focus on imporving reproductive health of women and lowering morbidity and mortality among infants and children; (c) a differentiated and disaggregated approach; (d) quality of care in service delivery and infrastructure; (e) improvement in contraceptive technology; (f) area-appropriate strategies; (g) alternative channels of service delivery; (h) strengthening of information, education and communication (IEC) activities; (i) freezing of population-based representation according to the 1971 Census till the year 2021; (j) incentives and disincentives; and (k) beyond family planning method and multi-sectoral coordination. The draft suggests that some innovative schemes need to be considered and evolved to explore the implications of promoting a China - style "one-child policy". Two new measure suggested in the draft are: emphasis on area - appropriate strategies; and concern for quality care. The draft has been under severe attack from several groups and experts. The debate ensued from circulation of the draft has once again shown importance of women's issues, environmental sustainability, poverty eradication, district level planning, fundamental rights and lessening of bureaucratic controls.

A document prepared by Indian Association for the Study of Population and The Population Council (Premi, 1993) has shown that if the growth rate in Uttar Pradesh has to be stalled from further rise and has to be curtailed, both the Central and State Governments will have to adopt several strategies simultaneously. Some of them are as follows:

1. The Centre should make it incumbant on the State to make it both a Plan and Non-Plan activity. The States must share the responsibility equally.
2. Literacy rates of women in rural areas, particularly among the weaker sections must be raised.
3. The quality of services and facilities for institutional deliveries should be improved.
4. Training of all types of health staff should be strengthened.

5. Teachers at the senior primary and secondary levels, all organised sector industries, trade union functionaries and Gandhi Kahdi Ashram should be involved.

Who can doubt that if people are literate, services are of good quality, IEC activities are adequate and community leaders are interested, family planning programme can improve acceptance level. Services offered by "providers" is only one part of the story. Socio-economic conditions, motivational factors and culture are other determinants of family planning acceptance. As a matter of fact the socio-cultural milieu decides how are policies implemented in practice and perceived by people. It is encouraging that planners have recognised importance of area-specific-approach (Misra, 1991) in health and family welfare. They should also examine people's perceptions and motivate them to accept family planning as part of a general policy to solve their socio-economic, political and cultural problems.

There is a need to explore role of values. After all people's perceptions and actions are heavily influenced by values. A generation ago, in India many people preferred to die rather than use allopathic medicines. Gandhi, the father of the nation, was only a representative of them. All the people do not believe in the utilitarian rational model of population scientists. Religion, ethics, material conditions and socialisation produce values and people act according to them . Thus for both theorising about action and intervention, values and their contexts should be properly understood.

Unfortunately, till this day population policy has aimed solely at reduction of birth rate. The issues of ageing, migration, urbanisation, inequality with respect to health facilities, employment, status of women, social mobility, etc. which are vital for population control have not been accorded similar importance. Is the fall in the birth rate in Goa, Kerala, Tamil Nadu, Punjab or in urban areas of other states due to better working of family planning programme there or is it largely due to fall in the demand for children? Obviously, at the State level the developmental factors have been more important than family planning. Moreover as stated in the beginning, development should be as important a goal as family planning. Commenting on the problems of population and backwardness among the people in Africa and Bangladesh, Paranjape (1993) says:

"We may have destroyed ourselves and them by then. We are the perpetrators of this senseless development; they the victims. What if they hold us responsible for messing up their lives. Just as we hold the colonists and the neo-colonists responsible for continuing to mess up the world. Who is responsible for whom? Are we not all responsible for all of us?

If so, then let us remember that development which leaves a majority of our population untouched or worse off, is no development. If we use Gandhi's words, we would say that it is a sin. Only by changing that model or pattern can we make a better tomorrow for us all.

By extending education and awareness, by re-prioritising our investments, by changing our emphasis, we will give these oppressed people more control over their bodies, over their lives, over their future. That is the solution to the problems of population."

With more than 40 years experience in population planning, time has come to rethink about the whole issue. Data show that total fertility rate in urban India is 2.8 only. Also, within urban India, besides Kerala and Tamil Nadu, West Bengal has reported a TFR of 2.1-2.2 during 1988-90. Has the urban West Bengal solved its population problem? Are the states of Kerala, Tamil Nadu, Goa and West Bengal which have undergone demographic transition recently more ready for development than population of U.P. and Bihar? Can we not say that the birth rate in Kerala has declined more because of poverty-aspirations syndrome than development? These are some questions to ponder. Extensive data collected in the National Family Health Survey (1995) on various aspects of health and reproduction in India can help in answering these questions and formulating appropriate strategies for holistic development.

It must be understood that population control can be achieved in several ways but achievements in this respect have ultimately to be translated in terms of levels of happiness, lest the population control and mechanisms of control lower social health and happiness in general. Family planning programmes are important. Over the years the providers have certainly become wiser. The strategies suggested above are comprehensive and can be effective. There is a general feeling among providers that what matters most today is the commitment with which the proposed strategies are implemented rather than alternative design or policies. But the real and long-term goal should be to promote positive values of peace, equality, non-violence and love. We should start working towards building a holistic theory of population in the light of which population planning can be given a new orientation.

REFERENCES

Misra, B.D., 1991, *Area Specific Approach in Health and Family Welfare-Uttar Pradesh,* State Institute of Health and Family Welfare, Lucknow (mimeo).

National Family Health Survey 1992-93, 1995, *India,* International Institute for Population Sciences, Bombay.

Paranjape, Makarand, 1993, *Decolonization and Development,* Sage Publications, New Delhi.

Premi, M.K., 1993 *Family Planning and MCH in Uttar Pradesh: A Review of Studies,* The Population Council, Asian and the Near East Operations.

Sharma, A.K., 1985, *Social Inequality and Demographic Processes,* Mittal Publications, New Delhi.

Sharma, A.K., 1989, *Issues in Social Demography,* Mittal Publications, New Delhi.

Visaria, Pravin, 1993, *A Population Policy of India: A Draft for Facilitating Discussion,* Nirman Bhawan, New Delhi.

BIBLIOGRAPHY

Adiseshiah, Malcolm, S., 1985, *Science and Technology for Women,* Tamil Nadu State Council for Science and Technology, pp. 1-3.

Agarwal, A., 1986, "Politics of Environment", *Gandhi Marg,* Vol. 87.

Agarwala, R.D. 1975, "Influence of Infant and Child Mortality on Fertility in India," paper presented at the *Seminar on Infant Mortality in Relation to Level of Fertility* , CICRED Series, Paris.

Agarwala, S.N. 1962, *Age at Marriage in India,* Kitab Mahal Pvt. Ltd., Allahabad.

—, —, 1970, *A Demographic Study of Six Urbanizing Villages,* Asia Publishing House, New York.

Agnew, Vijay, 1979, *Elite Women in Indian Politics,* Vikas Publishing House, New Delhi, pp. 34-61.

Ambedkar, B.R., 1982, *Annihilation of Caste.* Bhim Patrika Publications, Jalandhar, p. 159.

Ananta, Aris, 1990, "The Impact of Demographic Variables on the Quality of the Environment", *Indonesian Journal of Demography,* Vol. 17, No. 33, pp. 1-16.

Ananthu, T.S., 1990, "Going Beyond the Intellect: A Gandhian Approach to Scientific Education", in Sharma, Anuradha, and Sharan, Raka (eds.), *Social Responsiblilites of Technologists, Scientists and Managers,* Gian Publishing House, New Delhi.

Anonymous, 1987, "Islam and Family Planning", *Asia Pacific Population Journal,* Vol. 2, No. 3, pp. 78-79.

—, —, 1993, "Are There Two Many of Us?", *Population Headliners,* No. 222, September, p. 4.

Badry, M.A. E1., 1967, "Differential Fertility in Greater Bombay," *Contributed Papers: Sydney Conference,* International Union for Scientific Study of Population.

Bakshi, S.R., 1987, *Gandhi and Status of Women,* Criterion Publications, p. 103.

Bang, Thakurdas, 1984, *Kissan Mazdoor Ki Loot,* Sarva Seva Sangh Prakashan, Varanasi (in Hindi).

—, —, 1986, *Vigyan Ki Sahi Disha,* Sarva Sewa Sangha Prakashan, Varanasi (in Hindi).

—, —, 1987, *Swatantrata ke Char Daskak,* Sarva Seva Sangh Prakashan, Varanasi (in Hindi).

Barnes, Barry, 1974, Scientific Knowledge and Sociological Theory, Routledge & Kagan Paul, London.

Bandopadhyay, J., 1969, *Social and Political Thought of Gandhi,* Allied Publishers, New Delhi.

Barney, G.O., 1980, *Global 2000: The Report to the President Entering the 21st Century,* U.S. Government Printing Office, Washington D.C.

Berry, Thomas, 1988, *The Dream of the Earth,* Sierra club Books, San Francisco.

Bhargava, Gopal, 1981, "Slums of Urban India: Planning and Policy Framework", in Bhargava, Gopal (ed.), *Urban Problems and Polcy Prespectives,* Abhinav Publication, New Delhi.

Bhasin, Kamla, and Khan, Nighat Said, 1986, *Feminism*, KALI for Women, New Delhi, pp. 1-2.

Bhatia, P.S., 1990, "Population Growth of Various Communities in India-Myth and Reality, *Demography India,* Vol. 19, No. 1. pp. 121-30.

—, —, 1983, "Health for All by 2000 A.D.: Can India Achieve its Goals?" Paper presented in the *Ninth Annual Conference of the IASP,* Rajasthan University, Jaipur.

Bhave, Vinoba, 1989, *Stri Shakti,* Sarva Sewa Sangh Prakashan, Varanasi.

Bishop, D.H., 1976, "Science, Technology and Value" in Pandeya, R.C., and Bhatt, S.R. (eds.), *Knowledge Culture and Value*, Motilal Banarasidass, Delhi, pp. 51-52.

Blacker, C.P., 1947, "States in Population Growth", *Eugenics Review,* Vol. 39, pp. 81-101.

Bogue, D.J., 1969, *Principles of Demography,* John Wiley & Sons, New York, pp. 51-53.

Bongaarts, John, Mauldin, Parker W., and Phillips, James F. 1990, "The Demographic Impact of Family Planning Programs", Studies in Family Manning, Vol. 21, No. 6, pp.299-310.

Bose, Ashish, 1978, *India's Urbanization: 1901-2001,* Tata Mc Graw Hill Publishing Company Ltd., New Delhi.

—, —, 1980, "Return of Malaria in India? - Political Economy of the Mosquito", paper presented in the IASP *Conference on Population*

Distribution and Development, ISI, Calcutta.

Bottomore, Tom, and Himmelweit, Susan, 1983, "Population", in Bottomore, Tom (ed.), A *Dictionary of Marxist Thought,* Oxford University Press, Delhi, pp. 378-380.

Bourgeois - Pichat, Jean, 1957, " Utilisation de la notion de population stable pour measurer la mortalite *et al* ficundite" despopulation des pays sonsdeveloppe's, *Bulletin de 1 Institute International de Statistque* Tome 36, 2 Livraison, Stockholm, pp. 94-121.

Brahma, P.B., 1974, "Registration Scheme - Birth and Death Rates", in Bose, Ashis, Mitra, Ashok, Desai, P.B., and Sharma, J.N. (eds.), *Population in India's Development,* 1947 - 2000, Vikas Publishing House Pvt. Ltd., Delhi, pp. 425-30.

Bryson, Lyman, 1947, *Science and Freedom,* Columbia University Press, New Delhi.

Bumiller, Elisabeth, 1990, *May You be the Mother of a Hundred Sons,* Penguin Books, Calcutta, pp. 125-281.

Caldwell, J.C., 1978, " A Theory of Fertility: from High Plateau to Destabilization", *Population and Development Review,* Vol. 4, No. 4, pp. 553-77.

—, —, 1991, "The Soft Underbelly of Development, Demographic Transition in Conditions of Limited Economic Change", in Fischer, Stanley, Tray, Dennis de, and Shah, Shekhar (eds.), *Proceedings of the World Bank Annual Conference on Development Economics, 1990,* World Bank, Washington D.C., pp. 207-254.

Caldwell, J.C., Reddy, P.H., and Caldwell, Pat, 1983, "The Social Component of Mortalityu Decline: An Investigation in South India Employing Alternative Methodologies," *Population Studies,* Vol. 37, pp 185-205.

Camp, S.L., 1991, "Population, Poverty, and Pollution", *Forum for Applied Research and Public Policy,* Summer, pp. 5-15.

Capra, Fritjof, 1983, *The Tao of Phsics: Exploration of the Parallels between Modern Physics and Modern Mysticism,* Boulder Publications, Shambhala.

Cassen, R.H., 1978, *India: Population, Economy, Society,* The Macmillan Press Ltd., Hong Kong.

Census of India, 1977, *Paper 2 of 1977: Fertility Tables, 1971*, Seris 1, India, Office of the Registrar-General and Census Commissioner, India.

—, —, 1991, *Provisional Population Totals,* Paper-1, Registrar General & Census commissioner, India, New Delhi.

—, —, 1991, *Provisional Population Totals: Rural Urban Distribution*, Paper-2, Registrar General & Census Commissioner, India, New Delhi.

—, —, 1991, *Provisional Population Totals: Workers and Their Distribution*, Paper-3, Registrar General & Census Commissioner, India, New Delhi.

Chacko, K.C., 1986, *Metaphysical Implications of Gandhian Thought*, Mittal Publications, New Delhi, p. 63.

Chamberlin, N.W., 1970, *Beyond Malthus: Population and Power*, Basic Books, New York.

Chandra, Bipan, 1992, *The Epic Struggle*, Orient Longman, New Delhi, pp. 15-28.

Chandrasekharan, C., and Deming, W. Edwards, "On a Method of Estimating Birth and Death Rates and the Extent of Registration," *Journal of American Statistical Association*, Vol. 44, No. 245, pp. 101-15.

Chandrasekharan, S., 1972, *Infant Mortality, Population Growth and Family Planning in India*, George Allen and Unwin Limited, London.

Chattopadhyaya, Kamladevi, 1983, *Indian Women's Battle for Freedom*, Abhinav Publications, New Delhi, p. 107.

Chatterjee, Margaret, 1983, *Gandhi's Religious Thought*, The Macmillan Press Ltd., New Delhi, p. 61.

Chisholm, Roderick, 1966, *Theory of knowledge*, Prentice-Hall, Inc.

Chowdhury, Kunal Roy, 1993, "Gandhi's Theory of Sarvodaya Socialism, *Gandhi Marg*, Vol. 15, No.1, pp. 62-77.

Coale, Ansley J., 1963, "Estimates of Various Demographic Measures Through the Quasi-Stable Age Distribution, *"Emerging Techniques in Population Analysis*, Milbank Memorial Fund, pp. 185-86.

Coale, A.J., and Trussesll, J., 1974,"Model Fertility Schedules: Variations in the Age Structure of Childbearing in Human Popualtions," *Population Index*, Vol. 40, No. 2, pp. 185-258.

Commoner, Barry, 1991, "Rapid Population Growth and Environmental Stress", *International Journal of Health Services*, Vol. 21, No. 2, pp. 199-227.

Conway, G.R. and Edward B.Barbier, 1988, "The Green Revoltion: Sustainable and Equitable Agricultural Development", *Futures*, Vol. 20, Nov. 6, pp. 651-70.

Daly, H.E., 1971, "A Marxian - Malthusian View of Poverty and Development", *Population Studies*, Vol. 25, No. 1, pp. 25-30.

Dandekar, K., 1959, Demographic Survey of *Six Rural Communities*, Gokhale Institute of Politics and Economics, publication 37, Asia Publishing House, Bombay.

Dasgupta, Sugata, 1985, *Towards a Post-Development Era: Essays in Poverty, Welfare and Development*, Mittal Publications, New Delhi.

Davis, Kingsley, 1951, *The Population of India and Pakistan*, Princeton University Press, Princeton.

—, —, 1990, "Population and Resources: Fact and Interpretation, in Davis, Kingsley, and Bernstam, Mikhail (eds.), *Resources, Environment and Population: Present Knowledge, Future Option*, Population Council, New York, pp. 1-24.

Demeny, Paul, 1990, "Tradeoffs between Human Numbers and Material Standards of Living", in Davis, Kingsley and Bernstam, Mikhail S. (eds.), Resources, Environment and *Population: Present Knowledge, Future Option*, Population Council, New York, pp. 408-21.

Desai, M., 1973, *Day-to-day with Gandhi*, Sarva Seva Sangh, Varanasi.

Desai, Neera, and Krishnaraj, Maithreyi, 1987, *Women and Society in India*, Prentice-Hall, p. 394.

Dharmadhikari, Dada, 1983, *Sarvodaya Darshan*, Sarva Sewa Sangh Prakashan, Varanasi.

Dharampal, 1983, *The Beautiful Tree: Indigenous Indian Education in Eighteenth Century*, Biblia Impex Private Limited, New Delhi.

Dhawan, G., 1963, *Sarvodaya Tatva Darshan*, Nav Jivan Prakashan Mandir, Ahmedabad.

Diwakar, R.R., 1967 "The Relevance of Gandhi", in Ramachandran, G. and Mahadevan, T.K. (eds.) *Gandhi: His Relevance for Our Times*. Gandhi peace Foundation, New Delhi.

Dubey, B.R., 1969, "Gandhi's Views on Status of Women", in Biswas, S.C. (ed.), *Gandhi: Theory and Practice, Social Impact and Contemporary Relevance*, Indian Institute of Advanced Study, Simla, pp. 113-21.

Dube, S.C., 1988. *Modernization and Development*, Vistaar Publications, New Delhi.

Duncan, O.D., 1961,"Human Ecology and Population Studies", in Hauser, P.M. and Duncan, O.D. (eds.), *The Study of Population* Asia Publishing House, Bombay, pp. 678-716.

Elisa, Norbert 1982, "Scientific Establishments", in Elias, Norbert, Martins, Herminio and Whitley, Richard (eds.) *Scientific Establishments and Hierarchies*, D. Reidel Publishing Company, London.

Erikson, E.H., 1975, *Dimensions of a New Identity,* Light & Life Publishers, New Delhi.

Fisher, Louis, 1963, *The Essential Gandhi,* George Allen & Unwin Ltd, London.

Flank, P.W., 1961, "Ecology and Demography", in Hauser, P.M., and Duncan, O.D. (eds.), *The Study of Population,* Asia Publishing House, Bombay, pp. 652-676.

Fletcher, Ronald, 1974, *The Crisis of Industrial Civilization: The Early Essays of Auguste Comte,* Heinemann Educational Book Limited, London.

Forrester, J.W., 1971, *World Dynamics,* Wright - Allen Press, Canbridge, England.

Fradkin, N.G., and Mashbits, Y.G., 1975, "Capitalist Society" in Gerasimov, I.P. *et al., Man, Society and the Environment,* Progress Publishers, Moscow, pp. 45-55.

Freedman, R., 1986, "Theories of Fertility Decline", in Mahadevan, K., Reddy, P.J. and Naidu, D.A. (eds.). *Fertility and Mortality: Theory, Methodology and Empirical Issues, Sage* Publication, New Delhi.

Friedlander, S.L., 1969, "Demographic Responses and Population Change", Demography, Vol. 6, No. 4, pp. 359-81.

Gandhi, M.K., 1930, Young India, 10 April and 17 April.

—, —, 1957, *Satya Ke Prayoga,* Nav Jivan Mandir, Ahmedabad.

—, —, 1971, *The Collected Works of Mahatma Gandhi*, Vol. 43, Ministry of Information and Broadcasting, New Delhi, pp. 189-98, 350-60.

—, —, 1971, *Collected Works of Mahatma Gandhi,* Ministry of Information and Broadcasting, New Delhi, Vol. 44, p. 68.

Gandhi Peace Foundation and Centre for Science .and Environment, 1988, *Our Environment,* GPF and CSW, New Delhi.

Gandotra, M.M. and Das Narayan, 1983, "Impact of Health care Intervention and Nutrition on Infant Mortality in India", Paper Presented in *Ninth Annual Conference of IASP.* Rajasthan University, Jaipur.

Garland, H. K,. 1991, *Population, Resources Degradation,* Palms Press, Dora Creek.

G.B. Pant Institute of Himalayan Environment and Development, 1992, *Himalayan Environment and Development: Problems and Perspectives,* Gyanodaya Prakashan, Nainital.

Giddens, Anthony, 1989, *Sociology,* Polity; Press, 1989, pp. 156-80.

Goswami, C.L., and Sastri, M.A., 1982, *Srimad Bhagavata Mahapurana,* Gita Press, Gorakhpur.

Gotpagar, K.B., 1985, "Recent Trends and Defferentials in Mortality in

India", *National Seminar on the Utilization of Demographic Knowledge in Policy formulation and Planning,* IIPS Bombay.

Government of India, 1985, *Seventh Five Year Plan 1985-90, Vol. II,* Planning Commission, New Delhi, p.385.

—, —, (ed.), 1962, The Collected Wroks of Mahatma Gandhi, The Publication Division, Ministry of Information and Broadcasting, Vol. 8, p. 211.

—, —, (ed.), 1971, *The Collected Works of Mahatma Gandhi,* The Publication Division, Ministry of Informtion and Broadcasting, New Delhi, Vol. 44, p. 138.

—, —, (ed.), 1975, *The Collected Works of Mahatma Gandhi,* The Publication Divison, Ministry of Information and Broadcsting, Vol. 62, p. 223.

—, —, 1985, *Seventh Five Year Plan 1985-90,* Vol.1, Planning Commission, Government of India, New Delhi, p.5.

—, —, 1985, *Seventh Five Year Plan: 1985-90,* Vol. II, Planning Commission, New Delhi.

Goyal, R.P., 1975, "Shifts in Age at Marriage in India between 1961 and 1971, *Demography India,* Vol. 4 No. 2.

—, —, 1982, "Nuptiality Trends and Differentials", in United Nations, *Population of India,* Country Monograph Series No. 10, United Nations New York, pp. 109-134.

Goyal, R.P., and Desai, P.B., 1968, *Inter-district Variation in Mean Age at Marriage* -1961, Institute of Economic Growth, Delhi (Mimeo.)

Gupta, Ravindra, 1986, *Fertility Talbles: Uttar Pradesh Series 22, Part VI-A & B,* Registrar General and Census Commissioner, Government of India.

Habermas, Jurgen, 1970, "Knowledge and Interest", in Emmet, Dorothy, and Macintyre Alasdais (ed.), *Sociological Theory and Philosophical Analysis,* MacMillan, pp. 36-54.

Hajnal, John, 1953, "Age at Marriage and Proportions Marrying", Population Studies, Vol. 7, pp. 111-136.

Handwerker, W.P., 1986, "Culture and Reproduction", in Handwe4ker, p. (ed.) Culture and Reproduction: An Anthropological Critique of Demographic Transition Theory. Westview Press, Boulder & London.

Haribabu, E., 1990, "Economic and Political Dimensions of Pollution: Need for Political Action for Environment protection" in Sharma, Anuradha, and Sharan, Raka (eds), *Social Responsibilities of Technologists, Scientists and Managers,* Gian Publishing House, New Delhi.

Higgins, G.M., *et al.*, 1982, *Potential Population Supporting Capacities of Lands in the Developing World,* Food and Agricultural Organization, Rome.

Hill, Kenneth, 1991, "Approaches to the Measurement of Childhood Mortality: A Comparative Review", Population Index, Vol. 57, No. 3, p. 369

Himes, Christine L., and Clogg, C. C., 1992, "An Overview of Demographic Analysis as a Method for Evaluating Census Coverage in the United States", *Population Index*, Vol. 58, No. 4, pp. 587-607.

Holzner, Burkart, and Marx, J.H., 1979, *Knowledge Application: The Knowledge System in Society,* Allyn and Bacon, Boston.

Iyenger, K.R., 1972, Sri Aurobindo: A Biography and a History, Vol 1-2. Sri Aurobindo Ashram Trust, Pondicherry, pp. 837-875.

Iyer, Raghavan N. 1973, *The Moral and Political Thought of Mahatma Gandhi,* Oxford University Press, New Delhi.

—, —, (ed.), 1986, *The Moral and Political Writings of Mahatma Gandhi,* Vol. 1-3., Clearendon press, Oxford.

Iyer, Raghavan, 1969, *The Moral and Political Thought of Mahatma Gandhi,* Oxford University Press, Clarendon.

—, —, 1973, *The Moral and Political Writings of Mahatma Gandhi,* Clarendon Press, Oxford, Vol. 3, pp. 1-2, 394.

Jain, Anrudh K., 1989, "Fertility Reduction and the Quality of Family Planning Services", *Studies in Family Planning,* Vol. 20, No. 1, pp. 1-16.

Jain, Anrudh K., and Visaria, Pravin, 1988 (eds.) *Infant Mortaility in India: Differentials and Determinents,* Sage Publications, New Delhi.

Jain, Devaki, 1991, *Development,* Vol. 1, p. 75.

Jain, S.P., 1974, "Some Aspects of Mortality", in Box, Ashish, Desai, p. B., Mitra, Asok, and Sharma, J. N. (eds.) *Population in India's Development,* Vikas Publishing House Pvt. Ltd., Delhi, pp. 319-333.

Judith, Willer, 1971, *The Social Determination of Knowledge,* Prentice-Hall, Inc., Englewood cliffs, New Jersey, pp. 20-141.

Kahn, Herman, and Wiener, A.J., 1967, *The Year 2000: A Framework for Speculation on the Next Thirty-Three Years,* MacMillan, New York.

Kapadia, K.M., 1966, *Marriage and family in India,* Oxford University Press, Bombay.

Karkal, M. 1979, Child Mortality and Morbidity in Greater Bombay, IIPS, Bombay (mimeo).

Karlekar, Hiranmay, 1992. *Colonialism Redivivus: The Implications of Exploitative Development from Above.* Indian Express, November

28, New Delhi, p.8.

Kelien, Ethel, 1984, *Gender Politics: From Consciousness to Mass Politics,* Harvard University Press, p. 126.

Keyfitz, Nathan, 1972, "Population Theory and Doctrine: A Historical Survey", in Peterson, William (ed.), *Readings in Population,* The MacMillan Company, New York, pp. 41-69.

—,—, 1990, "Toward a Theory ofPopulation-Development Interaction", in Davis, Kingsley, and Ernstam, Mikhail (eds.), *Resources, Environment and Population: Present Knowldege, Future Option,* Population Council, New York, pp. 295-314.

—,—, 1991. "Population and Development within the Ecosphere: One View of the Literature", *Population Index,* Vol. 57, No.1, 1991, pp. 5-22.

Keyfitz, Nathan, Nagnaur, Dhruva, and Shrma, Divakar, 1967, "On the Interpretation of Age Distribution," *Journal of the American Statistical Association,* Vol. 62, pp. 870-871.

Khan, Irfan, 1991, *Fertility Behaviour and Birth Control among Muslims in India: A Study of a Village in Bihar State,* Unpublished Ph.D. thesis, HSS Department, IIT Kanpur.

Khan, M.E., 1976, *The Correlates of Muslim Fertility in Urban Setting: A Case Study; of Kanpur City,* Unpublished Ph.D. thesis, HSS Department, Kanpur.

—,—, 1978, *Birth Control Among Muslims in India,* Manohar Publication.

Kishwar, Madhu, 1988, "Nature of Women's Mobilisation in Rural India: An Exploratory Essay", *Economic and Political Weekly,* December 24-31, pp. 2754-2763.

Knorr-Cetina, .Karin D. and Michael, Mulkay, 1983, "Introduction: Emerging Principles in Social Studies of Science", in Knorr-Cetina, Karin D., and Mulkay Michael, (eds)., *Science Observed,* Sage Publications, New Delhi, pp. 1-18.

Kohli, K.L., 1977, *Mortality in India; A Statewise Study,* Sterling Publishers, Pvt. Ltd., New Delhi.

Korpardekar, H.D., 1986, *Social Aspects of Urban Development,* Popular Prakashan, Bombay.

Kuhn, Thomas, 1970. *The Sturcture of Scientific revolution,* University, of Chicago Press, Chicago.

Lala, E.S., 1989, "Nehru's Vision of Women, development and Family Planning", *The Journal of Family Welfare,* Vol. 35, No. 6.

Landry, A., 1935, *Las Revolution Demographique,* Sirey, Paris.

Leibenstein, H., 1975, "Relation of Economic Development to Fertility" in Tabah, Leon (ed.), *Population Growth and Economic Development in Third World,* IUSSP, Vol. 2, pp. 437-508.

Lovelock, James, 1989, "The Greening of Science", *Resurgence,* No. 138, pp. 12-19.

Madan, T.N., 1987, *Non-Renunciation: Thmes and Interpretations of Hindu Culture,* Oxford University Press, New Delhi.

Mahadevan, K. Reddy, P.R., Murthy, M.S.R., Reddy, P.J., Gowri, V., and Raju, S. Siva, 1986, "Culture, Nutrition and Infant and Childhood Mortality", in Mahadeven, K., Reddy, P.J., and Naidu, D.A. (eds.) *Fertility and Mortality: Theory Methodology and Empirical Issues,* Sage Publications, New Delhi, pp. 314-37.

Majumdar, D.N., 1960, *Social Contours of an Industrial City,* Asia Publishing House, Bombay.

Maitra, P., 1986, *Population, Technology and Development: A Critical Analysis,* Gower Publishing House.

Malaker, C.R. 1978, Study of Indian Nuptiality Ph. D. Dissertatoin, ISI Calcutta, pp. 78-105.

Malthus, T.R., 1965, *First Essay on Population 1798,* M. Kelley, New York.

Mannheim, Karl, 1973, "Sociology of Knowledge from the Standpoint of Modern Phenomenology: Max Scheler", in Remmling, G.W. (ed.), *Towards the Sociology of Knowledge,* Routledge & Kegan, Paul, London, pp. 187-201.

Margaret, Sanger, 1969, "A Summit Meeting on Birth Control", in Cousins, Norman (ed.), *Pofiles of Gandhi: America Remembers a World Leader,* Indian Book Company, New Delhi.

Marx, Karl, 1973. quoted in United Nations, *The Determinants and Consequences of Population Trends,* United Nations Publications, New York, pp. 47-50.

—, —, 1974, *Capital Vol. 1,* Progress Publishers, Moscow, pp. 574-600.

—, —, 1978, *The Poverty of Philosophy,* Progress Publishers, Moscow, pp. 112-17.

Mc Gee, T.G., 1979, *The Urbanisation Process in the Third World,* Bell & Hyman, London, pp. 13-30.

Meadows, D.H., Meadows, J.R. and Behrens, W.W. III, 1972, *The Limits to Growth,* Universe Books, New York.

Measavoric, M., and Pestel, E., 1974, *Mankind at the Turning Point,* E.P. Dutton, New York.

Mehta, Hansa, 1981, *Indian Women,* Butala & Co., Delhi, pp. 110-111.

Merton, R.K., 1973, *The Sociology of Science: Theoretical and Empirical Investigations,* University of Chicago Press, Chicago.

Misra, B.D., 1980, An Introduction to the Study of Population, South Asian Publishers Pvt. Ltd., New Delhi.

—, —, 1990, "Population, Eco-System and the Environment: An Indian Scenario", *Demography India,* Vol. 19, No. 1, pp. 59-64.

—, —, 1991, *Area Specific Approach in Health and Family Welfare-Uttar Pradesh,* State Institute of Health and Family Welfare, Lucknow (mimeo).

—, —, 1993, *Area-Specific Approach in Health and Family Welfare-Uttar Pradesh,* State Institute of Health and Family Welfare, Lucknow.

Misra, B.D., Ashraf, A., Simmons, R. and Simmons, George, 1982, Organization fort Change: *A Systems Analysis of Family Planning in Rural India,* Radiant Publishers, New Delhi.

Misra, R.P. and Lakshamanan, T.R., 1988, "Intorduction" in Misra, R.P. (ed.), *Gandhian Model of Development and World Peace,* Concept Publishing Company, New Delhi.

Mohan, Rakesh, 1985, "Urbanization in India's Future", *Population and Development Review* Vol. II, No. 4, pp. 619-646.

Morris, J.K., 1969, "Professor Malthus and his Essay", in Kammeyer, K.C.W. (ed.), *Population Studies: Selected Essays and Research,* Rand Mc Nally and Company, Chicago, pp. 54-75.

Morris, M.D., 1979. *Measuring the Condition of the Worlds' Poor: The Physical Quality of Life Index.,* Pergamon, Oxford.

Mukerji, S., 1987, "Applications of Operations Research Techniques in Demographic Analysis", in Saxena, P.C., and Talwar, P.P. (eds.) *Recent Advances in the techniques for Demographic Analysis,* Himalaya publishing House, Bombay, pp. 426-456.

Mukerjee, Radhakamal, 1930, "Optimum and Over-Population", *Indian Journal of Economics,* Vol. 10, No. 3, pp. 407-21.

—, —, 1933, "The Criterion of Optimum Population", *The American Journal of Sociology,* Vol. 38, No. 5, pp. 688-89.

Muttagi, P.K., 1989, "Urban Environment - The Bombay Scene", *Nagarlok,* Vol. 21, No. 2.

Myrdal, G., 1968, *Asian Drama: An Enquiry into the Poverty of Nations,* Vol. 3, Penguin Books.

—, —, 1970, *The Challenge of World Poverty,* Penguin Book.

Nagchaudhuri, B.D., and Bhatt. S., 1987, *The Global Environment Movement: A New Hope for Mankind,* Sterling Publishers Private Ltd, New Delhi.

Naik, J.P., 1982 "Education Planning after the Commission", quoted in Sundrum, R.M., *Growth and Income Distribution in India,* Sage Publications, New Delhi, 1987, p. 276.

Namboodiripad, E.M.S., 1959, *The Mahatma and the Ism.*, People's Publishing House, New Delhi.

Narayan, J.P., 1986, *Aamne Samne,* Sarva Seva Sangh Prakashan, Varanasi, (in Hindi).

Nargolkar, Vasant, 1957, *JP's Crusade for Revolution,* Ram Nagar, New Delhi, pp. 40-67.

National Institute of Urban Affairs, 1988, *State of India's Urbanization,* National Institute of Urban Affairs, New Delhi.

Nehru, Jawaharlal, 1972, The Discovery of India, Asia Publishing House, Delhi.

Ness, G.D., 1991, "Population, Development and Global Change", *Populi,* Vol. 18, No.1 pp. 24-33.

Norgaard, Richard B., 1988, "Sustainable Development: A Co-Evolutionary View", *Futures,* Vol. 20, No. 6, pp. 606-620.

Notestein, F., 1953, "Economic Problems of Population Change", *in Proceedings of the Eighth International Conference of Agricultural Economists,* London.

Oakley, Ann, 1989, "Women's Studies in British Sociology: To End at Our Begining", *The British Journal of Sociology,* Vol. 40, No. 3, p. 443.

Oberai, J.P.S., 1978, *Science and Culture,* Oxford University Press, New Delhi.

Oberai, A.S., 1989, "Rapid Population Growth, Employment and Housing in Megacities in Developing Countries" in IUSSP, *International Population Conference,* Vol. 2. IUSSP, Belgium, pp. 187-200.

Ojha, S.D., 1987, "Prachin Bhartiya Parampara Our Janasankhya Shiksha". in Misra, B.D. *et al.* (eds.), *Janasnkhya Siksha,* Population Centre, Lucknow.

Omvedt, G., 1991, "Rural Women Fight for Independence", *Economic and Political Weekly,* Vol. 29, pp. 910-33.

Oommen, T.K., 1979, "Rethinking Gandhian Approach", *Gandhi Marg,* Vol. 1, No. 7, pp. 416-23

Operations Research Group, 1972, *Family Planning Practice in India,* O.R.G. Baroda.

Pakrasi, Kanti B., 1970, *Female Infanticide in India,* ISI, Calcutta.

Panikkar, P.G.K., 1975,"Fall in Mortality Rates in Kerala: An Explanatory Hypothesis", *Economic and Political Weekly,* November 22, pp. 1811-18.

Panda, A.C., 1987, *Contemporary Social Movements in India,* Unpublished Ph.D. thesis, I.I.T. Kanpur.

Paranjuli, Pramod, 1991, "Power and Knowledge in Development discourse: New Social Movements and the State in India", *International Social Science Journal,* Vol. 127, pp. 173-90.

Paranjape, Makarand, 1993, *Decolonization and Development,* Sage Publications, New Delhi.

Patel, Bibhuti, 1988, "Emergence and Proliferation ofAutonomous Women's Groups in India: 1974-1984", in Ghadially, Rehana (ed.), *Women in India,* Sage Publications, New Delhi, pp. 249-56.

Patel, Sujata, 1988, "Consturction and Reconstruction of Woman in Gandhi", *Economic and Political Weekly,* February 20, pp. 377-86.

Patel, C. N., 1981, *Mahatma Gandhi in His Gujrati Writings,* Sahitya Akadami, Delhi, pp. 8-9

Pearce, David, 1988, "Economics, Equity and Sustainable Development", *Furutes,* Vol. 20, No. 6, pp. 598-605.

Petersen, William, 1965, *Population,* The Macmillan Company, New York, pp. 307-35.

Pethe, V.P., 1985, *State of Knowldege and the Demographic and Social Reality,* Poona, pp. 3-4.

Phillips, J.F., Ruth, Simmons, Koenig, M.A., and Chakraborty, J., 1988. "Determinants of Reproductive Change in a Traditional Society: Evidence from Matlab, Bangladesh, *Studies in Family Planning,* Vol. 19, No. 6, pp. 335-53.

Planning Commission, 1985, *Seventh Five-year Plan 1985-90,* Vol. II, Government of Indain, New Delhi.

Population Crisis Committee 1990, *Life in the World's 100 Largest Metropolitan Areas,* Population Crisis Committe, Washington.

Prasad, D.R., 1989, "Introduction", in Prasad, D.R. (ed.), *Urban Renewal: The Indian Experience,* Sterling Publishers Private limited, pp. 1-25.

Prabhu, R.K. and Rao, U.R., 1967, *The Mind of Mahatma Gandhi,* Navajivan Publications, Ahmedabad.

Pradhan, Benudhar, 1980, *The Socialist Thought of Mahatma Gandhi,* G.D.K. Publishers, Delhi.

Premi, M.K., 1993 *Family Planning and MCH in Uttar Pradesh: A Review of Studies,* The Population Council, Asian and the Near East Operations.

Premi, M.K., Ramanamma, A., and Bambawale, Usha, 1983, *An Introduction to Social Demography,* Vikas Publishing House Pvt. Ltd., New Delhi.

Preston, S.H., and Donaldson, Peter, 1986, "Population Growth and Economic Development", *Asia-Pacific Population Journal,* Vol. 1, No. 2, pp. 3-12.

Pyarelal, 1956, *Mahatma Gandhi: The Last Phase,* Navajivan Publishing House, Ahmedabad, Vols 1 & 2.

Radhakrishnan, S. (ed.), 1968, *Mahatma Gandhi-100 Years,* Gandhi Peace Foundation, New Delhi.

Radhakumar, 1969, "The Women's Movement", *Seminar,* March.

Raghavan, V. R., 1986, "Reflections on Gandhian Economics", *Gandhi Marg:* Vol. 7, No. 1, pp. 107-110.

Ratcliffe, J.W., 1983, " Toward a Social Justice Theory of Demographic Transition: Lessons from India's Kerala State", *Janasamkhya,* Vol. 1, No.1, pp.1-38.

Rele, J.R., 1963, "Fertility Differentials in India", *The Milbank Memorial fund Quarterly,* Vol. 41, pp. 183-85.

—, —, 1967, *Fertility Analysis Through Extension of Stable Population Concepts,* Institute of International Studies, University of California, Berkeley.

Rele, J.R., and Sinha, U.P. 1970, "fertility and Mortality in India, 1951-60", in Bose, Ashish, Desai, P.B., and Jain, S.P. (eds.), *Studies in Demography,* George Allen and Unwin Ltd., London, pp. 212-26.

Remmling, G.W., 1973, "Existence and Thought", in Remmling, G.W. (ed.), *Towards the Sociology of knowledge,* Routledge & Kegan Paul, London, pp. 3-43.

—, —, 1973, "The Significance and Development of Karl Mannehim's Sociology", in Remmling, G.W. (ed.), *Ibid,* pp. 217-28.

Repetto, Robert, and Holmes, Thomas, 1983, "The Role of Population in Resource Depletion in Developing Countries", *Population and Development Review,* Vol. 9, No. 4, pp. 609-32.

Rifkin, Jeremy, and Howard, Ted, 1980, *Entropy,* The Viking Press, New York.

Robbins, Lionel, 1927, "The Optimum Theory of Population", in Gregory, T.E. and Dalton, Hugh (eds.), London Essays in Honour of Edwin Cannan, Routledge, London, pp. 103-34.

Rodgers, G., 1989, "An Overview", in Rodgers, G. (ed.), *Population Growth and Poverty in Rural South Asia,* Sage Publications, New Delhi.

Rostow, W.W., 1978, *The World Economy: History and Prospect,* University of Texas Press, Austin & London.

Roy, Bhaskar, 1983, "Science", in Bottomore, Tom (ed.), *A Dictionary of Marxist Thought,* Oxford University Press, Delhi pp. 434-36.

Roy, T.K. and Mukerji, S. 1981, "Analysis of Maternity History Data: A Simulation Experiment", in Srinivasan, K., and Mukerji, S. (eds.) *Dynamics of Population and Family Welfare,* Himalaya Publishing

House, Bombay, pp. 15-29.

Ruzicka, G.T. and Kanitkar, T. 1973, "Infant Mortality in Greater Bombay", *Demography India,* Vol. 2, No. 1, pp.41-55.

Sarkar, Tanika, 1991, "The Women as Communal Subject: Rashtra-Sevika Samiti and Ram Janmabhoomi Andolan", *Economic and Political Weekly,* Vol. 26, No. 35, pp. 2057-2062.

Saran, A.K., 1978, "On the Promotion of Gandhian Studies at the University Level", *Gandhi Marg,* Vol. 7, No. 1, pp. 363-81.

—, —, 1987, "Traditionalism and Trancendantalism in Indian Society", in Hellen, G. C. (ed.) *Sociology in India,* Vol. 1, Rohini Publications, Meerut, pp. 336-44.

Saraswati, Swami Satya Prakash, and Vidyalankar, Satya Ram, 1977, *Rgveda Samhita,* Vol IV, Veda Pratisthana, New Delhi, P. 915.

Saseendran, P.P., and Kumar, Mithilesh, 1989; *Determinants of Family Welfare Programme in U.P. :An Analytical Study of CPR and Socio-Economic Variables,* Population Centre, Lucknow.

Sawhney, Nirmal, Mithilesh, Kumar, and Saseendran, P.P., 1990, *Socio-Religious Dimensions of Family Welfare Programme: A Case Study of Muslim Elite,* Population Centre, Lucknow.

Saxena, P.C. and Shrama A.K., 1976, "Population Projections for Cities of Maharashtra, *IIPS Newsletter,* No. 55, pp. 10-14.

—, —, 1976, "Projections of Rural and Urbn Population of Destricts of Maharashtra", *IIPS Newsletter,* No. 52. pp. 1-5.

Scheler, Max, 1982, "On the Positivistic Philosophy of the History of Knowledge and its Law of Three Stages, in Curtis, J.E., and Petras, J.W. (eds.), *The Sociology of Knowledge : A Reader,* Praeger Publishers, London, pp. 170-86.

—, —, 1982, "The Sociology of Knowledge: Formal Problem" in Curtis, J.E., and Petras, J.W. (eds.), *Op cit,* pp. 161-69.

Schumacher, E.F., 1979, Good Work, Harper and Row, New York.

Seers, Dudley, 1969. *The Meaning of Development,* Eleventh World Conference of the World Society for International Development, New Delhi.

Sharma, Kumud, 1992, "Contemporary women's Movement in India: Its Deialectics and Vilemmas", *The Indian Journal of Social Science,* Vol. 5, No.2, pp. 1-31.

Sharma, A.K., 1979, "Demographic Transition: A Determinant of Urbanization", *Social Change,* Vol. 9, No. 3, pp. 13-17.

—, —, 1984, "Aspects of Population Debate and Stratification", *The Journal of Family Welfare,* Vol. 31, No. 1 pp. 37-50.

—, —, 1985, *Social Inequality and Demographic Processes,* Mittal

Publications, New Delhi.

—, —, 1988, "Fieldwork in Large Scale Surveys", in Sawhney, Nirmala, Talwar, P.P., and Misra, B.D. (eds.) *Large Scale Surveys in Health and Family Welfare Programmes in India,* Population Centre, U.P., Lucknow.

—, —, 1989, *Issues in Social Demography,* Mittal Publications, New Delhi.

—, —, 1989, "Muslim Population in India", *The Eastern Anthropologist,* Vol. 42, No.4, pp. 353-64.

—, —, "Social Implications of Urbanization in India", *The Journal of Sociological Studies,* Vol. 6.

—, —, 1989, *Issues in Social Demogeaphy,* Mittal Publication, New Delhi, pp. 23-40

—, —, 1989, "Growth of Muslim Population in India: Some Policy Issues", *The Eastern Anthropologist,* Vol. 42, No. 4.

—, —, 1991, "Gandhian Theory of Population: Revelence and Implication", *The Journal of Family Welfare,* Vol. 37, No. 4, pp. 32-45.

Sharma, A.K., and Misra, B.D., 1978, "Fertility Defferentials in India-An analysis of Census Fertility Data", *The Journal of Family Welfare,* Vol. 25, No. 2.

Sharma, Anuradha, and Sharan, Raka, 1990, *Social Responsibilities of Technologists, Scientists and Managers,* Gian Publishing House, New Delhi.

Sharma, S.L., 1989. "Social Development: Reflections on the Concept and the Indian Experience", *Guru Nanak Journal of Sociology,* Nos. 1 & 2, pp. 37-53.

Shirk, Evelyn, 1988, "New Dimensions in Ethics: Ethics and the Environment", *The Journal of Value Inquiry,* Vol. 22, pp. 77-85.

Shiva Kumar, A.K., 1991. "UNDP's Human Development Index: A Computation for Indian States", *Economic and Political Weekly,* Vol.26, No. 41.

Shiva, Vandana, 1991, *Ecology and the Politics of Survival: Conflicts over Natural Resources in India,* Sage Publications, New Delhi.

Shryock, Henry S. and Siegel, J.S., 1973, *The Methods and Materials of Demography,* Vol. II, U.S. Government Printing Office, Washington, pp. 188-251.

Skolimowsky, N. D., *The Ecological Man* Eco-Philosophy Publication, Madras.

Skolimowsky, Henryk, 1981, *Eco-Philosophy: Designing New Tactics for Living,* Marion Boyans, Boston.

Simmons, G.B., and Bernstein, Stan. 1982,"The Educational Status of Parents and infant and Child Mortality in Rural North India", *Health Policy and Education,* Vol. 2, pp. 349-67.

Singh, S.N., Dwivedi, S.N. and Singh K.N. u.d. "Trend in Neo-natal and Post-natal Mortality Rates in India", *Centre of Population Studies,* BHU, Varanasi (mimeo).

Singh, Yogendra, 1973, *Modernization of Indian Tradition,* Thompson Press, Delhi.

Sinha, J.N. 1958, "differential Fertility in Uttar Pradesh", *Population Studies,* Vol. 2, p. 162.

Smucker, C., Simmons, G.B., Bernstein, S. and Misra B.D., 1980, "Neonatal Mortality in South Asia: The Special Role of Tetanus", Population Studies, Vol. 34.

Sorokin, P.A., 1947, *Society, Culture and Personality: Their Structure and Dynamics,* Harper & Brothers Publishers, New York.

Srinivasan, K., 1967,"Fertility Trends and Differentials in Athoor Block", *Bullentin of Institute of Rural Health and Family Planning,* Gandhigram, Vol. 2, No. 1, pp. 67-68.

Srivastava, Aseem, 1992, "Overpopulation: The Great Red Herring", *Economic and Political Weekly,* Vol. 27, No. 38, Sep. 19, pp. 2033-38.

Srivastava, H.C. 1979, "A Study of Fertility Differentials among Hindu and Muslim Women in Bhiwandi", in Srinivasan, K. and Mukerji, S. (eds.) *Dynamics of Popluation and Family Welfare in India,* Popular Prakashan, Bombay, pp. 284-92.

Srivastava, J.N. and Saksena, D.N., 1980, "Infant Mortality in an Urban Setting: Study of Socio-Demographic and Health Care Differentials", paper presented in The IASP Conference on Population Studies, No. 34, New York, p. 119.

Srivastava, D.N., 1989, "Hindu-Muslim Defferentials in Family Size Ideal by Socio-Economic Status", *The Journal of family Welfare,* Vol. 35, No. 4, pp. 38-48.

Srivastava, P.N., 1989, "Convocation Address", IIPS Newsletter, Vol. 30, No.3, p.2.

Srinivasan, K., 1986, " Has Modernisation Increased Fertility in Karnataka India", Demography India, Vol. 15, No. 2, p. 281.

Steinkraus, W., 1976, "Transcultural Value Pre-suppositions of Science", in Pandeya, R.C., and Bhatt, S.R.(eds.) *Knowledge Culture and Value,* Motilal Banarsidass, Delhi, pp. 63-66.

Stonich, S.C., 1989, "The Dynamics of Social Processes and Environmental Destruction: A Central American Case Study", Population and

Development Review, Vol. 15, No. 2, pp. 269-96.

Suman, Ramnath, 1969, *Samaj Sudhar: Samasyayen aur Samadhan,* Gandhi Sahitya Prakashan, Allahabad.

Sundrum, R.M., 1987. *Growth and Income Distribution in India: Policy and Performance since Independence,* Sage Publications, New Delhi.

Swee-Hock, Saw, 1989, "Muslim Fertility Transition", *Asia-Pacific Population Journal,* Vol.4, No. 3, pp. 31-40.

Templin, R.T., 1969, Gandhi Belongs to Tomorrow, in Cousins, Norman (ed.). *Profiles of Gandhi: America Remembers a World Leader,* Indian Book Company, pp. 114-16.

Thapa, G.B., and Weber, K.E., 1989,"Population and Environment in the Hills of Nepal", *Asia-Pacific Population Journal,* Vol. 4, No. 2, pp. 49-70.

Theis, Joachim, and Grady, H.M., 1991, *Training Manual: Preparing a Participatory Rapid Appraisal Training,* International Institute for Environment and Development, London.

Thompson, W.S., 1929, "Population", *American Journal of Sociology,* Vol. 34, pp. 959-75.

Thompson, W. S. and Lewis, D.T., 1965, *Population Problems,* McGraw-Hill Book Company, New York, pp. 37-54.

UNCED, 1992, *The Global Partnership for Environment and Development: A Guide to Agenda 21,* UNCED, Geneva.

United Nations, 1961, *The Mysore Population Study: A Cooperative Project of the United Nations and the Government of India, Population Studies,* No.34, New York, p. 119.

—,.—, 1967, *Manual IV: Methods of Estimating Basic Demographic Measures fromn Incomplete Data,* Department of Economic and Social Affairs, New York, pp. 22-28.

—,—, 1973, *The Determinants and Consequences of Population Trends,* Vol. 1, United Nations Publications, New York.

—,—, 1979, *Prospects of Population: Methodology and Assumptionns,* United Nation, p. 116.

—,—, 1981, *World Population prospects as Assessed in 1980,* United Nations, p. 2.

—,—, 1990. *Study on the Development of Quality of Life Indicators in Asia and the Pacific,* ESCAP, New York, p. 39.

—,—, 1991, *Notes for Speakers: Earth Summit 92: The United Nations Conference on Environment and Development,* United Nations, p. 14.

—, —, 1992, *Earth Summit in Focus,* No. 6, United Nations Department of Public Information.

—, —, 1992, *The State of World Population 1992,* United Nations Population Fund, p. 44.

United Nations Conference on Environment and Development, 1992, *The Global Partnership: For Environment and Development, A Guide for Agenda 21,* UNCED, Geneva.

United, Nations Population Fund, 1992, *The State of World Population, UNFPA,* New York, p. iii.

United Nations, n.d., *Report and Selected Papers of the Regional Seminar on Ecological Implications of Rural and Urban Population Growth,* Economic Commission for Asia and the Far-East, Bangkok.

Unnithan, T.K.N., 1979, *Gandhi and Social Change,* Rawat Publishers, Jaipur, p. 149.

Upadhyay, D. 1969, "The Family Planning Policy", in Daswani, P.R. (ed.), *Issues of National Policy,* Jaico Publishing Company, Bombay.

Urlanis, B.T., 1978, "World Population Growth", in Valentey, D.I. (ed.), *The Theory of Population,* Progress Publishers, Moscow, p. 231.

Vadekar, D.D., 1978, "Science, Technology and Value", in Pandeysa, R.C., and Bhatt S.R. (eds.), *Knowledge, Culture and Value,* Today and Tomorow Publishers & Printers, New Delhi, pp. 25-36.

Vaidyanathan, K.E. (ed.), 1972, *Studies on Mortality in India,* The Gandhigram Institute of Rural Health and Family Planning Gandhigram.

Visaria, Pravin, 1993, *A Population Policy of India: A Draft for Facilitating Discussion,* Nirman Bhawan, New Delhi.

Waites, Bernard,. 1989, "Social and Human Engineering", in Chant, Colin (ed.) *Science Technology and Everyday Life,* 1870-1950, Routledge.

Weber, Max, 1958, *The Protestant Ethic and the Spirit of Capitalism,* Charles Scribner's Sons, New York.

—, —, 1964, The Sociology of Religion, Beacon Press, Boston.

Woolgar, Steve, 1983. "Irony in the Social Study of Science", in Knorr-Cetina, Karin D., and Mulkay, Michael (eds.), *Science Observed,* Sage Publications, New Delhi, pp. 239-266.

Woolgar, Steve, and Malcolm, Ashmore, 1988, "The next Step: an Introduction to the Reflexivity Project", in Woolgar, Steve (ed.) *Knowledge and Reflexivity,* Sage Publications, New Delhi, pp. 1-11.

The World Bank, 1992, *World Development Report 1992: Development and the Environment,* Oxford University Press, New York.

—, —, 1993, *World Development Report 1993,* Oxford University Press, pp. 276-277.

World Commission on Environment and Development, 1987, *Our Common Future,* Oxford University Press, Oxford, p. 40.

World fertility Survey, 1984, *World Fertility Survey: Major Findings and Implications,* pp. 23-24.

Wyon, J.B. and Gordon J.E., 1971, *The Khanna Study: Population Problems in Rural Punjab,* Harvard University Press, Cambridge, p. 163.

Yadava, K.N.S., and Singh, Ram B., 1991, "A Probability Model for the Distribution of the Number of Migrants at the Household Level," *Genus,* Vol. 47, Nos. 1-2, pp. 1-20.

Zaba, B., 1981, "Use of Relational Gompertz Model in Analysing Fertility Data Collected in Retrospective Surveys, "*CPS Working Paper,* Series 81, No.2, London School of Hygiene and Tropical Medicine.

Ziman, John, 1984, An Introduction to Science Studies: The Philosophical and Social Aspects of Science and Technology, Cambridge University Press, Cambridge.

INDEX